Hidden Designs

JONATHAN CREWE

Hidden Designs

The critical profession and Renaissance literature

Methuen
New York and London

First published in 1986 by
Methuen, Inc.
29 West 35th Street
New York NY 10001

Published in Great Britain by
Methuen & Co. Ltd
11 New Fetter Lane
London EC4P 4EE

Phototypeset by AKM Associates (UK) Ltd
Ajmal House, Hayes Road, Southall, London
Printed and bound in Great Britain
at the University Press, Cambridge

Library of Congress Cataloging in Publication Data
Crewe, Jonathan V.
   Hidden designs.

   Bibliography: P.
   1. English literature - early modern, 1500–1700 –
History and criticism. - theory, etc.   2. Criticism –
history - 20th century.   3. Historical criticism
(Literature)   4. Theater – political aspects.   I. Title.
PR69.C74   1986   820'.9'003   86-16262
ISBN 0-416-92350-X

British Library Cataloguing in Publication Data
Crewe, Jonathan V.
   Hidden designs: the critical profession and Renaissance literature.
   1. English poetry – Early modern, 1500–1700
   – History and criticism
   I. Title
   821'.3'09   PR531

ISBN 0-416-92350-X

Contents

Acknowledgments

The time-span covered by this book is roughly that between 1980 and mid-1985, during which I was a member of the English Department of the Johns Hopkins University. The acknowledgments I make, as well as the history I record in the book, may seem excessively domestic, giving unwarranted scope to an eccentric or self-serving view of the world from Baltimore. Believing, however, that one must begin where one is, and not from some hypothetically all-encompassing vantage point, I must identify the place in which the book was written as well as the names of people who have been important in its inception.

I want to record above all my appreciation of colleagues and students in the English Department and the neighborly Humanities Center. The institution endures, but a number of those who defined this Hopkins phase have moved on to other places, so this appreciation also commemorates one of those fleeting human combinations that constitute the best meaning of the academic life. I also want to record a continuing debt to friends and former teachers from Berkeley.

Of the particular debts I have incurred, intellectually and for help and support, the largest are those owed to Sharon Cameron, Michael Fried, Jonathan Goldberg and Stephen Greenblatt. The presence of Stanley Fish in the following pages will testify to a special and complicated form of indebtedness (sometimes that of resistance), but I want to record here my gratitude for his friendship, unique intellectual example and unfailing generosity. What Johns Hopkins and the profession in general owe to him – a debt in which I also participate – is as well known as it is difficult to overestimate.

Others who have been stimulating companions and/or generous, exacting readers include Jerome Christensen, John Coetzee, John Hollander, Stephen Orgel, Mark Seltzer and Michael Warner. I am conscious of a special debt to the members of a graduate seminar I conducted during 1983/4 in the poetics of the sixteenth century. Some debts to members of this group are recorded in the footnotes, but there is no way of footnoting the fluent general interaction that made this seminar productive. No blame sticks to any individual or group named above for the faults of this book or for my failures to benefit from enviable opportunities.

Finally, I want to acknowledge my own family's tolerance of the antisocial activity of critical writing, pursued often at its expense. I also record with admiration the skill and pleasure with which all its members have, while giving moral support, conducted the business of their own lives.

The author and publishers wish to thank the editors of *English Literary Renaissance* for permission to reproduce on pp. 21–34 "The hegemonic theater of George Puttenham", which originally appeared in vol. 16, no. 1 (1986), pp. 71–85.

The illustrations on pp. 96, 104, 107, 109, 111, 113 and 115 from "A theatre wherein be represented as wel the miseries and calamities that follow the voluptuous worldlings, as also the great joyes and plesures which the faithful do enjoy . . .", devised by Jan Baptiste van der Noot, 1569, are reproduced by permission of the British Library.

Prehistory

My theme turns in on itself – I do not know whether everyone will
accept it.

(Montaigne, "Of Experience")

He will be the enemy of those he loves and of the institutions that
have produced him.

(Nietzsche on Schopenhauer in *Untimely Meditations*)

Terror and a broader poetry

(Flaubert, planning a novel about chivalry)

Since it diverges from some scholarly and professional norms, this
book needs more justification than most. But even if the justifications
were superabundant, the book would still have to speak for itself, so
I will confine myself to the minimum of necessary explanation. I would
like to say that it came to me to write a book in this form when I realized
that a certain history, which I will try to record as a medium rather
than as a significant actor, had suddenly taken shape for me. The fairly
brief critical history that I had lived, in other words, without any
particular informing sense of order or mission, took shape in the light
of the apparent discovery with which my account ends. Only in the
light of that discovery, which can be said to have a literal and a
conceptual aspect, could there be a critical history; not, admittedly, a
finished one, but one that had now taken form in relation to a definite
point.

This history isn't one that can be presented to any hypothetical general
audience or readership, since its events *are* events only in the context of
academic criticism and indeed within a fairly restricted professional
field, that of the English Renaissance. It is in that field, by the same token,
that the book must stake its claim to make a critical contribution. And
although I deal with the major figures of Shakespeare, Sidney and Spenser

(a "dispersed" or fragmented representation of Spenser constitutes the principal matter of the book), George Puttenham, putative author of *The Arte of English Poesie* (1589), remains a key figure in the argument. His work is familiar only to a very specialized academic readership. The readers, therefore, to whom this history will readily be accessible are close colleagues; they may feel that they know it already and may also prefer to get their professional business done without diversion or redundancy. (Everyone is the subject of his/her own history of course, but that is professionally irrelevant.) So the enterprise of writing such a history may seem to be forestalled by the simple questions "for whom?" and "why?"

Not only does any appeal from inside the profession to a hypothetical general readership now seem impractical, but any claim to cater at the same time to professional and so-called general concerns must confront the probability that those separate concerns, if both exist, are now irreconcilable. The existence of any general readership or disinterested intelligentsia is itself questionable, and any claim that such a category exists would now immediately be seen as an ideologically motivated falsification, designed to give a spurious look of universality to limited interests. The same objection would probably meet anyone's claim to speak for general "human" interests. Principled objections aside, more-over, critics like the Leavises and the Trillings who could hope (however one may assess the outcome) to mediate effectively between perceived academic and general concerns have left no recognizable progeny, and with their disappearance the role of the *critic* – of criticism – in at least one traditional sense of the word has come into question. On one hand, the institutionally defined and contained work of the profession, and on the other – what?

Spoken, no doubt hubristically, from inside the profession (and the productions of contemporary poets, playwrights and novelists aren't at issue here), the answer seems increasingly to be "nothing." Although it might be courteous to make an exception of some well-known reviews, some non-professional publications self-defined as intellectual, and some famous book reviewers, the truth is that the work of the professional collectivity now proceeds in a state of almost complete indifference to all of these, and does so without fear that there may be another game in town, or, for better or worse, any form of interpretive rigor other than its own. The professional community of readers is now large and confident enough to subsist without fear of an authoritative readership other than the one it comprises. Those who oppose to the authority of this academic-professional community the higher sanction of an implicitly leisure-class, non-professional intelligentsia or of the "Renaissance" generalist in *litterae humaniores* have recently had their bluff called by Stanley Fish, who is also the professional academic author who has most effectively called the bluff of anti-professionalism.[1] I take Fish's arguments at present to remain unrefuted if not unchallenged.

So a history that isn't professionally called for, that can only in a rather paradoxical way style itself a professional contribution, and that can't appeal to a general audience (in the existence of which belief is hardly possible) may seem condemned from the start to perfect redundancy. But in J.L. Austin's much-quoted dictum about philosophical arguments, there is the part where you say it and the part where you take it back. Since the title of this book contains the phrase "The Critical Profession" (by which I don't mean quite the same thing as "critical professionalism") it may already have been inferred that the preceding objections will be overridden. Yet I take the objections seriously, and don't seek to *override* them. This book could simply become a revelation of the impossibility of "the critical profession" – of nostalgia for a critical role no longer even capable of being attempted. The book might thus serve to elicit a recognition, but only at the price of its own exemplary failure.

Preferring if possible to forgo the martyrdom of failure, I must appeal to colleagues; first to colleagues (under which heading I include graduate students) in the field of the English Renaissance on the strictly professional basis that this is a book within the field. Still addressing those colleagues, but also now broadening the professional appeal somewhat, I want in writing this history to attempt certain forms of avowal that have become difficult under normal conditions of professional relevance. What I want to avow, and perhaps it is little more than that, is an unerased conception of the critical profession as an activity, a name, and even an object of worldly faith distinct from, though not necessarily opposed to, critical professionalism. To avow, moreover, a belief in the critical goal, however problematical or "impossible," of disinterestedness, and in the obligation of criticism *to* criticize without conceding or claiming any form of privileged immunity, professional or otherwise. To suggest, finally, that these terms and conditions just aren't politically negotiable if criticism is to be professed and practiced, however tactfully, or with whatever degree of respect for constructive achievement. In making this avowal I appeal for confirmation or denial, and thus implicitly for a disclosure of this continuing faith if it exists. Implicitly, too, I want to test the generality of this "profession" in the sense of its ability to traverse disciplinary, institutional and political boundaries, and thus to constitute a community self-defined, even if not exclusively so, as "critical."

I shall also attempt to pose the question of criticism within the profession. Does criticism, as distinguishable from regular professional work, from interpretation, and perhaps from theorizing, but informing and informed by all three, still constitute a part of the activity we pursue, of the self-definition we embrace? (Since it obviously does so in such phrases as "school of criticism and interpretive theory," it remains for me to explain why the commitment or its generality are to be doubted.) Is it possible within the profession to regenerate both a distinction and an interchange between the particularities of the scholarly field and the generality that has been the critic's traditionally professed concern? Is it possible that the community of academically employed or affiliated readers is large enough, heterogeneous enough, and sufficiently well informed or concerned to sustain a critical discourse of higher generality than that of the field? And how literal is it necessary to be about the existence of different audiences? Was the old specialist–general reader antithesis ever more than a fiction, albeit perhaps one necessary to the practice of criticism? And if so, can a doubling and interchange of critical positions or roles be regarded as professionally legitimate – even as necessary?

In a way the practical answer to some of these questions is already "yes," since it can hardly be said that academic discussion, informed as it has been by powerful theoretical models, has restricted itself during the past few decades to narrowly delimited fields and technical concerns. But the continuing viability of theory as the medium in or through which general concerns can be articulated now seems questionable. The present exhaustion of the theoretical impulse, manifest in the diminishing returns, scholastic defensiveness, and/or dutiful repetition of much work done in the name of theory suggests that, far from constituting a high and continuing discourse of generality or of critical force, theory as we know it now reveals its finite and partial character – its temporality and even its mortality. And the assertion by Stanley Fish and others[2] that theory is simply inconsequential, although sometimes resulting in a summary and premature reification of practice, suggests nevertheless that theory has lost its grip. The possibility of going "beyond" theory also now gets entertained even at the risk of falling back into a pretheoretical position. And if theory fails in that sense – or has already done so – a great deal of credence must be given to the claim of Stanley Fish that the stakes, interests and concerns of the profession are finally not those of any broader community, of any public or general interest, or of any particular intellectual or moral order, but simply and materially those of the academic institution as such. What must then be accepted is that the stake for which the game is played is – and can be – nothing but the continuation of the game, with its contingent benefits or sole real products of institutional triumph and material advancement.

It is true that in Fish's terms the rules of the game appear to be negotiable and an historical rise of the profession can be charted. Yet the existence of an *ideal* professionalism, always and already preceding this material embodiment, is also regularly implied in Fish's arguments. Wherever Fish sees interpretation occurring – and he does so, practically speaking, always and everywhere, even before modern professional institutions come into being – professionalism is also there as its visible or invisible complement. The modern profession is thus to be seen as the full materialization of this hitherto imperfectly embodied ideal, not something new at all. And if the name of the game is "interpretation," its unalterable point is to perpetuate itself while producing winners and losers according to prevailing institutional–material criteria of success and failure.

My own aim isn't to propose as alternatives to this game a renewed hypocritical amateurism or squeamish spirituality, but rather to acknowledge the moment of truth in Fish's arguments and then take it from there. I would also suggest that the professionalistic argument faces at least two embarrassments of its own once it has been enunciated in its full purity and rigor. The first is that of outliving its own culmination by going on redundantly to insist that the profession *is* the sole object and content of its own activity. The second is that of replacing one form of idyllic false consciousness with another, here involving the belief that the profession, like the old "leisure class," is an ideally self-sustaining and self-serving phenomenon, never more than nominally connected to any history but its own.

Still pursuing Fish's primary argument, however, it must be added that participation in the game, which also means in a very strong sense belonging to the institution, implies participation in the larger worldly system that contains both – a system, in Fish's terms, unequivocally corporate, capitalistic and imperialistic, any appearances to the contrary notwithstanding. This claim, which I take to be stronger than any claims of which I am aware to serve purposes transcending or subverting those of the institution or of the larger "system" from within, renders the question of criticism (of *its* possible independent stakes, motivations or professions) moot. Without suggesting that Fish's view now uncontentiously prevails, it is a view that will continue to trouble my own account. Insofar as I try to confront this compellingly categorical claim, I shall not do so in the name of anti-professionalism, but of a renewed commitment to the critical profession. Implicitly, I shall also consider whether the claim exclusively to interpret forestalls criticism rather than enabling it.

A renewed commitment to the critical profession can't include any attempt to revive the critic as a Coriolanus figure able or even wanting to go it alone, nor can it entail relinquishment of the resources, standards and collective enterprises of the profession. Nor can there be any question of reinstating old critical dictatorships of taste or opinion, or of claiming to mediate "the best that is thought and felt." Conceptions of critical activity as that of the poet *manqué* or of the ostensibly disinterested leisure-class reader are also not to be contemplated, any more than is the simplistic notion of the critic as licensed butcher of sacred cows. Yet the disavowal of these possibilities as defining ones for the critical profession shouldn't blind us to the persistence of some of the underlying impulses – "imaginative," affective, evaluative, mediatory – as ones continuously repressed or merely unacknowledged in the current practice of professional criticism. (Even Paul de Man's supercilious dismissal of the "chitchat of evaluation" is a contribution to that chitchat.)[3] Disclosure of these atavisms, as well as a possible self-criticism or attempted transformation arising from the disclosure, might paradoxically constitute a more accountable and self-interrogative criticism than that now generally practiced, in which responsibility is either diffused throughout the institution, subordinated to one or other partisan claim, or relinquished to one or other supposedly constraining "discourse." To require accountability isn't necessarily to reinstate the individual critic as the perfectly free agent determining his/her own practice, but rather to insist on the recurrent and possibly obscure *volition* that binds us individually to these practices even as we are shaped and bound by them.

In addition to imagining this "responsible" criticism, however, and perhaps as its corollary, I envisage the persistence of a relatively unconstrained critical function (or "will") in the profession, in doing so formally acknowledging or if necessary reinventing the critical function as one of free general commentary – of exploration, assent, dissent, and judgment – but also as one existing in no systematically corroborative or adversarial relation to professionalism and its institutions, which, as Fish unassailably points out, are enabling as well as restrictive. It is a function that implies no attempt on the part of the critic to assume a fixed position outside the system, however the system is conceived – a position almost pathetically claimed by some of Fish's antagonists[4] – but does allow for periodic questioning of the professional canons, for moments of un-authorized commentary, and for periodic departures from a professional interchange now increasingly taking on the look of highly ritualized display – all the more so for its now strictly codified transgressions. Fidelity to the essay as the definitive working form of the critic, a form committed in its very name to the enactment of the critical process and/or to the acknowledgment of doubt, may also be seen as a token of commitment to the critical profession.

The critical function I advocate may further be envisaged as one permitting a certain interplay between naive seeing (or perhaps tabooed empirical knowing) and authorized discourse, an interplay, fictional or otherwise, without which the critical principle succumbs helplessly to a powerfully renascent institutional authoritarianism. The function of criticism at the *present* time may thus include speaking naively against particular theoretical or institutional conceptions of abstract generality or constraining necessity – of which the self-proclaimed sophistication is often the one supposed immanent guarantee – but also *for* particular conceptions as the case might require, even if the condition of doing so is to engage in a certain primitive fundamentalism. And it might finally include some consideration, however unpoverishing, of what "we" might be capable, not of assimilating theoretically, but of embodying or acknowledging in fact. It is precisely in the context of a hegemonizing professionalism and/or of a masquerade of positions within it that the fiction, if that is what it must be called, of the unconstrained critical profession might regain its vitality and even re-establish its value. If these prospects are illusory, it will not take long for that to appear, but their preemptive denial might lead one to suppose that a fundamentally anti-critical regulation of professional discourse is now in the making. (In the name of what, if not of the profession itself?) To suppose, moreover, that the one interest never for a single moment negotiable by "us," whatever our possible claims to the contrary, is that of the professional hegemony itself.

Whether the critical function I have sketched can produce results of any value remains to be seen. I do however contend for the notion of temporality and hence for a local history of critical phenomena including that of theory; it is in the context of that local history that I present my own case, one comprising both a series of critical attempts ("essays") and a linking narrative. My purpose is to suggest how these critical attempts, making their appeal within the particular field, are also attempts through the encounter with literary texts in a given field to uphold the critical function defined above. Some disclosure of motive and situation, normally assumed to exist but not recognized as pertinent to the professional result, may also facilitate an answer to the question, "Do we still want to speak of ourselves as critics?" Perhaps, too, an answer to the questions: "Who are 'we' that profess to be critics?" "Who are we *now*, that profess to be critics?" Or yet again – and perhaps this is the most appropriate way of asking the question – "Who or what is at present identified by the ubiquitous 'we' of critical discourse?"

To take the plunge, then, I will begin by recording that, while working on a book on Spenser, I unexpectedly found the critical and scholarly aspects of the undertaking splitting apart (the taken for granted critical-scholarly-theoretical synthesis also resolving again into its elements), and not only splitting apart but polarizing themselves in terms of the now outmoded and professionally almost unintelligible antithesis between criticism and scholarship. Confronting *that* antithesis was to recall, not without uneasiness, some of its half-forgotten contexts.

It was for a start to recall the intensely suspicious and finally quixotic attitude to "scholarship," maintained in the name of criticism, of F.R. Leavis and *Scrutiny*. That attitude could, it is true, be expressed as a mild counsel of perfection; it was so, for example, by R.G. Cox in a *Scrutiny* review of Rosamund Tuve's *A Reading of George Herbert*.[5] Taking it that Tuve "stands squarely for *control* of criticism by scholarly information" (my emphasis), Cox observes that "Tuve's optimism hardly allows for the many instances of scholarship used to support critical prejudices which remain unconscious or unacknowledged."[6] If this domination of criticism by scholarly "information" had therefore to be repudiated in principle, the benign relationship between criticism and scholarship was envisaged by Cox as a mutually supportive one between "informed criticism and scholarship which answers genuine critical questions." In practice, however, this formula hardly constituted a solution ("genuine" critical questions, for example, here being understood to mean almost anything but institutionally generated ones) and the priority as well as privilege of criticism was the bone of violently exhilarating contention for Leavis himself.

To recall that was also to recall what had facilitated this elevation of criticism, namely a general devaluation of supposedly empty ideas or theories as opposed to lived experience, the latter taken to be *embodied* in literature and revealed by an analytical practice for which prior real-life experience was the inescapably tautologous prerequisite. To recognize the "life" of the literary text, in other words, or to distinguish between texts possessing life and those lacking it, prior firsthand experience of life "itself" was indispensable. Those who had not really lived (intellectuals as a class, for example) were called on to admit their incapacity, but were given the paradoxical reassurance that the deficiency could be remedied, not by plunging belatedly into life, but by reading the works of fiction (notably those of D.H. Lawrence, of course) in which the presence of life intensely manifested itself. Under these circumstances, however, the prospect that criticism could ever seriously be informed by scholarship was illusory; the real informing presence and adjudicating principle was that of an imperiously asserted life.

Repetition of this history was one of the threatened unappealing consequences of reinvoking the criticism–scholarship distinction. (Scholarship however being defined by Cox in unproblematic terms that I will accept for the duration as a knowledge- or information-producing practice.) Reopening Leavis's war on two fronts, first against the supposedly moribund conventionalism of practically all institutional learning, the language of which was to be regarded quite simply as the language of death, and then against the pseudo-intellectual production of "mere" ideas, would not just have been quixotic in itself but would have been to confront the demand, repeated with ever greater insistence throughout Leavis's career, that he come through with something positive or concrete to justify his critical negativism. It was a demand Leavis himself recognized:

> It would be very innocent of us to be surprised by the frequency with which we are asked to "show our colours" . . . indeed, this very formulation came first from Mr George Santayana, and others whom we respect have repeated it in substance, since. We should have thought that we had amply made out our case (if one were needed) for holding the assertion and application of serious standards in literary criticism to be an essential function.[7]

Yet it was precisely the essentializing of the "function" – the action that gives Leavis an argument but also takes it away – that can be said finally to have done the project in. Not only was a critical practice conducted in the name of principle rather than of methodological first principles institutionally discounted, but the requirement that the critic ·come through with something more than a name or a recurrently asserted principle could even be reapplied to fictional characters, as it was by Hugh Kenner in 1955. Writing about Stephen Dedalus as the figure of the failed or blocked artist, Kenner complained that "the meaningless word *life* recurs and recurs [in Dedalus's speech]."[8]

None of this made for comfortable recollection. Nor did the alleged existence of an English *critical* style per se as opposed to an American theoretical or professional one. In the terms of this opposition, the Anglophone critical phenomenon as such was to be identified with a certain "English" *sprezzatura* and belle-lettrism, with disdain for so-called pedantry, with free and easy social as well as literary criticism, and with sublime indifference to theory, to sustained analysis, and to the articulation of any coherent critical position. Such was criticism. Whatever it was that went on in American universities could be regarded only as a phenomenon of indiscriminate production, of conspicuous, justifying, and preferably endless work, and of fully articulated but always equally academic positions. This kind of distinction could still belatedly be invoked by Empson in a review of essays written for the Marvell tercentenary in 1978 – belatedly no less in the context of prevailing *English* criticism than in any other – as could the supposition that criticism written by Englishmen about "their" own literature is the only kind normatively at home with its subject: "Most of the critics I blame here are foreigners [i.e. Americans] . . . the English have not the American theoretical drive."[9] (The latter phrase was not of course meant to diagnose a failing of English criticism.) If anything was importantly at stake for Empson in this nationalistic opposition, his reinvoking it in 1978 entailed the pathos of doing so after history had already decided against the (always implicitly class-determined) English thing, apparently in favor of the American and/or cosmopolitan one.

Going through any of that again would not only have been pointless, but it might have meant embarking on an endless regression in quest of the true critical principle. A regression, in other words, through the positive phase of a criticism practiced in the name of life, through the negative phase represented by Arnold's "criticism of life," through possible earlier phases marked by canonical names (Coleridge, Johnson, Dryden, Sidney), and all in quest of a principle becoming increasingly dehistoricized, decontextualized, disembodied and finally occult. A principle tending, moreover, to become increasingly withdrawn from defining oppositions such as those to "theory" or to "scholarship." Persistence in this quest promised to result, at best, in the positing of a principle that might result in a critical dialectic of giving and withholding, of showing forth and occulting, but never in a practice capable of delivering the goods. And if there were other routes along which the professed critic might travel, it seemed as if the destination would always be the same: the critic as poet doubly *manqué*; as Dedalus doubly blocked.

There is no doubt a way in which the question can be turned around to make it one about professedly *un*principled activity going on under the name of criticism – activity of the kind that has in recent years been advocated from various devil's disciple positions and characterized as "rhetorical" or "political," but with a sophistical razzle-dazzle that has characteristically not known quite what to make of itself. The question can also be turned around to make it one about what, in the absence of principle, enables criticism to distinguish itself, for instance, from interpretive theory – and about what would make one even want to hold onto the distinction. Attempting to turn the question round promised no very gratifying result, however, since good "unprincipled" answers (political, institutional, or methodological ones anticipating the question) are on record, and the question of principle is very widely taken to have been mooted.

And yet criticism is the thing continuing to be professed or willed here, difficulties notwithstanding. The context rather than the cause to be invoked is that of the present, and of my own perception of a weakening and temporal deracination of theory, especially where theory can be translated to mean institutionally contained, gutted or already-circumvented radical critiques. The loss of critical point if not of refinement *in* the field of theory not only gave a fundamentalist turn to my own interests, but seemed to bring up the question of self-constituted critical principle and practice all over again, as if it were new, and as if it had been submerged in that of theory all along. It might, I thought, be worth risking the charge of presumption in trying to deal with the case as I was beginning to perceive it (or in constituting myself as a medium), but could the somewhat aberrant critical form of my narrative be recognized as legitimate?

At the time of writing, there were of course precedents for anomalous forms, for so-called marginal or preliminary texts, and for aberrant performances. The fallout from Derrida's stylistically explosive performances and from deconstruction generally was still to be seen everywhere in the profession, not least at its highest level. But precedents of that kind were no longer helpful, either in general (what were those forms now doing for anyone?) or in the particular case. Although the critical language of poststructuralism, deconstruction above all, could be said to have emerged as the dominant cosmopolitan one, having irreversibly and enrichingly pervaded Anglo-American critical idiom after the initial overblown afflatus of too-literal translation had diminished, punctilious observance of the forms at this stage could serve no imaginable purpose. Given the existence of a new situation, moreover, or the possibility of defining one, what would meet it?

The temporizing solution that suggested itself was that of writing a critical case history. To do so would be to display some evidence without claiming either to determine its final significance or to draw irresistible conclusions. In the medical sense of the term, a case history may or may not possess general significance, may or may not allow a textbook pathology to be established, and this provisional quality seemed most appropriate in the given circumstances. Limited interpretation of that history, such as I have in fact undertaken, would hardly preclude further or other interpretations, assuming that the case was of any interest at all. The idea of the case history, with critical essays constituting the "evidence," is therefore one to which I have partly adhered. Yet the term "case history" is at least potentially ambiguous, allowing criminal as well as pathological investigation to be invoked. (The two procedures are not wholly unrelated, and the ambiguity allows a degree of suspense about whether "crime" or "illness" is in question when the same evidence can point in both directions.) So the investigative sense of the term is also one that I invoke, almost, it might be said, to the exclusion of the medical one since the *polis* rather than the *psyche* is the subject of this book. Yet if I seek to retain a double sense of the term, it is partly to preserve its vital indeterminacy and partly because it allows for some shuttling between the roles of agent and patient, another form of critical interchange that I would want to advocate.

The *narrative* form of the investigative case history recommended itself to me partly because of the unexpected oddity of a conclusion to which I had come about Puttenham,[10] a conclusion that seemed to call for some backtracking of the route along which I had travelled, but also because the critical history I ("we"?) were now living seemed to be in increasingly urgent need of recontextualization and reappraisal. One of many occasions on which this was brought home was that of a panel discussion at Johns Hopkins in 1984. A distinguished Parisian who may benefit from anonymity in this instance still spoke of "May 1968" as an epochal unmasking of bourgeois democracy, the beginning of a *novus ordo seclorum*. This "mistake" was, it is true, corrected by Richard Rorty, who suggested that the events of May 1968 don't count, and never did so, in the history of expanding freedom and perpetual betterment that we, as liberal democrats, prefer to tell in a world in which one fairytale is as good as another. Yet both the Parisian error and its Princetonian correction left room for further discussion, either because there are other stories that it might be possible to tell or because of the difficulty of lending any conviction to those still being told in the names of the radical and liberal visions respectively. Even while continuing to "do" criticism or philosophy as the case might be, a stronger effort to contextualize these doings seemed incumbent if this fatigued repetition were to be avoided – or if overwhelming intellectual reaction were to be admitted as the possible truth of "our" history.

I use the term "case history," then, primarily to describe my own effort, the appropriateness of which it is not for me to judge, to reappraise a particular critical history from the vantage point of my own experience. But is the case that of criticism in general or of the particular critic?. Of a developing individual pathology or (to extend the normal use of the term "case history" somewhat) of an investigation in progress? This remains to be seen. I shall add only that the case implicitly under investigation, within admittedly narrow limits befitting the activity of literary detection, is that of the English Renaissance author – of the meaning of his (her?) literary performance and also of "our" present ability to construe it.

I may have been led without realizing it towards academic detection, and hence to a form of criticism not professionally institutionalized, by having read Leonardo Sciascia's admirable novellas, *The Day of the Owl* and *Equal Danger*, shortly before making my own "discovery."[11] These works, particularly *Equal Danger*, are detective fictions written very atypically from a left standpoint, and among the possibilities they include is that of the detective's becoming virtually a surrogate for the criminal he hunts, or of seeing his own image momentarily but exactly reflected in the face of the killer. (Detective in the work of Sciascia meaning professional policeman rather than the elegant amateur, "supplementing" the always inadequate regular police, of reactionary fantasy.) The logic of this situation, which includes the oedipal possibility of the detective's double role as pursuer and criminal, began to seem compelling. Sciascia's prompting results in my own work, it is true, in a procedure of reversed priorities, since it is as if the investigation, spurred only by a taint in the air, begins before the existence of any crime has been demonstrated. In the order of my presentation, unlike Sciascia's, the quest for a criminal is also a quest for a crime. Yet this inverted order of priorities has its own logic, and may even claim a small share in the legitimacy conferred by *Hamlet*, which, as a work of detective fiction, proceeds in the same order.

Although recourse to the detective format may seem to require that something will eventually be proved beyond shadow of doubt, the models referred to above are ones that may be taken to question the possibility of such an outcome. In *Hamlet*, what is proved in the mousetrap-play is only what Hamlet knows long before it is proved, and the proof (apart from the curious motivations that lead Hamlet to acquire it) seems to make no fundamental difference to the situation. In Sciascia, moreover, it isn't what can be proved but what can't that becomes the object of interest. If there is a conceptual aspect to the "discovery" that begins to be made in the course of my own book, and is finally claimed towards the end of it, it is the discovery of the "unprovable" as a category. A forever dubious category, no doubt, since the unprovable can always be dismissed as the merely unproven, yet I don't take this category to be a stable, metaphysical one. I take it rather to be an institutional-political category: the "unprovable" is what can't be proved – or can barely be shown – given existing discursive and evidential conventions, but also given a particular institutionalized structure of legitimation, reward and punishment. What is "unprovable" may thus be insusceptible to proof either for methodological reasons or (relatedly) because it would make no political sense to try and prove it. Proof would either make no difference in the particular circumstances or else be attainable only at seemingly prohibitive cost. Whether the category of the unprovable is accordingly one of virtual nullity or of disturbing import remains in question, and this indeterminacy will undoubtedly be reflected in the shape and tone of my argument.

Although some further justification for the critical anomaly of detection (or of yielding to the detective impulse) will appear in due course, some questions of legitimacy raised by the form of this book can't be settled in advance or perhaps even after the fact. The book of critical essays, with or without linking narrative, is properly conceived at present as the form suitable to the critic of assured eminence. The interest of the case is understood to reside in the reflections, underwritten by exceptional accomplishment and significant experience, of the particular person; entitlement to the privileged form is implicitly taken to be earned through incontestable prior achievement in more regular forms of systematic professional investigation (in the field of the provable). Frequently, moreover, the essays collected are already ones that have exerted an influence powerful enough in their fields to make their permanent availability in a collection desirable. None of these conditions, of course, applies here. In seeking to make this form one of paradoxical anonymity despite recourse to the first person, I hope to suggest that there is at least a certain level at which the critical act can be conceived as impersonal in principle; as strictly anonymous in the sense that the "I" who speaks is not so much a "real presence" or a possessor of his/her own critical discourse as its medium. Only on the basis of that entitlement – the acceptability of which must remain precisely one of the things in question – can the discussion proceed without succumbing to fatal accusations of bad form. And insofar as the form of the essay is here taken seriously as an exploratory one, entailing both the activity of reviewing and of tentative critical rehearsal, its justification must arise from the defined circumstances under which the *given*, both ideologically and professionally conceived, is exactly what constitutes the ongoing major problem.

Although unavoidably particular, and personally formulated, then, the history to follow aims without undue "personality" to be that of criticism during the past decade, particularly criticism written about the English literature of the sixteenth century. As a history of this criticism, it might be said to have begun in 1980, in a conversation I recall with Stanley Fish. The subject was that of the paradigms available for interpreting sixteenth- and seventeenth-century English literature respectively, and it seemed that while there were strong paradigms for reading the English seventeenth century (including ones established by S.F.!) the same could not be said for the English sixteenth century. Terms like "the language of prose comedy," "the eloquent 'I'," "self-consuming artifacts," "the reader in the text," "voices of melancholy," and "the illusion of power" all stood for critical names and projects that had within reasonable limits, and for the moment, mastered the canonical literature of the seventeenth century.[12] Each phrase also represented a "trenchant distinction" of the kind that Fish has more recently although not explicitly promoted as the definitive mark of critical achievement.[13] But none of this applied to the sixteenth century. Although there was no shortage of good work on particular sixteenth-century texts and authors – on Raleigh, Spenser, Sidney and Lyly for example[14] – a certain lack of critical perspective still seemed to characterize discussion of sixteenth-century literature. The "plain style" and the "drab" versus "golden" paradigms of Yvor Winters and C.S. Lewis respectively had long since yielded all they were capable of yielding (not programs for reading, as it turned out). William Empson's work in *Seven Types of Ambiguity* and *Some Versions of Pastoral* had inaugurated a program of close reading and of attention to the pastoral genre that had resulted in notable work on Spenser by Harry Berger, Jr and Paul Alpers, but long before 1980 the impetus given by Empson had waned. Radical critiques of high-cultural artifice, of urbane pastoralism, and of ideological fabrications of the natural had also fundamentally challenged the categories of this enterprise, bringing it at least to a temporary halt. (Very temporarily if at all in the case of Berger's protean work.) And while good non-programmatic work on sixteenth-century authors and topics appeared, as it regularly did, something still seemed to be missing. The mass of critical theory that had accumulated by 1980 promised successful applications, but these had been slow to appear. (Perhaps the most notable such application appeared shortly afterwards, however, with Jonathan Goldberg's pathbreaking discussion of Spenser in *Endlesse Worke*.)[15] If "self-fashioning" as a key term for understanding the literary goals and performances of sixteenth-century authors had begun to make an impact – Stephen Greenblatt's book generally enunciating that conception and also, interestingly, avowing its author's own stake in it, had appeared in 1980 – its full assimilation had not yet taken place. Even when it did so there were important aspects of Greenblatt's case that seemed, as I will suggest in due course, to go unnoticed.[16]

It may seem to readers that only dogmatic slumberers could still in 1980 have been complaining about paradigm deficiency in the criticism of sixteenth-century English literature. It may also seem as if the complaint was invidious or prejudicial to much work that had by then been done with sixteenth-century texts; prejudicial even to the enormous achievements of Renaissance scholarship in the fields of rhetoric, iconology, intellectual history, and comparative literature, in comparison with which the presence or absence of simplifying critical paradigms might be insignificant. But such facts are to be recorded in a case history. More to the purpose, that complaint was very quickly overtaken by the triumphs of feminism and historicism, particularly the latter, in the field of sixteenth-century literature.

As a history, the narrative that follows is to a significant degree one of encounter with, and ambivalence towards, historicism. The historicism in question isn't one that I will try to define in advance except to say that it entails the now-familiar supposition that the definitive contexts of literary interpretation are historical ones. This supposition, which might still be called that of the "old historicism," is, however, complicated in the "new historicism" by the poststructuralist critique of any belief in history or context prior to textualization and hence self-imposed rather than interpretively constructed or always and already *written*. Historical texts, narratives, or reconstructions (always plural) are, in other words, incapable of determining literary meaning, though they may inform and be informed by literary texts. Varying degrees of accommodation to this poststructuralist critique are apparent in the practice of historicism, which, as Louis Montrose has recently pointed out, tends to be theoretically reticent.[17] I will suggest, I think justifiably, that recent historicist *practice* in the criticism of English Renaissance literature has been sufficiently sustained and productive to call for recognition beyond the boundaries of the field (not to say that it hasn't already, and hasn't been practiced in other fields as well) but that recognition can now profitably be accompanied by appraisal.

One prompting, from my own point of view, to engage in appraisal arises from the fact that no special criteria, no proper discourse, and above all no autonomy of the literary work are acknowledged in historicism, which accordingly seeks to absorb literary texts into the total ensemble of political discourses and/or ideological significations at a particular historical moment. The threatened disappearance of the literary – however idly threatened while the convention persists that the works in question, although no longer called literary or invidiously segregated, must be discussed in an atemporal mode designated by the present tense of critical writing – this *threatened* disappearance is what prompts a return in some of the ensuing chapters to temporarily suspended rather than superseded questions of classical poetics; to reconsideration, moreover, of strategies, powers and impulses that reveal their effect in literary composition. This re-engagement implies no logical commitment to the text as self-sufficient object or to any particular list of canonical works, but rather to the literary or specifically poetic phenomenon, capable in principle of manifesting itself in any work even if it is characteristically avowed, consciously embodied, or foregrounded in many works that we already designate as "literary." *Contra* historicism, in other words, the *object* of literary criticism is not the historical period or its particular ensemble of significations and cultural–political strategies, but rather the phenomenon of *poesis* both in and *as* those significations and strategies. In principle *poesis* can, in other words, manifest itself in any form of discursive practice although the determination of its presence, as well as the revelation of its powerful and continuous manifestation within the work, may remain the contentious task of criticism. And if working definitions of *poesis* are needed to get on with, I take them to be more than adequately supplied in the Renaissance works to which I will be referring: vaticination as prophesying and hence willing the existence of that which may come to be (poetics is future-oriented or it is nothing); *poesis* as "making;" *poesis* as personifying; and *poesis* as representing that which is normally mute, absent or un-conceived (*prosopopeia*). Without *poesis* as its object, literary criticism can hardly be professed, and even if constructive faith in this object can't continuously be sustained or insisted upon, its prolonged absence or diplomatic denial eventually renders the literary-critical position untenable. At a certain moment, which I take to have arrived, the profession has explicitly to be renewed or abandoned. Once this profession is made, moreover, criticism forfeits the luxury of any theoretically independent position from which it may, dispassionately survey the literary phenomenon.

In keeping with these assumptions and professions, I will adhere as far as possible to the term "construe" rather than "interpret" to describe the activity of critical reading, partly because "construction" is akin to poetic "making," but also because interpretation, whether in theory or observable practice, implies the priestly–political–legalistic activity of going between the pre-constituted source of authority (the text, for example) and its lay recipients. Admittedly, the *institutionalized* intermediary position of the interpreter can be reconceived in at least two ways: first, as the politically strong one from which the form of authority and the nature of the recipient community can be dictated, and, second, as one at the center of a closed field in which interpretations circulate and hierarchies are established with only nominal acknowledgment of the go-between role. Yet even these reimaginings do not change the commitment of the interpreter to the principle of authority, and hence to the justification of established power. It is with this perpetual justi-fication of power that criticism simply cannot afford to identify itself, no matter how problematical its relationships to established forms of power are bound to remain.

For practical purposes, each of the documents constituting the following case history can be read independently of the critical narrative, though each is also contextualized in the narrative. I have not included any work, published or unpublished, that I would now reject in its own terms; it would be insulting to expect readers to take seriously work reclaimed from a discard file. So even if particular essays represent "mistakes" from the standpoint of the narrative conclusion, they don't on that account fall by the wayside. A foreclosure of critical possibilities isn't the purpose of this narrative. The structure of this book implies, moreover, a certain need by indirections to find directions out – a process in which no direction is proven wrong until *one* direction is proven right, and in which initial skepticism about the supposedly right directions (the map or instructions as given) may remain unconquered to the end.

It remains now only to be said that my narrative incorporation of this series of essays brings with it at least one intractable problem. Given that the separate essays were written at different times and for different occasions, while the framing narrative incorporating them was written last and with the benefit of hindsight, the book embodies different temporal perspectives: those of a succession of lived moments and that of a general retrospect. The essays were certainly not written under any prophetic conception of a history in which they were always and already subsumed, nor with any claim to privileged distance from the scenes of critical action in which they were produced. Correspondingly, the narrative could be wise only after the event. Yet this distinction is less than perfect. No single essay was written (how could it be so?) without being informed, in whatever limited degree, by a notion of its temporality and by a distinction between critical means and ends. And the narrative retrospect doesn't belong to a wholly different order of time and purpose from that of the essays. Moments of temporal merging and/or indeterminacy can't therefore be wholly eliminated from the book. All I can repudiate in advance is an unwanted formal effect of privileged insight or foresight attending these mergers, an effect proper only to the kind of teleological plot that this book emphatically does not embody.

1
The politics of theater (I)

This paper, which for merely chronological reasons appears as the first document in the history to be recorded, was written in the flow of discussion, published and otherwise, about the nature of Renaissance theatricality and about the politics and/or cultural anthropology of Renaissance theater. If this discussion can be said to have developed under a general rubric, it was that of "the powers and limits of subversion." The rethinking of subversion can by the same token be identified as an important revision through which radical (sometimes Marxist) literary criticism of the sixties becomes a different kind of criticism, one to which the term "reactionary" may or may not be appropriate, but which in any case has a significant bearing on the question of who "we" may claim to be or to work for. The issue of subversion remained frequently if not always explicitly at stake in discussions of the political functioning of the English public theater, of the centrality of theatrical forms and practices to the cultural politics of Renaissance England, of role-playing and theatricalization of the "self."[1] All these were developing topics, taken to be of fundamental importance in any attempt to read Renaissance texts in their historical setting. If the importance of these topics had to a very significant degree been established by the work of Stephen Greenblatt, it was he, too, who had most powerfully inaugurated a reconsideration of apparently subversive, countercultural and/or counterauthoritarian representation in important Renaissance works, including those of Shakespeare.[2]

The result of this questioning wasn't to affirm the subversive power of the works or particular representations in question (both "subversive" and "power" needing to be taken as operative words here) but rather to suggest the ability of dominant cultural structures and/or political formations to generate and absorb their own forms of subversion. If Shakespeare's own allegiances, for example, were impossible to determine, his plays might nevertheless display both the prevailing forms of subversion and the ability of the "system" to assimilate and neutralize them. Or, to put it in slightly different terms, Shakespeare's plays could not fail to participate in a cultural dialectic in which the moment of subversion would be a moment only, not a politics (let alone a fixed authorial stance) in its own right.

Such arguments obviously constituted a critique of claims widely repeated in the previous two decades (broadly "the sixties") about the powerfully subversive or essentially countercultural nature of major literary works. If the revisionary arguments of Greenblatt and others have in turn been criticized as ones reifying the forms of order and authority that generate and successfully absorb their own subversion[3] – if they have, in other words, been criticized as a quasi-totalitarian misrepresentation of political situations in which power is always divided and resistance is unforeclosed – they have nevertheless compelled a close re-examination of Renaissance texts and have in salutary fashion challenged the sentimental and ultimately sterile mystique of pure subversion.

Dealing with the "politics of theater" question in this essay amounted to a tacit acknowledgment of the extent to which that topic had become compelling in the Renaissance field, but what was on the horizon at that time, and remains so throughout this book even if its recognition was delayed in the writing, is the question of whether the only kind of thinking now capable of being effected is the counterrevolutionary thinking of containment – the thinking contingent, that is to say, on the fact if not always on the recognition of failed or thwarted revolution. By "thinking of containment" I now mean not only the process of thinking or legislating new forms of containment into existence (a process that occurs simultaneously in the fields of theory and institutional–political management) but of the mere supposition of containment that is now apparent across practically the entire academic spectrum (is indeed so pervasive as to have become virtually naturalized).

If the "thinking of containment" as a positive enterprise is one that can be associated with the name of Foucault, it was paradoxically in criticism self-defined as radical or liberating that the mere supposition of containment first struck me as most damagingly revealing itself. "Problematization," "subversion," "contestation" and "transgression," for example, all began to seem like terms in the ordinary use of which prohibitive containment, and sometimes the unalterable lawfulness or fatefulness of that containment, are virtually conceded. The terms thus seem logically to facilitate only trapped, guilty, or masochistic dis-courses, not liberating ones, while the actual discourses in question are ones in which a power or principle of transformation seems seldom to be desired or imagined. None of these putatively liberating conceptions can, in other words, ever suffice, since they are, and seem destined to remain, governed by disabling presuppositions.

Even in Marxist critical discourse, it appears that the uses to which Gramsci, Bakhtin and Althusser, for example, have been put (and maybe those authors themselves) facilitate a transition to undialectical thinking, thus saving/betraying a Marx suspected, perhaps with secret unease, of lacking "sophistication" (it has been said) or of being timebound. ("Marxism exists in nineteenth-century thought like a fish in water," wrote Foucault, forestalling, one would have thought, any Marxist attempt to co-opt his work or finesse the question, "[it is] unable to breathe anywhere else.")[4] Betraying a discourse in order to save it may admittedly have to be regarded as an inescapable condition of its prolongation – if it is to remain the same, it can do so only by becoming other – but the question of whether this diplomatic betrayal constitutes a fatal departure or contradiction of logical principle must remain under periodic review if the enterprise is to be worth pursuing.

"Worth pursuing" is the implied answer to the still-unasked question in the following essay, although the explicit questions of the essay as well as its conclusions were overwhelmingly determined by the state of play in the Renaissance field. In that context, George Puttenham's *The Arte of English Poesie* (1589) could be read as a pertinent work – as one embodying, as if in anticipation of Vico, a general anthropology to which the forms of art are central. It also presented models of poetic and dramatic containment that could be brought into play in the discussion of cultural politics, not indeed as explanations but as mediations between modern anthropological and/or political discourse and the phenomenon of the sixteenth-century theater. My own paper implicitly considers "the limits of subversion" from the standpoint of this sixteenth-century text on cultural politics.

The hegemonic theater of George Puttenham

In *Homo Ludens*, Johan Huizinga practically dismissed the Renaissance notion of the theater of the world as an effete topos of Neoplatonism – implicitly, as debilitated metaphysics even in its most worldly guise as political theater.[5] In doing so, he opened the way to his own quasi-anthropological treatment of play as a phenomenon no longer theatrically determined in the first instance. Whatever we may think of the outcome, his restoration of theater to a place *in* the world may prompt us to reconsider the extent to which we, by contrast – even in our most apparently unrelenting analyses of the Elizabethan and Jacobean political scenes – have again become prisoners of the topos. Do we, on one hand, exaggerate the explanatory power of the theatrical metaphor, and on the other effect a totalizing assimilation of the political order to the theatrical one – virtually to that of court theater – and in doing so suppress other categories of political interpretation? Or simply lose sight of everything that courtly "theater" fails to include?

If George Puttenham, nominal author of *The Arte of English Poesie* (1589), enables us to pursue such reflections as these, he does so in a very limited and paradoxical way. His own *Arte* testifies as strongly as any document of its time to the intense theatricality of Elizabethan courtly-political life,[6] and hence to the possible constitutiveness of the theatrical "metaphor." Yet Puttenham doesn't lose sight of the phenomenon of theater as one material institution among others in the world. Nor does he evade recognition of what, with glancing reference to the terminology of Antonio Gramsci,[7] we might call the hegemonic *necessity* inherent in any enduring situation of political inequality or class antagonism, a necessity by no means fully discharged by public spectacle and the opulent theatricalization of royal power.

To say this isn't to claim Puttenham, of all people, as a Gramscian before his time, nor is it to suggest that we find in Puttenham's work any full-scale anticipation of Gramsci's conception of hegemony. It is only to suggest that Puttenham's account – which is also categorically an account of theater *in* the world – implies a view of theater as a major hegemonic institution of the state; as one more important, in a sense, than the state's formal apparatus of legal, educational and bureaucratic institutions. The arresting implication arising from Puttenham's history of the dramatic forms is that public drama – and hence public theater – alone possesses the ability to institute hegemonic control in a situation otherwise insusceptible to "enlightened" or "lawful" rule, albeit rule in the manifest interests of a ruling *class*.[8] By dramatic and hence theatrical means alone can the otherwise ungovernable populace be persuaded to relinquish its own desires, to suppress its antagonism to its self-elected rulers, and to become essentially self-regulating.

Puttenham's discussion of drama is of course only a part (even a small part, though that isn't without significance) of a larger discussion of poetry in the world. This discussion is informed at every point by commonplace Renaissance–neoclassical conceptions of poetic form and function, and the affinities between Puttenham's conceptions and those of Sidney, for example, are obvious.[9] But the value of Puttenham's discussion from my point of view arises from his narrative rearticulation of these commonplaces in such a way as to present a unified theory of cultural politics, and it is in the course of that rearticulation that his conception of a "hegemonic theater" emerges. After attempting a critical rehearsal of Puttenham's exposition, I shall try to suggest some ways in which Puttenham's account may inform, if not form, our own conceptions.

The Arte of English Poesie begins, as readers will recall, by narrating the origin and succession of the poetic genres. This narrative of origin also discloses the logical necessity under which the poetic forms subsist in the world, and is thus capable of being described, albeit erroneously, since a poetic onto-theology is involved, as an evolutionary narrative by Puttenham's modern editors. As Puttenham conceives them, the poetic forms (hymn, epic, pastoral, etc.) are transcendentally founded, and they persist culturally in the context of certain timeless occasions – such as those of heroic action, love, marriage, and death – to each of which a proper decorum corresponds. The dramatic genres, in contrast to the poetic ones, are *politically* instituted from the beginning. The standard dramatic genres, which, for Puttenham, are those of satire (*sic*), comedy and tragedy, originate in typical, successive phases of communal development leading from the most primitive to the most sophisticated of human polities. Not only does a particular dramatic form correspond to each phase of development, but each form arises only in reaction to a radical threat to the maintenance of "good order" in the particular community. By implication, the persistence of any dramatic form is not the result of its ontologically determined necessity, but of the persistence of typical threats to good order. There is thus a fundamental difference in the character and status of the poetic and dramatic genres. This difference remains ineffaceable despite Puttenham's attempt to incorporate both within the same history and despite his characterization of authentic dramatic forms as those of dramatic *poesie*, thus bringing them under a general poetics.

For Puttenham, as for many of his humanist contemporaries, "poesie" originates in, or recapitulates, the creative will and/or inspiring presence of the Divine Mind:

> A Poet is as much to say as a maker ... . Such as (by way of resemblance and reuerently) we may say of God: who without any trauell [work, or movement away from itself into the temporal spacing of representation] to his diuine imagination, made all the world of nought ... Euen so the very Poet makes and contriues out of his owne braine, both the verse and matter of his poeme, and not by any foreine copie or example ... If they do it by instinct diuine or naturall, then surely much fauored from aboue.[10]

Whether this "poesie" manifests itself as vatic utterance or through the faculty of the poetic "maker," its good origin secures it in its essence throughout its subsequent history. But the same does not apply to drama, not even in its guise as dramatic poetry. In the beginning, there is no drama. What first constitutes the human polity (if polity is the word for it at this stage) is an essentially pure force of poetic persuasion. Puttenham tells us how it is "fayned," albeit authoritatively, that Amphion and Orpheus were the poets of "the first age."[11] It is also "written" (by Ovid among others, though Puttenham hardly needs to tell his audience so) that "Poesie was th'originall cause and occasion of [the] first assemblies, when before the people remained in the woods and mountains, vagarant and dispersed like the wild beasts, lawlesse and naked . . . ." While Amphion "builded vp cities, and reared walles with the stones that came in heapes to the sounde of his harpe," Orpheus instituted civility in the wilderness by his "discreete and wholsome lessons vttered in harmonie and with melodious instruments."[12] In the state of civility and humane rule thus established, the poets remained, again by virtue of their God-given faculty, the first systematic observers of the natural order, the first prophets, priests and lawgivers, the first "Philosophers, Astronomers, Historiographers and Oratours and Musitians."[13] Neither drama nor theater is yet in evidence, the malign necessity under which both emerge not yet having disclosed itself.

So the familiar story goes, in a canonical humanist poetics to the persistent cultural authority of which Rilke among others still testifies in the twentieth century in his "Sonnets to Orpheus." "In the beginning," the poet is the universal man, at once the founder and acknowledged legislator of human society, while the pure force of harmonious *language* at once constitutes and circumscribes the human community. But what is true in the beginning is ideally *always* true, and the original condition of human civility remains throughout Puttenham's account the ideal condition, one never to be superseded in the course of time. More than this, it remains the permanent if subsequently *recessive* (unacknowledged?) condition of any community that can lay claim to lawfulness or civility, and the founding poetic priesthood continues, any appearances to the contrary, to retain its prerogatives and functions even when a recognizably political order has supervened.[14]

Immediately after Puttenham's opening exposition, a break threatens to disclose itself in the narrative. It does so when Puttenham has to negotiate the transition from authoritatively "fayned" preliterate antiquity to written history; from the world of the poetic founders to that of political record. The poetic form that Puttenham situates on the threshold between two worlds is the archaic hymn sung by the primitive community to its god(s). This form is before writing; it is also written down for the first time rather than always and already written in such poems as the Psalms and Homeric hymns. Implicitly, poetry enters history uncontaminated, while the archaic poetic theocracy remains close to the world of the poetic founders. But the narrative rupture is only briefly postponed, though Puttenham finesses both it and its possible implications.

"Some," writes Puttenham, "perchance would thinke that next after the praise and honoring of their gods, should commence the worshippings and praise of good men,"[15] but this step, which might seem to be called for by the logic of poetic descent, has to be postponed on account of an unforeseen contingency. What has immediately to be reckoned with, both in the history of literary forms and in the world fashioned by the poetic priesthood, is the unaccountable manifestation of communal "vice" and "idleness."

Even if Puttenham writes as a Christian in a post-lapsarian world, and even if a Fall predating the foundation of the poetic community would have been taken for granted by Puttenham's readers (it is explicitly invoked by Thomas Wilson in his *Arte of Rhetorike*),[16] we as readers have been led to suspect no failure or *lack* in the ideal community of the poetic founding fathers. Suddenly, and perhaps catastrophically in both senses of the word, that community is one in which authority is challenged and vice threatens virtue:

> ... before that came to passe [i.e. the praising of famous men], the Poets or holy Priests, chiefly studied the rebuke of vice, and to carpe at the common abuses, such as were most offensiue to the publique and priuate, for as yet for lacke of good ciuility and wholesome doctrines, there was greater store of lewde lourdaines then of wise and learned Lords, or of noble and vertuous Princes and gouernours.[17]

Here we manifestly enter a new, bad economy, or an economy *per se*, in which a "lacke" of civility produces an unwanted surplus of "lewde lourdaines." This compensatory economy is also a *political* economy in which distinctions have appeared between the realms of public and private interest and to which the notion of the unitary "commonwealth" no longer seems to apply.

If we can perceive the moment of awkwardness for Puttenham, we can by the same token appreciate his finessing of it. He implies that no problem exists except in the mind of a reader capable of being surprised by the mere local contingency of vice or disorder in the ideal poetic commonwealth. For Puttenham, only a minor deviation in the no doubt wrongly expected course of the master-narrative is required to accommodate this contingency. It is, however, in response to *that* contingency, and within a bad political economy of lack and surplus, that drama is somewhat inauspiciously born.

Confronted by an unpersuaded and unmollified (unpropertied?) mob, the "priests" invent the first form of dramatic "reprehension," in doing so constituting drama as "reprehensive" in principle. In their attempt to curb "vice," the priests at first devise only the satirical diatribe in "plaine meetres, more like to sermons or preachings then otherwise," but the ineffectiveness – the lack of *authority* – of this form is almost immediately evident. It is in recognition of this lack that a theatrical supplement fatefully gets introduced. The "hallowed places dedicate to their gods," in which the people had assembled "because they had yet no large halles or places of conuenticle" are implicitly transformed into theaters in which the poets – or a new class of functionaries known as "recitours" – can appear masked and amplify the power of the invective:

> ... the first and most bitter inuective against vice and vicious men, was the *Satyre*: which to th'intent their bitternesse should breede none ill will, either to the Poets, or to the recitours, (which could not haue been chosen if they had bene openly knowen) and besides to make their admonitions and reproofs seeme grauer and of more efficacie, they made wise as if the gods of the woods, whom they called *Satyres* or *Siluanes*, should appeare and recite those verses of rebuke, whereas in deede they were but disguised persons vnder the shape of *Satyres*, as who would say, these terrene and base gods being conuersant with mans affaires, and spiers out of all their secret faults.[18]

In what is, for Puttenham's narrative, the unacknowledged moment of truly *political* inception, the place of communal devotion in which the people are present to themselves, their fathers and their gods, is transformed into the site of a theatrical masquerade. The moment in which the priests or their surrogates become maskers is also the one in which they decisively alienate themselves as a ruling class from the community, irrevocably politicize their own existence, and substitute the power of theatrical mechanisms for the primordial authority of the word. The transparency and immediacy of "good government" are simultaneously lost, and representation is inaugurated as misrepresentation.

Theatricality, as well as the originary dramatic form of "satyre," begins in the moment of this fall into politics (the occurrence of which it also signifies) and it remains wholly excluded from the "fayned" condition of true civility. To say now that drama is born as the *hegemonic* instrument of the ruling caste in Puttenham's account is to draw attention to its unique capacity to induce consent, or at least to institute effective control short of direct violence. The intense hostility of the populace to their self-elected rulers – a hostility that Puttenham attributes to the power of vice – necessitates the use of the mask in the first instance as a means of self-protection, shielding the "recitours" from identification, but the mask is then also found to invest the reproofs of the rulers with a "grauetie" and "efficacie" otherwise unattainable. The impersonation of the "Satyr" invests the players (as well as the puppet-masters) with a supernatural authority to which they cannot presume in their own persons, and it invests the wearers with a semblance of worldly omniscience as "spiers out" of mortal transgressions.

If Puttenham can silently approve the tactics of the rulers, it is partly because of his access to commonplace moral categories under which idleness and rebellion are *ipso facto* vicious, and partly because the political order in the process of being constituted – or hegemonically reconstituted – remains contained in its own inferior sphere, its own narrative loop. The entire history of the dramatic forms, and of everything that they imply, is encapsulated within the history of poetic forms, the integrity and magisterial succession of which it is not allowed to disturb. No "other" origin of drama, and hence no radically other way of comprehending the history of literary forms, is acknowledged by Puttenham; no doubt such possibilities are unthinkable by him, though not undreamt of by some of his dramatist contemporaries.

Drama thus remains a form of convenience in more ways than one: politically convenient in Puttenham's version of the lawful common-wealth and convenient, too, in that certain embarrassments are averted in Puttenham's own history of the poetic forms. Both the poetic persona and the phenomenon of (mis)representation enter the history of "poesie" only via the dramatic back door; to the extent that performativeness, deception or even "reprehension" might also manifest themselves in poetry, they would do so only after they had been inaugurated as phenomena of outsidedness and fallen secondariness. They would not be part of the original constitution of the poetic, nor would they ever be of the poetic essence. The integrity of poetic forms, and the integrity of the true civility that they reciprocally guarantee, remain inviolate.

As a form of convenience, drama remains bound, as one might say, to the original sin that elicits it. It remains not only bound to the forms of evil that it combats, but becomes increasingly bound to *represent* the evils that it seeks to overcome. As its forms develop beyond that of "satyre" (satire/satyr play), the "good" of drama, unlike that of poetry, comes to consist in its conquest of the evil that is present within it from the start. The defense of drama, which is never capable of embodying ideal forms for emulation,[19] accordingly becomes a more sophisticated undertaking than the defense of poetry, since it must concede the claim of Elizabethan antitheatricalists that drama is an "infectious"[20] staging of vice and promiscuity. Puttenham's implicit defense of drama concedes, in effect, that vice is always the thing represented, but it locates the salutary effect of the representation in an audience response that becomes predictable and hence capable of being engineered. This response is one in which the audience, far from being seduced by the appeal of staged vice, will imaginatively reconstitute and internalize the *law* under which criminal licentiousness remains effectively prohibited.

But this is to anticipate: such sophistications as these are latter-day ones, not foreseen in the phase of "satire." The second phase in dramatic "history" begins when the priesthood recognizes the relative ineffectiveness of satire as a form of control. Drama thus progresses, just as it originates, only when a particular lack has disclosed itself. The section on comedy (in which Puttenham distinguishes between Old and New) is introduced by the heading: "How vice was afterward reproued by two other maner of poems, better reformed then the Satyre, whereof the first was Comedy, the second Tragedie."[21] It is only after recognition of an insufficiency has occurred that it becomes possible to inaugurate the more sophisticated (better reformed) comedy. Yet this development does not occur simply as a technical adjustment. What renders satire ineffective, and at the same time creates a situation favorable to the emergence of comedy, is an advance in the form of society itself.

No longer does an embattled "priesthood" confront an unruly populace; division of labor manifests itself in the stereotypical characters of comedy that Puttenham enumerates, and a world of trade and industry has silently been inaugurated. (Apparently, too, a parasitic class of petty criminals has also arisen; Puttenham mentions, in addition to legitimate "marchants, souldiers [and] artificers," whole classes of "bawds, brokers [and] ruffians.") Perhaps the satyr-hegemony has made this social advance possible, but if so it has rendered itself obsolete. In the newly advanced society that manifests itself, "rebuke, vttered by the rurall gods out of bushes and briers" understandably produces little effect. Something more urbane is called for, and the "finer heads," as Puttenham now calls his poet-priest-politicians (or perhaps only an inner cabinet), invent comedy: "The Poets deuised to haue many parts played at once by two or three or foure persons, that debated the matters of the world ... but neuer medling with any Princes matters nor such high personages . . . ." Recognizing the gaucheries not only of the undivided satirical persona and rustic *mise-en-scène*, but also of the reprehensive dramatic monologue as a form (which is "not so popular as if it were reduced into action ... or by many voices liuely represented,") the plotters of public restraint *devise* comedy as a dialogic and fully representational form, one so naturalistic that "a man might thinke it were euen now a doing." Accompanying the emergence of comedy, pleasure and profit make their first separate appearance among the categories of Puttenham's discussion. The desired *utile* comes paradoxically to depend on *dulce* instead of remaining hopelessly at odds with it: "It was also much for the solace & recreation of the common people by reason of the pageants and shewes."

What has happened is that an irrevocable concession has been made to "popularity" – to the populace, to the "vicious" popular demand for pleasure – and the regulative power of drama must now be detoured through the process of gratification. Yet this concession is highly productive; it not only attenuates an unconquerable antagonism, but allows for far more sophisticated control. The ventriloquism of the rulers is more effectively camouflaged than it can be in the satirical masquerade, and the audience is solicited to engage itself in the issues debated in the onstage dialogue – issues that are of course presented as debatable, but of which the dramatized resolution remains under the control of the "finer heads." Finally, the audience is invited to see its own image(s) rather than those of dubious authority in the ludicrous representations of comedy; the application is left to the audience, as is the internalization of the law and of the forms of "perfection" under which vice remains effectively prohibited.

In the moment in which the audience succumbs to comedy, the hegemonic institution of theater is apparently perfected – yet this appearance is premature, since perfectedness would also imply a termination in the process of social change. What can apparently never be foreseen at any one stage is simply the next stage, the beginning of which will be marked by an unexpected deficiency. The insufficiency of comedy is discovered when, for no apparent reason, certain individuals acquire fame and hence power (forms of excess) beyond the limits of the still implicitly local or organic community; the individual as a new and paradoxical *type* also emerges to supersede the castes and classes that have hitherto been in evidence. This acquisition of individual eminence turns out to be nothing more than a prelude to the indulgence of "lusts and licentiousness" of hitherto unprecedented magnitude – ones manifestly beyond any power of comic containment. The political form of tyranny rather than of popular misrule threatens by the same token to gain possession in place of any "lawful" form of government including that of the priestly caste.

Before considering the tragic response devised to meet this new contingency – one so drastic and disorientating as to threaten the "composure" of Puttenham's narrative of succession – we must recall that the priesthood now coexists with a latter-day state apparatus comprising kings, titular lords and governors, and preachers and educators of the vocational rather than poetic variety. Indeed, as Puttenham dutifully proclaims, "princes and gouernors of the earth [possess a] souereignty and function next vnto the gods,"[22] and the poetic priesthood as a now unacknowledged legislature has receded from the forefront. Yet even if the priesthood has effaced itself (been effaced) and the nominal divinity of kings *does* require acknowledgment, the exercise of its hegemony remains compatible with the existence of a legitimate state apparatus. But the rise of the lawless individual to eminence and even "soueraignetie"[23] is perceived as a greater threat to this hegemony than even popular misrule would be. It is as if the dispersed power and desire of the populace were concentrated, and thus rendered effective, in the person of the individual tyrant, a being capable either of living beyond the law or of becoming a law unto himself.

By the logic of Puttenham's argument, it is necessary that this lawless individualism rising to the power of tyranny should fully manifest itself before the dramatic response can be fashioned. So Puttenham rather bleakly acknowledges that during the ascendancy of the tyrant nothing can be done to restore either civility or legitimacy. The tyrannical individual simply exerts a power beyond the control of any law or hegemonic device. During the reign of the tyrant, the poets themselves are silenced (or implicitly reduced to flattery) while in his "great prosperitie" the tyrant will be "feared and reuerenced in the highest degree."[24] Only posthumously can tyrants' "infamous life and tyrannies" be "layd open to all the world, their wickedness reproched, their follies and extreme insolencies derided, and their miserable ends painted out in playes and pageants." Lacking the power to oppose entrenched tyrannies, the poets can only (and quite literally) re-present the career of the dead tyrant in such a way as to make it odious and exemplary. Tragedy is always thus a revisionist portrayal of an ostensibly prosperous career (now a career finished and cast in definitive form by its providential ending) and it always anatomizes (lays open) an evil formerly hidden by good appearances. Tragedy comes after the event of tyranny, and the repetition of tragedy in the theater seeks to forestall the repetition in political reality of tyrannical rule.

Readers familiar with sixteenth-century poetics will not of course be surprised at this iconoclastic treatment of the tragic protagonist – by Puttenham's denial to that figure of any pathos, nobility or serious ability to contest either the decrees of fate or the laws of God. It will also surprise no informed reader that Puttenham is more indebted to medieval "tragic" notions of fortune's wheel and the fall of princes than to classical conceptions. Even by the standards of his contemporaries, however, Puttenham's account of tragedy may seem reductive. Sidney, for example, includes "wonder" among the appropriate responses to tragedy, and seemingly tries to conceive of tragedy as therapeutic as well as exemplary spectacle. A *pathology* of the tragic protagonist as well as of the spectators is implicit in Sidney's reference to "... the high and excellent Tragedy, that openeth the greatest wounds, and showeth forth the ulcers that are covered with tissue."[25] Cauterization vies with anatomization as a possible aim of tragedy, and the recuperability of the patient(s) seems to be envisaged. But in his relentlessly monocular account of tragedy – the form of which remains strictly related to the *function* of demystifying the tyrant – Puttenham conceives of a spectacle that will unequivocally cut the protagonist down to size. No sympathetic appeal, no countercurrents, and no superfluous effects are admitted within the tragic experience.

In presenting his necessarily reductive, consistently functionalist account of tragedy, an account focussed exclusively on the tragic protagonist, Puttenham cannot but betray his consciousness of a contest for power and legitimacy occurring between the idealized ruling caste and the sovereign tyranny that at once mirrors and opposes it; i.e. of a division and contest for priority *within* the symbiosis of the "ruling class." Abruptly, the designated audience is no longer necessarily popular, although the upstart character of the tyrant means that his career is implicitly open to anyone at all, and a timely warning need not be lost on any member of the audience. But the critical tradition Puttenham shares with Sidney, as well as the actuality of Elizabethan playgoing, make the sovereign himself (herself) the proper witness of tragedy: "Tragedy ... that maketh kings fear to be tyrants, and tyrants manifest their tyrannical humours."[26]

As the form of last resort and of veiled political contestation within the "ruling class," however, Puttenham's "tragedy" understandably lacks the full rationale, corresponding to a transcendent intention, that can be imputed to comedy in his account. Indeed, Puttenham's account makes tragedy seem almost like a crude regression to farce; an atavistic resurgence unaccountably occurring at the end of the succession. Denied any capacity to excite pity or terror, the protagonist is exposed and even pilloried before a vulgar audience seemingly afforded no interpretive latitude about the laws that apply in his case. Yet countering this movement of degradation, a marked elevation of decorum also occurs: "the Poets stile was also higher and more loftie, the prouision greater, the place more magnificent"[27] than they had hitherto been. Paradoxically justified by the bad eminence of the principal character, the entire representation becomes literally more stilted: "These matters of great Princes [*sic*] were played vpon lofty stages, and the actors thereof ware vpon their legges buskins of leather called *Cothurni*, and other solemne habits, & for the speciall preheminence did walke vpon . . . high corked shoes."

Contradictory and even bizarre as this form may appear, one thing that seems clear is that the demystification of the "tyrant" is accompanied by an elevating mystification of theatrical representation itself; of the *institution* that has acquired its own cultural place and relative political autonomy. Yet even this "positive" development – no doubt representing, although couched in classical terms, the developing institutionalization of the public theater in Elizabethan England – is not enough, since the tragic performance still can't be staged at all without revealing the impotence of any *human* law to contain the passion of the tyrant. What apparently has still to be risked in the last resort is the audience's identification with represented unpunishable "lusts and licentiousness" (their own writ large) and hence *with* the tyrant-sovereign.[28] The very coarseness and violence of the tyrant's exposure seem designed to break this romantic identification, arising from his ability to act out the prohibited ["alienated"] grand desires of those who observe him. All that tragedy can do is capitalize on the *end* of the tyrant's career and allude to interpretive schemata under which that ending is to be understood as providentially "bad;" it remains for the audience to make the leap of faith that will reaffirm the providential necessity to which the tyrant succumbs, and to which *it* implicitly remains subject.

It goes almost without saying that Puttenham's attempt to tell the whole story of drama in a particular temporal order is – whatever its interest in comparison with subsequent attempts, including our own – a conceptual spacing and hence representation of a single phenomenon (drama) that can't be "thought" all at once. A comparable spacing of the cultural and political orders is also evident in the *Arte* as a whole. If this attempt is manifestly problematical – or manifestly "ideological" – it also reveals the difficulty of fully rationalizing dramatic forms in which archaic and ritualistic survivals remain incorporated; satyr-play, ritual regicide, scapegoating. My point, however, is that the *consistent* claim throughout Puttenham's account of drama is that its function is hegemonic, and what does evolve smoothly in his narrative, emerging finally into prominence in its own right, is the physical institution of theater. Following the conversion of rustic places of devotion into impromptu theaters-in-the-round, *ad hoc* "floores" and "scaffolds" emerge as the settings of comedy, while these in turn are superseded by the permanent "lofty stages" and magnificent "place" of tragedy. A progressively evolving institution of theater remains, in Puttenham's account, both the instrument and the sign of effective hegemonic rule. Nothing, it seems, compromises that success.

I began by suggesting that Puttenham restores the perspective of a theater *in* the world, in doing so going somewhat against the grain of our own criticism as well as against that of Elizabethan plays (notably Shakespeare's of course) in which an attempt is made to think and keep on rethinking the implications of supposing that all the world *is* a stage. I also suggested that Puttenham allows us to consider from the outside, so to speak, the character of theater as an institution within the political domain rather than as one encompassing it. Yet the attractions of this approach aren't obvious. Puttenham might be called crudely reductive in ways that prevent him from doing justice to English Renaissance drama. A more serious objection concerns Puttenham's qualifications to interpret the Elizabethan theater at all. *The Arte of English Poesie* postdates the establishment of the public theater in 1576, but its own appearance in 1589 (it must have been *written* earlier) makes it virtually coincide with the earliest performances of Marlowe's work. Puttenham does not therefore write as a longstanding witness to the Elizabethan drama that we now designate major; he does not write as a longstanding witness to the peculiarly Elizabethan mutant of "revenge tragedy;" he does not write as a witness to the increasingly complicated involvement of the players in court life; and, even more disastrously than the maligned Sidney, he remains a prisoner of his own neoclassical categories in approaching such native or romantic drama as he might have been able to witness. (Significantly, Puttenham can't name a single English dramatist or "dramatic poem" worthy of the name, while even Sidney can acknowledge the propriety of *Gorboduc*.) As a commentator before the event on both the dramatic forms and the institution of theater after 1590, Puttenham seems positively to disqualify himself.

Yet the hypothesis offered by Puttenham, in the teeth of the facts to come, is that public or communal theater, insofar as it exists at all as an institution in the world, can function *only* in the hegemonic way I have outlined. While it would not be necessary for that theater to represent any particular form of government as good, it would be bound to the task of representing – and of inviting spectators to participate in the defeat of – threats to the hegemonic *status quo*. The audience is invited not merely to acknowledge but imaginatively to embody the law of which *it* is the ultimate subject. In Puttenham's terms, an unbreakable reciprocity exists between the public institution of theater and the possibility of "good government," and no other theoretical or practical possibility exists for that theater. The consistency and intransigence of this implicit claim constitute its force, and the claim itself might be read as a prophecy of what occurs when, under Jacobean and Caroline rule, a hegemonic public theater is weakened and partly appropriated for the purposes of the sovereign-tyrant.[29] In Puttenham's terms, the institution of drama (and of theater) is essentially denatured or radically misconceived in becoming the mirror of a wished-for tyranny, while the hegemonic principle is also fatally betrayed.

From our own standpoint, of course, Puttenham's claim has to be reinterpreted and perhaps "corrected," yet the utility of considering his thesis may be somewhat heightened by the fact that the role of theater in *Elizabethan* society is manifestly at issue in his "history." Although his history moves by implication from "fayned" antiquity via Greece to Rome, it reveals itself in its many anachronisms as a history of the present and future; it also emphasizes the development of the theatrical institution accompanying or subtending the succession of dramatic forms. The three phases of social and dramatic development projected into the past coincide in the present in which Puttenham writes, just as the three dramatic forms – satire, comedy, tragedy – coexist and retain their functions in the stratified society Puttenham inhabits. The point is that the institutional apparatus of the state alone remains, in Puttenham's view, insufficient to establish effective control of a divided society or to hold it together as a community; what is called for, either in fact or in principle, is the powerful hegemonic institution of theater as a political "conventicle." The history of the dramatic forms thus doubles as an explanation of successful rule in general and of an always-possible Tudor "good government" in particular; the phenomenon of theater as a major public institution carries with it this one inescapable meaning for Puttenham.

No doubt it is possible for us to think otherwise, particularly in a Gramscian framework in which theater might be reconceived (some modern commentators have done so)[30] as a site in which contestation of the dominant ideology is capable of occurring, and in which forms of cultural and political transgression may be staged to subversive effect. Yet in a sense it is *this* claim that Puttenham anticipates and, perhaps heuristically from our standpoint, rewrites as a hegemonic one, implying that such stagings can only, in the last resort, reinstate the law that is transgressed.

2
Sympathy

This chapter moves away from the very basic questions of theatrical and political principle rehearsed in the first one, but for reasons that will emerge, the "politics of theater" is a topic that comes back to haunt the book. As questions of almost "pure" principle, those of the first chapter are difficult to resolve or develop, and, as previously suggested, their rehearsal was in some ways the rehearsal of a "radical" impasse. Getting around the impasse, meaning also, in terms of the detective fiction, finding new leads, depended on serendipity. The event at which this power came opportunely into play was that of the Shakespeare Association meeting at Boston early in 1984. If mention of its proceedings is necessary to sustain the narrative here, those proceedings deserve notice on their own account.

The event was significant because it was the first-ever meeting of the Association at which "Shakespeare and Poststructuralism" had formally appeared on the agenda. While the interest of the Shakespeare Association in this topic, and reciprocally of poststructuralists in conducting their proceedings under the auspices of the Shakespeare Association, had to be regarded as healthy (in fact the proceedings justified the faith of the organizers), the occasion served to raise as well as to answer questions. Although this conference suggested that an "applied" poststructuralism would significantly revise traditional readings of Shakespeare in the near future, in doing so possibly altering the character of a Shakespeare Association still barely touched as an institution by more than a decade of critical theory, the question of what this embarrassing success might mean to poststructuralists became my concern as a respondent on one of the relevant panels. How could a hegemonic rather than "subversive" poststructuralism conceive of itself? Could it acknowledge its hegemonic rather than suppressed condition, its stunning and increasingly recognized effectiveness as the *defense* of poetry and of the high canon in our time rather than as a threat to either? Could it adjust itself to a situation in which it could hardly claim to be dislodging entrenched pieties and might indeed have become the fountainhead of piety – of the law itself?

What, furthermore, could be read in the new conjunction, not just between "Shakespeare and Poststructuralism," but between poststructuralists and the Shakespearean establishment? Did this conjunction portend a new Shakespeare criticism, different from the old yet taking the place of the old in a line of legitimate descent? Was poststructuralism in the role of upstart/bastard/outsider rather than of effete pretender soon to be revealed, in a dénouement not unfamiliar to readers of romance, as the true heir? And would the moment of inheritance turn out to be one of strange emptiness or gratifying possession?

To ask these questions was in effect to register some misgivings; it was also to suggest the need for continuing reservations, chiefly because a trade of critical force and self-consciousness for institutional authority might be entailed in the reconciliation between poststructuralism and the Shakespeare establishment. Given the institutional impetus of poststructuralism and given that its legitimation in fields other than that of Shakespeare criticism was also implicitly at stake at this meeting, it would have been perverse to wish for any thwarting of the process of reconciliation. An effort to hold poststructuralism to a permanently marginal or antagonistic position, or to insist, for example, on the prohibitions upon *any* institutionalization or methodization built into Derridean procedures, would probably have been to adhere to "principles" incapable of being fully sustained by their originator. The need to build in such prohibitions, which in a sense anticipate their own violation, implies a foreconsciousness of the hegemonizing, self-canonizing or lawgiving dynamic of the procedures in question. Yet the development of a certain false consciousness under a *ruling* poststructuralism appeared to be on the cards.

There were indications of an emergent poststructuralism unmindful of its own contingent history or present cultural circumstances, and with claims to represent a timeless ("enduring") enlightenment now manifesting itself under the appropriately favorable conditions. Accompanying this development, a significant poststructuralist interest in unreservedly reviving the topics and assimilating the gigantic repertoire of classical rhetoric was also discernible, and if this development too seemed plausible – intellectually justified and challenging, in fact – it was one that seemed increasingly mismatched with any countercultural or even political militancy. A powerful and self-empowering poststructuralism seemed in other words to be the thing in question, but if blindness or amnesia were to be the accompaniments of its rule, it might become, in quick succession to its phase of militancy and exclusion, a prematurely old poststructuralism, not a "mature" one.

Reservations noted, it remains also to be said that among the topics interestingly discussed under the "Shakespeare and Poststructuralism" rubric was that of literary representation. Not a new topic, but one that acquired some new urgency in the encounter between different critical generations and/or schools. The discussion of Shakespeare's traditional claims as well as those of tragedy as a genre to represent the generality of the human condition led to the conclusion that any such representation had now to be conceived paradoxically as a deficient or "failed" general representation.[1] The point, it should be emphasized, wasn't that Shakespearean tragedy has to be reconceived positivistically, empirically or historically as the adequate representation of particulars (though tragedy might also be that), but that it has to be conceived, perhaps for the first time ever, as *deficient* general representation, the only now thinkable kind of general representation. This (specifically Lacanian) thinking of tragedy had necessarily to stage itself as a transformational critique of traditional claims about Shakespearean representation, but also of Aristotelian poetics, and it ruled out any further claim that full general representation (of the human condition or whatever) is to be found in Shakespeare. Tragedy, it was argued, and *Hamlet* in particular, can enact only an agonized consciousness of this lack – of its own partiality, and of necessarily diminished claims. No such construct as the "concrete universal" is capable of effacing this manifest deficiency, nor can general representation ever be established either by analogical likeness or by synecdochic substitution of part for whole. The tragedy of tragedy, so to speak, is that of failed general representation; of absent wholeness and an accompanying violent exclusiveness.

If it seemed that Shakespearean tragic representation could hardly be thought otherwise, given certain premises widely accepted in poststructuralism, one unheralded effect of the argument was to reinstate tragedy in the privileged position in the hierarchy of genres, at the same time facilitating the claim that a bleak necessitarianism (bondage to the eternal law of lack) is the authentic expression of Lacanian poststructuralism. The troubling preemptiveness of this result was partly responsible for the concern of the following paper with representation, as was the prima facie commitment of Spenser, with whom I had been dealing, both to romance and to "sympathetic" representation. Bracketing the question of tragedy – or at least not necessarily conceding its generic privilege – would it be possible to conceive of poetic representation as that defined, perhaps uniquely so, by its sympathetic representation of the other(s)? To what extent could sympathy be conceived as the catholic if not quite "general" medium of poetic representation, or as the power informing it – as that which might allow representation to be thought of in terms other than that of pure lack?

The problem with asking this question is that logical rigor – perhaps just a certain idea or form of logical rigor – has to be sacrificed in answering it affirmatively. The logic of tragic deficiency, meaning also of lordly tragic acceptance and stoical renunciation, can still be said to have captured the institutional high ground, and contestation of that ground accordingly becomes prohibitively expensive if not absurdly paradoxical. An inferior or necessarily question-begging method is thus relied on in this attempt to sustain a conception of "sympathetic" representation, yet the hoped-for method is one that I take to be finely articulated in a recent essay by Thomas Greene.

Although hardly concerned with sympathy – Machiavellian *virtù* is in question! – Greene deals with the vexed issue of the signifier *virtù* in *The Prince* by pointing out that, although soon over-extended or dangerously hollowed out, it does nevertheless function successfully as an operator in the text and does constitute a nexus of significations rather than a simple, recurrent (one could almost say "mindless") marking of the *aporia*. And even to the extent that it does periodically designate a lack, it doesn't invariably, uniformly or irreparably do so:

> If the signifier *virtù* is vulnerable through its simultaneous superfluity/emptiness of meaning, then like other problematic signi-fiers it calls for the intervention of the reader to drain and fill it, to penetrate its opacity and grasp the emergent integrity of its incom-patibilities . . . *something* is there in the text, something not wholly unstable; that sort of thing we look to culture to provide.[2]

This is the kind of consideration that I would want to apply to my own use of "sympathy." The intervention of the reader is solicited to imagine what it would mean for something to be *there* in the text and/or the inseparable context rather than for something merely to be lacking; it is solicited to conceive of something capable of being put there ("intro-jected" may be the technically correct term), even if only intermittently so, by the reader whose "response" might then be subject to the criterion of (good) will.

If the ensuing discussion fails to make a *case* for sympathy, or makes it practically in reverse, this problematical signifier may still help to establish the historical ground of Spenser's poetic operations; it may also establish an imaginable alternative to the current thinking, not just of the tragic representation previously alluded to, but to another influential notion, which is that any possible representation of the other (in which "feeling for" or "entering into" might be implied) is a form of unmitigated violence or destructive penetration – virtually a form of demonic possession. This widespread anxiety of Elizabethan poets, playwrights and antitheatricalists is taken with appropriate seriousness by Stephen Greenblatt, who conceives of Iago, destructively penetrating and eventually possessing Othello, virtually as the incarnate principle of Shakespearean representation and western imperialism alike.[3]

I have spoken of an imaginable alternative, but it is one that remains to be imagined against all odds, as Spenser's work makes clear despite its apparent commitment to desired forms of chivalrous, humane, or compassionate representation, particularly of the woman as other. The "odds" represented in *The Faerie Queene* include numerous instances of destructive penetration, recurrently literalized as actual or attempted rape, an almost grotesquely frequent event in the narrative.[4] It need hardly be said that narcissism recurrently manifests itself at the narrative and representational levels of the poem alike, threatening always to restrict any poetic of sympathy to the (short) circuit of the divided, self-pitying and exclusively self-regarding subject. But in speaking of these only as the odds, I wish at least to postpone and at most to transform the foregone conclusion that the discourse of sympathy belongs either to history or to vulgar sentimentalism alone.

The nature of sympathy

To consider Spenser under the rubric of "sympathy" is to do so without strong authorization. By this I don't mean that the approach is prohibited by the traditions of Spenser criticism (no one would deny the possible pertinence of "sympathy"), but that the attempt isn't a mainstream one. In fact, the issue comes up virtually as a negative function of traditional idealizing approaches to Spenser. What this means in practice will emerge to some degree in the discussion; in the meantime it need only be said that the perspicuousness of the issue and its compelling nature are negatively dependent on the broadly established traditions of Spenser criticism. My approach is also, however, dependent, perhaps as a parasitic overgrowth, on some recent historicist and theoretical work that will be noted where appropriate. The point of my saying this is that the issue of sympathy in Spenser, for which no established place exists, must be articulated in this negative and/or superinduced relation to existing work. Despite this, or because of it, a fundamental rooting of the issue has to be attempted.

One prompting to take the question of sympathy seriously as a phenomenon specific to the Renaissance has been forthcoming from

Michel Foucault's discussion of the Renaissance *episteme* in *The Order of Things*.[5] Although the topic is not what Foucault has in mind, his work nevertheless prompts consideration of what it would mean for poetic representation to be situated in a closed field of Renaissance "sympathy." Conversely, the work of major Renaissance authors, including Spenser, prompts reconsideration of the account offered by Foucault, including reconsideration of its closure. I shall accordingly begin by rehearsing, in a way strongly informed by Foucault, a preliminary understanding of Renaissance sympathy.

For the Renaissance, "sympathy" is in the first instance an animistic phenomenon, one that implies the existence of occult powers of attraction joining like to like throughout the cosmos. Bound up with this attraction are natural forms of fellow-feeling, kinship and pity, but beyond these static bonds or forms of identification sympathy must logically entail a kind of harmonic repetition, of likeness repeating itself either vertically up the scale of being or horizontally through a seemingly endless mutation of forms. We may consider this sympathy a naturalistic counterpart to the mystical Pythagorean harmonics from which, in the Renaissance, it isn't necessarily or consistently distinguished;[6] we may also consider it as an affective force or principle binding like to like despite apparent differences throughout the cosmos, but also incipiently *undermining* the stable autonomy of apparently distinct forms (possibly including individual human selves). A universe of sympathy isn't one of isolated monads but of forms traversed by a power or principle of affinity, hence the action of sympathy is or appears to be benignly inimical to that of any absolute individuation or separation – to any absolute identity, in short.

But is the question of this sympathy closed – or wholly enclosed in the Renaissance *episteme* it helps to define? Can we proceed from the consideration of Renaissance sympathy to that of sympathy "in general"? The only extensive modern treatment suggesting that we can is Max Scheler's *Wesen und Formen der Sympathie*, translated by Stephen Heath as *The Nature of Sympathy*.[7] This work may be regarded in the Spenserian sense as a "moniment": aide memoire, landmark, but also warning. As a warning, it reveals some of the difficulties of attempting a general phenomenology of sympathy as well as the propensity of the attempt to lapse into reification and pseudoscience. But instead of dwelling on the limitations of the attempt, I shall occasionally appeal to its useful observations, distinctions and definitions, merely noting that the more phenomenological or "general" the consideration of sympathy becomes, the more elusive and problematical the phenomenon itself becomes.

A history rather than a general phenomenology of sympathy would, in fact, suggest that, even if sympathy has its prehistory in the Renaissance, its real emergence and disappearance coincide almost exactly with those of the European Enlightenment. As recent work, particularly that of David Marshall, has shown, sympathy gets rigorously thematized but also apparently played out in theories of the moral sentiments, particularly in the work of Hume, and Adam Smith.[8] Given this *clear* history, the general "nature" of sympathy begins to look like a nebulous topic, and it is unquestionably difficult to establish whether in any period in which the term is used, with the exception of the eighteenth and early nineteenth centuries, it designates a condition of the natural world or of human existence that is taken to be substantially more than a benign fiction.

Even during the Renaissance, in which commonplace ideas of natural sympathy (occult attraction between physical bodies) informed cosmological thinking, governed certain homeopathic practices, and were widely assimilated to demonology,[9] it can't be said that these ideas, however widely received, possessed the highest cultural authority. Sympathy is a concept marginal to "serious" Renaissance theology, to the medical practices derived from Galen and/or Paracelsus, to the political science of Machiavelli and Bodin, to the philosophy of Montaigne and Bacon. So if sympathy is accepted by Spenser as a good or fundamental condition, a profoundly critical consciousness of its paradoxes and limitations, and perhaps of its relative lack of authority, is apparent in his work from the start. Our own sense that "sympathy" is either a superficial term, a vulgar one, or one contaminated by blind egoism (that it belongs to a realm of *bad* sentimental fictions) is anticipated, although the conception itself remains apparently enabling, in the work of Spenser and other major Renaissance authors, notably including Shakespeare.[10]

Given these preliminaries, is there any way of mediating between several versions of "sympathy" – between the sympathy of the closed Renaissance *epistemé*, the sympathy that remains a closed historical phenomenon of the Enlightenment, and sympathy-in-general? Rigorously, the answer may simply be "no." Yet the assumption, for example, that the phenomenon of sympathy can fully be contained in Foucault's model of separate, discontinuous epistemic fields would tend to prohibit acknowledgment of the paradox that *each* of the epistemic fields in question can be penetrated and reconstructed from the single standpoint of the modern philosopher of knowledge. What Foucault projects as a diachronic succession of unlike knowledge-producing systems may thus also be regarded as a synchronic repertoire of epistemic possibilities thinkable (inhabitable, capable of being re-presented) by a contemporary philosopher of knowledge. What is absolutely other is, by the same token, *absolutely* impenetrable and uninhabitable – productive of wonderment, no doubt, in the moment in which it is "witnessed," but also of laughter on the borderline of the hysterical the moment after – as Foucault's Borgesian anecdote of the "Chinese Encyclopedia," the work embodying a truly unthinkable and hence uninhabitable system of classification, brings home:

> In the wonderment of this taxonomy, the thing that we apprehend in one great leap, the thing that, by means of the fable, is demonstrated as the exotic charm of another system of thought, is the limitation of our own, the stark impossibility of thinking *that*.[11]

The point having been made, however, it is time to spoil the story with the observation that the taxonomy of this "Chinese Encyclopedia" isn't so alien after all. If it classifies animals under such bizarre "oriental" headings as "embalmed" and "belonging to the Emperor," it also less perspicuously embodies in Foucault's citation a familiar if arbitrary "occidental" system of classifying that goes [a], [b], [c], [d], etc.[12] Finding this instance of the familiar (the naturalized) in the very place of supposedly ultimate strangeness suggests that a "hidden" principle of sympathy, likeness or affinity is operative in Foucault's own undertaking; it suggests too that whatever is capable of being represented fully or extensively is already *sympathique* – not absolutely other if also not identical. Not only is the containment of "sympathy" in the Renaissance *epistemé*, however methodologically justified for Foucault's purposes, incomplete, but even this attempted containment forestalls consideration of what it is *about* Renaissance sympathy that gives it an historical afterlife in the European Enlightenment.

For Foucault, sympathy remains an important feature of a Renaissance epistemic system in which *likeness* is generally privileged: a "becalmed sea of analogies." Sympathy belongs to this order of sameness but paradoxically threatens to disturb the calm:

> Sympathy plays through the depths of the universe in a free state ... [it] is an instance of the *Same* so strong and insistent that it will not rest content to be merely one of the forms of likeness; it has the dangerous power of *assimilating*, of rendering things identical to each other, of mingling them ... [it] alters but in the direction of identity, so that if its power were not counterbalanced, it would reduce the world to a point .... [13]

At once elastically pulled together and terrifyingly threatened with implosive contraction by sympathy, the cosmos needs, according to

Foucault, a countervailing power of antipathy, and this duly manifests itself in the natural "hatreds" commonly believed in the Renaissance to exist between various plants and animals. Foucault cites Renaissance authorities to the effect that antipathy is widespread in the natural world ("The rat of India is pernicious to the crocodile"[14]), and that there is something magically potent about the invisible forces that unite and divide the creation.

Is it definitively "the Renaissance" that speaks here – is it in fact the authentic *voice* of the Renaissance that Foucault ventriloquizes as "other?" Yes, insofar as supporting citations can be produced from works of natural magic or natural history (for Foucault, the decisive evidence); yes, insofar as it may be thought in the Renaissance that the occult powers can be manipulated or harnessed by the natural magician, one of whose avatars is the poet; but no, insofar as we don't necessarily discern in Foucault's fantasy of implosion (for which no explicit Renaissance confirmation is forthcoming) the full interest or subtlety of Renaissance intelligence as we are capable of recognizing it; of its play around the ideological margins, so to speak.

To say this isn't to attempt a refutation of Foucault. His argument could be that Renaissance intelligence, if that term means anything at all, is constituted only inside the epistemic parameters disclosed in such works as those he cites, and within which it remains ultimately confined. My point would, however, be that even in the space allowed a practice of skepticism and imaginative reconstruction, sufficient to make a difference, is discernible. Taking the phenomenon of sympathy *as* a problematical one, or skeptically mastering belief in sympathy rather than being possessed by it, the authors with whom I am concerned function neither in the domain of credulity nor that of knowledge, but of "poetic" construction and reconstruction. If their capacity to function in this area, *never* recognized by Foucault, can be claimed to make a difference, it is that of initiating *change* within the otherwise stable system and/or of crossing the threshold of the particular epistemic enclosure. In fact it is only the existence of that capacity (a necessary condition if not a sufficient one) that can account for a "rise" of sympathy in the sixteenth century continuing into the Enlightenment. The manipulation of Renaissance sympathy (as well as Renaissance "intelligence") can briefly and canonically be exemplified in the work of Montaigne.

It is virtually a given of traditional Montaigne studies that the "Apology for Raymond Sebond" renders the operation of the divine nominal and thus in a sense moot, while the late essays, especially "Of Repentance," movingly invite reconciliation with our natural condition.

In "Sebond," Montaigne's humorously bizarre denigration, verging on craziness, of the human condition, places man first of all under the good laws governing the animal creation, but then suggests that only a negative transcendence (a falling away from) those laws defines the human condition. Degradation becomes, in other words, virtually the sole and paradoxical form of human distinction. The inescapable context of the *human* becomes that of natural law, of which positive law (hence political society) can at most be a fallen imitation.

In this context of secular naturalism – of natural powers and laws only nominally determined by a theological origin – it isn't surprising that the question of sympathy arises in various forms. It does so in the crucial essay "Of Friendship," but does so, surprisingly at first sight, only to be disavowed and seemingly annulled. What defines human friendship (*amitié*) for Montaigne as the *summum bonum* isn't natural sympathy and/or the incomplete identification that would always imply (Montaigne, let us recall, quotes Aristotle's saying, "O Friends, there is no friend") but absolute identity: the complete annihilation of difference:

> In the friendship I speak of, our souls mingle and blend with each other so completely that they efface the seam that joined them, and cannot find it again. If you press me to tell you why I loved him, I feel that this cannot be expressed except by answering: Because it was he, because it was I [*Par ce que c'estoit luy; par ce que c'estoit moi*].[15]

Such is the virtually inexpressible and atemporal condition claimed by Montaigne in his friendship with de la Boétie, one which only the reference of the opposed pronouns "lui-moi" to a common, undifferentiated "ce" and a chiastic syntax can be summoned up to "explain." To this alone the name of friendship properly belongs. Insofar as both sympathy, difference and Montaigne's selfhood enter the situation, they do so together, but only after the friendship has ceased with the death of de la Boétie. They then manifest themselves both in and *as* the essay "Of Friendship."

As Montaigne criticism has it,[16] the death of Étienne de la Boétie is the enabling loss in which Montaigne's entire project of writing ostensibly arises as one of endless supplementation, *différance* and memorial inscription. (The loss, however, being made complete in Montaigne's text by the eventual omission even of surviving works by de la Boétie that that text was "intended" to incorporate). Only in this condition "after" the claimed perfect identity of friendship does an inferior sympathy manifest itself in the guise both of mourning and self-mourning, while a difference grows between the one arrested in death and the one who, to his shame, lives on to harvest the fruits denied to the other.

This commonplace shame is implicitly exacerbated by the fact that the fruits include for Montaigne the literary project of *self*-inscription as well as a career of public influence and literary success not only possible to the survivor but his unrivalled prerogative in the absence of the friend with whom he was identical. What thus manifests itself in the essay (in time; and in the writing of friendship) is paradoxically not friendship as defined, but rather its enabling lack. All that can now appear is the difference and contingent self-interest that are denied in the ideal state of friendship, remembered (or is it misrecalled?) as one in which selves and interests were identical. So this essay (trial, probing) of friendship asserts a definitive likeness but also manifests a difference – an ineffaceable prior difference and self-interest – that belongs to a world of sympathy or incomplete identification with the other. Sympathy implies something both less and more than *amitié*, and it is the condition of the essayist. Can that inferior or untrustworthy sympathy be transformed or rehabilitated?

Sympathy becomes explicitly an issue in "Of Cruelty," in which it is repeatedly *confessed* in a represented context of barbarous cruelty, such as that arising in the course of the religious wars, in the apparently ordinary proceedings of criminal justice (about which Montaigne has humane suggestions to make), and in the noble pastime of hunting, in which Montaigne acknowledges his own participation. (He is implicitly on the side of the stag at bay; he cannot "bear" the scream of the dying rabbit even as his hounds savage it.) This sympathy, now so named (*cette sympathie que j'ay avec elles*), is "confessed" as an historical anomaly by Montaigne:

> . . . I sympathize very tenderly [*je me compassionne fort tendrement*] with the afflictions of others, and would readily weep to keep others company, if I could weep for any occasion whatever. There is nothing that tempts my tears but tears, not only real ones, but all sorts, *even the feigned or the painted* [my emphasis].[17]

Without "put[ting] much stock in" the notion of "cousinship between ourselves and the animals,"[18] Montaigne nevertheless discovers in himself a certain compassionate kinship, however incomplete, with other natural beings. This discovered *benign* anomaly is also then professed as one that calls for normalization in generally more humane social and punitive practices.

Montaigne recounts with abhorrence some instances of torture and execution (instances of the kind described with a certain manic relish by Foucault in the opening of *Discipline and Punish*, but which are also noted, along with their accompanying terrors, in a recent essay by Thomas Greene).[19] In recounting these, Montaigne prefigures an enlightenment that will eventually do away with (or, in Foucault's terms, mask, disperse and institutionalize) certain barbarisms. The very act of recurrently confessing to the anomalous feeling tends in Montaigne's argument to establish its irrepressible force, while a certain ethical value begins to be attached to it, allowing Montaigne to sketch a secular program.

Both the essay "Of Friendship" and the example of the hunted rabbit no doubt betray the inadequacy or duplicity of sympathy, and even when Montaigne envisages humane execution, the execution itself isn't negotiable. The Enlightenment prophesied in the name of sympathy thus has its limits, and indeed a more efficient as well as better masked violence may be all that is eventually called for; thus far Foucault's post-Enlightenment strictures appear justified. But in Montaigne the represented *total* failure of the supposedly higher sanctions of religion makes even a limited, contradictory sympathy a thinkable alternative. If Christians distinguish themselves only by behaving much worse than everyone else, and by possessing a grand conception to which they cannot even for a second rise in practice, the "discovery" of sympathy as a possible ground for limited amelioration – precisely for limited *change* – is timely. It is a solution on the level of the proposer as well as those to whom it is proposed, as Christianity manifestly is not. And if this discovery (both finding and revelation) is only a fictional profession of Montaigne's (painted tears) it nevertheless occurs in a represented context in which otherwise only a cruelty beneath that of beasts prevails, doing so most virulently in the name of Christianity itself. Montaigne does not, then, just reveal as a man of the Renaissance the inert epistemic lodgment of sympathy claimed by Foucault, but testifies also to the conditions of its manipulated "rise."

Montaigne, but also Spenser and other major Renaissance authors committed to "sympathy", suggest in fact that a *structural* opposition between sympathy and antipathy, implied in the work of Foucault, is an untenable simplification. Sympathy implies within itself, as a putatively originary term, a prior *difference* that is always being overcome but never is so. Sympathy always operates, so to speak, from a distance, and positive antipathy is really secondary, external, or beside the point. An endless repetition or reaching rather than implosive closure or absolute identity with the other is precisely what characterizes sympathy, so there is a note of melodrama both in Foucault's ventriloquized anticipation of a terminal point and in his invocation of antipathy to keep things apart. If there is one paradoxical reassurance that Renaissance sympathy apparently brings, it is that the differences are in place.

* * *

Before considering Spenserian sympathy, I shall for the sake of clarity pause over two moments in the historical "afterlife" of Renaissance sympathy and then conclude by noting the "nexus of significations" (semantic complex) associated with the term. First, the moment in which a "theater of sympathy" is conceived by Adam Smith. David Marshall has recently argued that, in *The Theory of the Moral Sentiments*, Smith conceives the sympathetic condition to be essentially theatrical.[20] In other words, this sympathy becomes constructively, ethically, thinkable for Smith only in the setting of universal theater, not universal nature. There is then, in effect, no *nature* of sympathy. The condition of any individual in Smith's "theater of sympathy," whether he nominally occupies the position of the sympathizer or of the sufferer, is always simultaneously one of performance and spectatorship, of imagined suffering and projected sympathy. Not even the most intense pain, according to Smith, enables the sufferer (or the spectator, which the sufferer also remains of his own suffering) to transcend the sphere of theatrical mediations or to attain either self-identity or full identification with another. In the work of Smith, the field of sympathy ceases to be that of nature and becomes definitively that of culture – of a radically theatricalized culture, what is more.

In some ways Smith's argument can be regarded as one in which he radicalizes and systematizes Renaissance sympathy (implicitly subjects it to a transformational critique), in doing so making perspicuous the way in which an unacknowledged theatricality enters into Renaissance conceptions of sympathy. The *distance* that constitutes sympathy in the human realm, which is also that of language and representation, also constitutes spectatorship and "pathetic" performance. Something like a formalization of this inescapably theatrical sympathy enters from the start into the Renaissance rhetorical discipline on which poetic practice is founded.[21] To take a familiar example, in the exercise of *argumentum in utramque partem*, a student (implicitly male) might be asked to imagine the speech of Dido to her betrayer Aeneas; in thus learning to argue the case forensically from both sides, a constitutive if unacknowledged exercise in theatrical identification and "pathetic" speech was also being undertaken.

Theatricality and sympathy also enter together into the conceived ethical function of the Renaissance poet, who stands on no neutral ground in relation to his subject. As one who publicly praises or blames, the Renaissance poet enacts the relations of sympathy and antipathy to whatever he addresses (represents), and those relations ground his ethical discourse of praise and blame even as it rationalizes them. In further rationalizing and apparently "denaturing" sympathy, however, Smith also identifies it more exclusively with the principle of theatricality than is the case in the Renaissance. Or rather, he reconstructs "theater," on Marshall's showing, as a space of pure spectacle in which both "rhetoric" and difference (at least the difference figured by gender) are wholly elided. Whether or not we might conclude that the unheralded exclusion of women and language – and of poetry as "the language of women"? – is the prime unacknowledged condition on which Smith's ethical theory depends, it represents a fundamental departure from Renaissance sympathy, which plays out in a field both of represented difference and of "pathetic" speech.[22] It is with the operations of sympathy in *this* field that Spenser, for one, is concerned, and the particularity of this concern is evident, for example, in *The Ruines of Time*, in which the *poetic* persona, the female *genius loci* who mourns the destruction of the Anglo-Roman town of Verulamium, is simply on the scene and part of the scene prior to the arrival of the implicitly male narrator, whose function becomes solely a mediating and critically transforming one – as indeed it appears to be in Spenser's seminal first work, derived from Petrarch's Canzone 24, in *A Theatre for Voluptuous Worldlings*. The ontological primacy of the female figure both in the theater of sympathy and in poetic discourse – likewise the ontological primacy of mourning and complaint – are crucial concerns for Spenser, for whom a certain representativeness can be claimed in this respect.[23]

Second, the phenomenon of a constitutive difference from which sympathy arises or to which it remains bound – the difference that also constitutes the possibility of sympathetic representation – is strongly confirmed by Max Scheler's twentieth-century account. Deriving his observations partly from Adam Smith and his precursors, Scheler implies that human sympathy entails a condition of separation or incomplete identification with the other. But a *transcendence* of sympathy as envisaged, for example, by Schopenhauer, for whom the ground of human being and hence of fundamental non-differentiation is pain, remains for Scheler a condition of pathological or primitive ecstasy, forever to be distinguished from the condition of sympathy:

> For the positive moral value which Schopenhauer ascribes to pity does not primarily reside in the constituent function of *fellow-feeling*, but in the *suffering* inherent in it . . . since suffering represents, for him, the essential "way of salvation," it is only as a form of suffering and a mode of apprehending its ubiquitous presence that pity acquires the positive value that he attributes to it . . . but despite its appearance of nobility and pathos, this consummation is rooted in an emotional experience that is far from valuable . . . for even if the world *were* ultimately

reducible to a single, self-mortifying Will, such vicarious intimation of our unalterable fate ... would simply throw us back into the misery we had hitherto discerned only by inspection, as it were, and would automatically provoke a further instinctive struggle to escape it, so that mankind would be forever enmeshing itself in what Schopenhauer, following the Indian writers, calls "Sanasara" . . . Moreover, the presentation of the theory takes on a character which betrays a hidden element of sadomasochistic glee in the affliction of others.[24]

The saving difference that constitutes sympathy *per se* is thus also the difference that constitutes sympathy as a condition of unsullied spectatorship; namely, of only partial, non-exploitative identification between the sympathizer and the represented object of sympathy. An element of theatricality accordingly enters, *desirably* so, into Scheler's conception of sympathy, which, although based on a post-Nietzschean critique of any ethical theory grounded in sympathy, nonetheless prohibits its "savage" extension into full identification, beyond theater. Yet if it is in the "nature" of sympathy to want to go beyond itself, one implicit condition of its doing so is evidently that of risking sado-masochistic contamination and radical atavism, unacceptable to Scheler, yet not to be ruled out as possible extensions of Renaissance sympathy.

Finally, a "nexus of significations." In supplying a glossary to his translation (without committing Scheler to any of these particular usages, some of which indeed are excluded), Stephen Heath lists a number of terms that might logically be, or may historically have been, subsumed under "sympathy": fellow feeling (*Mitgefühl*); community of feeling (*Miteinanderfühlung*); empathy (*Einfühlung*); identification (*Einsfühlung*); benevolence, humanitarian sentiment (*Menschenliebe*); pity, commiseration (*Mitleid*). All these terms (German and English) have some critical utility in my own attempt to define the field of sympathy, yet for the sake of historical precision it is necessary for us also to recognize sixteenth-century usages, which are often stronger than the ones listed. Deriving the English word proximately from late L. *sympathia*, *OED* gives as its primary sense (operative in the sixteenth century): "A (real or supposed) affinity between certain things, by virtue of which they are similarly or correspondingly affected by the same influence (esp. in some occult way), or attract or tend towards each other." "Conformity of feelings," "community of feeling," "harmony of disposition," "affected by the sorrow or suffering of another" are also listed among the common senses of the word in Spenser's time. Spenser's "Hymne to Heauenly Beavtie" is cited as an authoritative source for one particular usage: "Loue is a celestiall harmonie,/ Of likely harts . . . Which ioyne together in sweete sympathy,/ To work ech other ioy and true content." The significance of this usage from my point of view is its tendency to *derive* the "celestiall" from the workings of natural sympathy rather than the other way round. It might also be suggested that a certain conscious poetic artifice is also foregrounded by Spenser's characteristically idio-syncratic spellings: sympathy is being consciously textualized, or found(ed) in the text. Finally, it needs to be said that both the common and the Spenserian usages are subject to extended construction, both critically and in Spenser's own work. This is especially true where terms like "supposed" (operative in sixteenth-century poetics) and "occult" are concerned.[25] Nothing but extended critical construction of primary terms can, in fact, yield the hoped-for poetic of sympathy, or perhaps account for the extendedness of Spenser's own poetic constructions.

Spenserian sympathy and the case of "Mother Hubberd"

A certain commitment on Spenser's part to natural sympathy can be inferred from a passage in his *View of the Present State of Ireland* that has always provoked comment, sometimes irritatingly to the exclusion of any other comment on this text. This is the passage in which Spenser represents through one of his fictional speakers the almost unspeakable plight of certain Irish rebels in the late stages of the Earl of Desmond's rebellion (*ca.* 1580). "How," the question usually goes, "is it possible for Spenser to witness (or gratuitously bear witness to) this abomination and yet justify British rule?" Or, in possibly more sophisticated terms, "Why does Spenser allow us an unforgettable view of Irish suffering when his ostensible purpose is to alienate sympathy from the Irish and present the British cause in the best possible light?"

These questions are deceptively simple, and an attempt to answer them (we will consider the passage itself shortly) can lead in various directions.[26] William Renwick, the editor of the *View*,[27] suggests, even while objecting to critical decontextualization of the passage, that it embodies something forever unassimilable. Such at least is the impli-cation of his unelaborated claim that the vision of horror haunted Spenser throughout his life.[28] At the risk of recasting Spenser's *View* as a sixteenth-century *Heart of Darkness*, we might then infer that the nightmare, if such it was for Spenser, might recurrently threaten every daytime vision of a benign civil and/or poetically constructed order. At the same time, Spenser might be seen as a martyr to an ineradicable and anomalous sympathy (*Mitgefühl*) with the victims of the very order that he inhabits and to the extension of which he contributes; perhaps as one exiled by his very sensibility *within* an order founded upon the infliction of suffering. It might further be assumed that the mere shock of witnessing almost inconceivable suffering and degradation, perhaps together with the sympathy such suffering might elicit beyond any possible rationalization, would be enough to prohibit further willed participation in the system under which such results become possible. A revelation of the *groundlessness* of civil claims or fictions might additionally be supposed to forestall any further constructive engagement in the civil order, taken by Spenser to be irreplaceably represented in Ireland by English law and administration.

It is true that all these suppositions may be anachronistic in relation to Spenser. Yet even in their own terms, the assumptions are probably back to front. Granting the, by definition, "weak" or "abnormal" possibilities of traumatic arrest or indeed of madness arising from a vision of the horror, the normal result (indeed, the very condition) of sympathetic observation can only be a continuing distance from the plight of the other. Overwhelming sympathy approaching full identification would imply nothing less than political, cultural or individual collapse, while the negation of sympathy may, under the same logic, become the *rigorous* condition of a continuing "civil" order and hence of stable, individualized existence. If the nightmare recurs, perhaps always as a liminal phenomenon just beyond or just within reach of cultural control and appropriation, its very power, which has inescapably to be risked, is also what makes possible the (re)assertion of cultural and/or political will. We may therefore take it that the moment of sympathy in Spenser's *View* is, however compelling, not incompatible with the continuing objectives both of British imperialism and of powerful if "ungrounded" Renaissance poetic production.

The passage comes after Irenius and Eudoxus, the represented speakers in the *View*, have been discussing whether winter favors the Irish rebels or the British occupiers, and it is eventually concluded that it might be made to favor the British, who, by campaigning in winter, could reduce their enemies to utter impoverishment and helplessness. (A strategy that was indeed successfully pursued by Lord Mountjoy in his campaign in Ulster in 1600, leading to the temporary pacification of the whole of Ireland by 1603.)[29] Irenius proposes that at the beginning of a campaign, while provisions for both sides are still abundant, the rebels should be given a chance to submit unconditionally to British rule, but that those who fail to submit should be pursued to their utter destruction. It is in the context of this discussion both of the alleged self-destructive practices of the Irish rebels and of the capacity of the British to harass and starve them that Irenius anticipates a final solution:

The end I assure me will be very short and much sooner than can be in so great a trouble (as it seemeth) hoped for. Although there none of them fall by the sword, nor be slain by the soldier, yet thus being kept from manurance, and their cattle running abroad by this hard restraint, they would quickly consume themselves and devour one another. The proof whereof I saw sufficiently ensampled in those late wars in Munster, for notwithstanding that the same was a most rich and plentiful country, full of corn and cattle, that you would have thought they would have been able to stand long, yet ere one year and a half they were brought to such wretchedness, as that any stony heart would have rued the same. Out of every corner of the woods and glens they came creeping forth upon their hands, for their legs could not bear them. They looked anatomies of death, they spake like ghosts crying out of their graves, they did eat of the dead carrions, happy were they could find them, yea and one another soon after in so much as the very carcasses they spared not to scrape out of their graves, and if they found a plot of water cress or shamrocks, there they flocked as to a feast for the time, yet not able long to continue therewithal, that in short space there was none almost left and a most populous and plentiful country suddenly left void of man or beast. Yet sure in all that war there perished not many by the sword, but by all the extremity of famine, which they themselves had wrought.[30]

The passage includes a claim, however trickily phrased, that the action or feeling of sympathy ("rue") in the face of this extremity is irresistible. That assertion of irresistible compassion is enough to invest the sympathetic "circuit" of appeal and response with an almost magnetic or reflexive inevitability, and to assert a condition under which a failure of sympathy is literally inconceivable.[31] In a sense therefore an ineradicable or compelling sympathy is asserted by the speaker; not by "Spenser," of course, but nevertheless in terms that prophesy both its recurrence and its power of disturbance.

What can we learn from this example? It will escape no one that sympathy for the suffering Irish is claimed by a speaker who is prepared systematically to inflict more of the same, and for whom the spectacle of misery gives rise not just to sympathy but to a virtually genocidal strategy under which the Irish as "other" will be destroyed and/or incorporated. While the speaker will admit, moreover, that not even a heart of stone could be unmoved by the plight of the victims, he will also speak from a standpoint other than that of the heart (or the sympathizing stone, an object not unknown to Renaissance natural science, which cannot *but* be moved). He, in contrast, is either *not* moved or something other than sympathy has supervened. If the speaker has been drawn into sympathy with the Irish, the distance apparent at the beginning of the passage diminishing as he enters into their plight, that "reflex" has been superseded by the conscious reassertion of a difference that coincides with the reinscribed *boundary* between the productive, civil and law-abiding man and the ostensibly self-consuming outlaw. The apparent withdrawal of sympathy is also a withdrawal *into* a purely civil and political community as opposed to one of natural sympathy, and this reasserted difference justifies any harsh treatment that might be required either to eliminate the outlaw or bring him under the law. It is the "civil" rather than the natural definition of man that prevails, and this definition alone becomes the one in terms of which any real community or kinship can be established.

A sentimental reading of the *View* would be one that failed to acknowledge both the historical provenance of this attitude (a widespread concern about civil versus natural definitions of man reveals itself in many Renaissance texts other than Spenser's) or to acknowledge that a mindless and impotent sympathy might indeed prolong a situation that quick, brutal action could bring to an end. (Sympathy itself might dictate that course.) The possible cogency of the "civil" argument also deserves acknowledgment; a field of natural sympathy and humanity beyond the law (or against it) becomes virtually unthinkable when it takes the form that it would have to take according to the *View*: regression to the point at which human culture sinks back into an abysmal human nature that itself declines into animal nature as the victims pitifully try to graze where their flocks had once grazed. But even as we acknowledge that the speaker has his reasons, or that his options are historically limited, we find ourselves in the posture in which we first find the speaker himself: "I assure me" that this is so. These rationalizations not only represent an attempt to heal an inner separation (between rigorous "I" and pitying "me") but are also deployed in a closed circuit of persuasion into which no deciding principle can make its way. The discourse proceeds both in the circuit of rationalization and as an *interminably* counter-sympathetic (anti-natural) rather than an unsympathetic (unnatural) one. The acknowledged oppression and disturbance of natural sympathy are progressively absorbed into a legalistic rationale that can mask guilt or anger under the pursuit of a justified policy of ruthlessness and transfer to the victims the entire burden of responsibility. "Which they themselves had wrought," the passage breathtakingly concludes, with the speaker suddenly pivoting from the stance of the sympathizer to that of the accuser, in doing so enacting a defensive rebound from sympathy to aggression, here directed against the victims.

If the speaker can't abandon himself or fully enter into the plight of the other when "moved" by sympathy – if, on the contrary, a violent reinstatement of boundaries arrests sympathetic identification and seemingly precludes its recurrence, it is partly because the pitiable spectacle is obviously at the same time one of threateningly repellant horror; the liminal *play* of sympathy, then, is also a play of profound cultural, political and personal choice; choice of the contingent particular over the general, but also re-election of the cultural, political and individual rather than the "natural" as the categories of being. Such, it might be said, is the law of sympathy – not just the law governing its operations, but also the law perpetually founded and refounded on its negation. (The scandalous Book V of *The Faerie Queene* may be read as an extended gloss on this principle.) Yet it is in representing the plight of these victims that the *View* attains its one universally acknowledged and never-forgotten moment of negative sublimity.

To account for this if need be in terms other than that of the passage's manifest content – of its *witnessing* of the unutterable – one might say that the rapid, conscious development of religious and secular prose in the late sixteenth century (including that of Biblical translation) makes syntactic and cadential effects of the kind Spenser attains here available, yet it would remain to be said that it is in the dislocating interplay between the prosaic discourse of scientific husbandry ("manurance") and that of prophetic lamentation in the face of apocalyptic extremity that the passage gains its disconcerting elevation. Generalized, familiar idioms of "civil" pastoral and courtship ("rich and plentiful country, full of corn and cattle;" "there they flocked as to a feast for the time;" "a most populous and plentiful country;" the Petrarchan trope of the stony heart) get transported, moreover, into a context not only of the utmost horrific strangeness, but one in which their presence is itself strangely dissonant, again contributing to a "negative sublime" that surpasses, perhaps ironically but also significantly, anything in the enormous body of Spenser's signed and official poetry. It is in other words *only* in representing the "unspeakable" condition of the other, here meaning of the abased Irish victims, beyond the pale in every sense of the word – or rather, it is only in the strange double-voiced, criss-crossing condition of sympathizer and aggressor, pleader and judge, outlaw and in-law – that Spenser gains full access to these almost scandalous, unofficial or "unclean" poetic powers.[32]

The result of all this, following the critique of Scheler, might at once be to intensify distrust of "sympathetic" representation and lead to a recognition of its access to otherwise unavailable powers and possibilities, a double view in which Spenser himself may turn out to participate. Such a conclusion would however be premature at this stage, since it depends both on an isolated passage that one is reluctant to turn purple and on isolating Spenser from the multiple contingencies, cultural, political and poetic, of his more regular poetic vocation. It is to these that we now turn in considering "Mother Hubberd's Tale," a poem that, if for no other reason than that of its critical history, needs somewhat fuller contextualization than we have thus far attempted with Spenser.

This poem, possibly circulated in an early form *ca.* 1579-80, apparently as patriotic, anti-Catholic satire at the time of Queen Elizabeth's marriage negotiations with the French Catholic Duc d'Alençon, but published only in the 1591 *Complaints* volume, is a well-known *locus classicus* for discussion of Spenser's relations to the court, to Leicester, to Burghley, to the Sidneys, and to Elizabethan politics in general.[33] Yet while the poem has mainly been taken as an index of Spenser's *early* career and position *vis-à-vis* the Burghley and Leicester factions,[34] few discussions have fully taken up the question of the poem's "late" reappearance in the 1591 *Complaints*, or of that volume's implicit disavowal of royal patronage, its author's claim to literary property in its contents, and its complicated, overt patronage maneuvers following the deaths of Leicester, Sidney and Walsingham. In a strongly autonomizing but by no means irrevocable gesture, Spenser proclaims himself, in the wake of the 1590 *Faerie Queene*, no longer the nameless "Immerito" of *The Shepheardes Calender*, but also not the incorporated Elizabethan court poet, and he aggressively repossesses his early work as his own property, also now claiming title to hitherto anonymous or unpublished imitations of Petrarch, du Bellay and many others. Although responsibility for the publication of the volume is taken in the preface by the printer, ostensibly capitalizing on the success of *The Faerie Queene*, manipulation of the circumstances by Spenser may reasonably be inferred from comparable instances in the presentation of *The Shepheardes Calender* as a volume and in the posthumous (1609) "Mutabilitie" cantos.[35] I shall, however, make one point only about the circumstances of this volume and of the possibly belated appearance in print of "Mother Hubberd."

It is that, questions of revision aside, the poem could not mean or have meant in 1591 what it could have meant *ca.* 1580. It would itself have been "informed" historically and contextually in ways different from those of 1580. If Spenserian poems are "context specific," in the language of current historicism, they are not "context bound" in the same language; their revision and/or recycling in contexts other than those of their origin begins well before Spenser dies and posterity takes over. The possibility of both manuscript and print circulation facilitates this contextual indeterminacy and iterability of the poem. The immediate point, however, is that if the 1580 "Mother Hubberd" is encoded with anti-French and anti-Catholic meanings, other codings or contextual investments, whether intentional or merely accruing to the poem in time, must be inferred in the 1591 "Mother Hubberd." Among these, I would suggest, is a possible ironic coding, in the poem's narrative of the rascally Fox and Ape, of Spenser and Raleigh's 1590 pilgrimage to the English court.

The evidence for this is necessarily tenuous (not more so, however, than that available for other "identifications" of the poem's protagonists) but the acceptability of my suggestion depends not so much on clues as on a willingness just to think of the public Spenser as an ironist or as the conscious subject of significant historical and cultural ironies. (How is that to be proved?) Another condition is willingness to recognize that related events become the subject of more overt, though hardly unironic representation in Book IV of *The Faerie Queene* and *Colin Clouts Come Home Againe*, in which Queen Elizabeth, Raleigh and Spenser all figure. Indeed, a general turning towards the autobiographical and the self-centered is evident in the works (or *volumes*) Spenser published during the 1590s, including that of the so-called marriage poems. The successful, named author of *The Faerie Queene* cannot, by the same token, fail increasingly to be *seen* (to see himself) as the subject of his own fictions and the bearer, as one might say, of a poetic fate.

Where, now, does the sympathy come in? The two principals in the story told by "Mother Hubberd," the Fox and the Ape, begin their rapacious adventures on the basis of their alleged sympathetic affinity. This assumption of likeness, despite the manifest difference of "kind" between the two, is encouraged by the narrator, and is grounded in the apparently equal fortune (or misfortune) of the two:

> Whilome (said she) before the world was ciuill,
> The Foxe and th'Ape disliking of their euill
> And hard estate, determined to seeke
> Their fortunes farre abroad, lyeke with his lyeke:
> For both were craftie and vnhappie witted;
> Two fellowes might no where be better fitted.[36]

Likeness of circumstances (between Raleigh and Irish neighbor-in-exile Spenser?) is emphasized but also questioned by the pun made available to Spenser through his own Chaucerian archaism: *ly-eke*= like/ lie, also. Each party is discontented with his own condition and an apparent sympathetic reciprocity arises between the two, with each in the double role of sufferer and sympathizer. Yet this *Mitgefühl, Miteinanderfühlung*

– these "forms" of which sympathy is the presumable essence – are *illusorily* grounded in fortune rather than nature, and, perhaps more importantly, both parties constitute themselves as victims in what must be seen as an endless *process* of complaint and sympathetic response. A process of constitutive self-persuasion and maybe of radical self-deception precedes, in other words, the appeal of the principals to others more "fortunate" than they. The Fox and the Ape don't just rehearse their cant, taking that word in its primary and literal sense as professional beggars' jargon, before embarking on their adventures, but they also assume a new selfhood that marks a departure from their given identities in the animal kingdom:

> Neigbour Ape, and my Gossip eke beside,
> (Both two sure bands in friendship to be tide,)
> To whom may I more trustely complaine
> The euill plight, that doth me sore constraine,
> And hope thereof to finde due remedie?
> Heare then my paine and inward agonie.
> Thus manie yeares I now haue spent and worne,
> In meane regard, and basest fortunes scorne. . . .
>
> Ah, my deare Gossip, (answer'd then the Ape,)
> Deeply doo your sad words my wits awhape,
> Both for because your griefe doth great appeare,
> And eke because my selfe am touched neare. . . .
>
> Surely (said th'Ape) it likes me wondrous well;
> And would ye not poore fellowship expell,
> My selfe would offer you t'accompanie . . .
> Abroad where change is, good may gotten bee.
> The Foxe was glad, and quickly did agree.[37]

Responding to the Fox's appeal for sympathy, the Ape doesn't strictly deny self-interest. On the contrary, while giving credit to the magnitude of the Fox's alleged distress, the Ape acknowledges that he is "touched neare," thus in effect claiming his own part in the Fox's misery. But an implicit distinction is embodied in his response between an *appearance* of distress ("your griefe doth great appeare") on the Fox's part, despite the Fox's claim to be baring his soul, and the inwardness of his own distress. The very language of the Ape's response, while claiming reciprocity, reserves to him both a difference and a privilege, and it also bears witness to a "great" performance at once admired and seen through – or seen as exaggerated. In terms of an everyday psychology, but also of Max

Scheler's anecdotal observations on the subject,[38] the effect of a recital of misfortune is rapidly to call forth a self-pitying counter-narrative (the truly authentic one!) from the listener, and this narrative is forthcoming from the Ape.

But the question goes beyond that of a commonplace psychology of sympathy. The rhetorical self-constitution of the victimized subject (can the subject *as* subject ever be other than "victimized"?) is under way. The speech of the Fox becomes a performance of grief (grieving, grievance) to which the Ape responds by discovering *himself* in the performance. The Fox's complaint, in other words, evokes only a cursory expression of sympathy for *his* situation, or with him, but produces an extended repetition of itself, now become the complaint of the Ape. The almost instant rebound of the Ape's identificatory sympathy is evident, as is the process whereby sympathy for another converts itself almost instantly into a fiction, experienced as the most profound self-recognition, of the self-as-victim. If this newly constituted *selfhood* supersedes an identity and fate conferred by kind – the "species-being" of the Ape – it might be supposed to embody a narcissistic yearning that finds in the language of complaint the uniquely satisfying means of its own objectification and reappropriation as subjecthood. A "bad" process of self-constitution (or of what Scheler might call sympathetic genesis), in which the complaint of the other is appropriated as the very language of the self, is thus apparent in the response of the Ape to the Fox. An endless chain of fraudulent self-discoveries, resulting in a multitude (ostensibly a community) of pseudo-victims, is consequently the product of *this* sympathy, or more precisely of the situation in which a rhetoric of complaint is deployed. The linguistic mirroring and repetition evident in the dialogue of the Fox and the Ape also establishes them as victims in an order of spurious likeness superimposed on difference, yet difference will reassert itself later in the violently amplified form of reclaimed selfhood, self-interest.

In quoting quite extensively from what may be, among other things, a schematized version of a "sympathetic" exchange between Raleigh and Spenser in Ireland, I take the sardonic humor of the representation to be self-evident. Yet what guarantees the possibility of this kind of humor is either an ideal case with reference to which this one may be stigmatized as spurious, or else an assumed priority of natural kinds and differences, natural and hence *just* places in the scheme of things, from which the Fox and the Ape willfully depart. Without those underpinnings, to the radical insecurity or absence of which the poem eventually testifies, *irony* undoubtedly remains, but remains to testify only to a more troubling situation than one of simple fraud, however brilliantly executed. We will shortly see some of the things that this situation entails.

Before proceeding, however, I want simply to list for convenience a number of "sympathetic" assumptions that surface in the exchange between the Fox and the Ape. These are that once fellow-feeling is recognized, its scope will tend to expand as more and more affinities are discovered, here for example those of neighborhood, gossiphood, etc.; that in principle sympathy forms a bond while lack of sympathy isolates and divides; that the discovery of sympathy either facilitates or is co-extensive with the discovery of trust and friendship; that victimization constitutes the most powerful or reliable bond of sympathy, taken in the sense of being and feeling alike; that what lies "inward" is a normally inexpressible pain or "agonie," capable of being uttered only in the sympathetic setting that also elicits its disclosure; that the *language* of this undisclosed agony is what constitutes a true exchange, enabling one sufferer to "find" another and to strike upon his "wit" with irresistible force (as if there is a natural affinity between the expression of pain and the human understanding).

Just listing these assumptions is almost enough to specify the terms of a sentimental poetics in which language functions in or as the medium of sympathy, and to which (now hidden) pain is again fundamental. To list these *assumptions* of sympathy is, however, virtually to list its deceptions and ruses – or at least that is so in "Mother Hubberd," in which Spenser as poet represents them in the exchange between charlatans. Is there something other than sympathy, or "another" sympathy, to which recourse may be had in the poem?

It could be argued that in terms of a rigorous Calvinistic theodicy available to Spenser[39] there is simply never and nowhere any ground for complaint. (In slightly different terms, complaint would always beg the question of true culpability). So if from a skeptical point of view it might be impossible ever to distinguish between proper and improper forms of complaint (with all the contingent differences between proper and improper selves, friendships, communities, etc.), from the standpoint of this theodicy it might hardly matter if one could, since, if the difference were not rendered irrelevant by the doctrine of election, any such condition would be culpably remote from that of penitence and understanding. From this standpoint, the Fox and the Ape as "guilty" selves, friends, victims, etc. might paradoxically emerge as morally superior to those whose unhappy but also "stupidly good" plight they seemingly exploit, rendering "sympathy" inappropriate.

Setting out in the somewhat Chaucerian disguise of soldier and yeoman, but also in the guise of an established (and pitiable) Elizabethan "ciuile begging sect,"[40] that of unprovided old soldiers, the Ape and the

Fox assume their respective theatrical roles as actors. The Fox also assumes the role of scenarist and director:

> Be you the Souldier, for you likest are
> For manly semblance, and small skill in warre:
> I will but wayte on you, and as occasion
> Falls out, my selfe fit for the same will fashion.[41]

Here no doubt we enter the field of Elizabethan theatricality and improvisation, but also of cultural fashioning and self-fashioning,[42] that may begin virtually at the level of street theater but which will, as the poem progresses, manifest themselves all the way to the top. (Is Raleigh the *miles gloriosus*, Spenser the deferential underling really in control of the production?) This "parasitic" order of theatrical deception is still ostensibly contained within an ontologically grounded order of degree and kind. Adhering somewhat to the structure of medieval estates' satire, Spenser takes his protagonists up a social ladder at every rung of which "abuses" disclose themselves, but at which it is also, it seems, possible to find examples of "good" shepherds and courtiers, if not of clerics.[43] Yet this goodness seems inseparable from inertia and even from nullity, a condition that seems also to have overtaken the passively "good" poetic persona at the start of the poem.

In contrast to those who stay at home, knowing their places and kinds, the Ape and the Fox are committed from their ostensibly marginalized start to fortune, to self-fashioning, and to boundless desire rationalized by an equally unlimited claim to prior unjust deprivation. If this is also the inescapable dynamic of the Spenserian career (to which endless "complaint" testifies, always perhaps to be regarded as voiced in the [mis]appropriated language of the woman) it is one that is strongly disavowed in "Mother Hubberd," in which the authorial persona asserts his distance from the protagonists and even from the "folk" art of Mother Hubberd as narrator.

Yet this withdrawal or ostensible paralysis of the poetic persona tends only to reinforce our perception that the Fox and the Ape are more than just subversive actors. They are the sole *agents* in a world otherwise characterized by stasis; they are even the sole *moral* agents in a world in which "good" exists only in forms of gullibility, corruption, or virtually suspended animation. (The latter is notably the case with the "ideal" courtier poet represented in 717-792 and often taken for a complimentary representation of Sir Philip Sidney.) The performance of suffering and the appeal for sympathy seem to belong entirely to an order of vigorous deception in which sympathy is always a contradictory appearance, and in which moral action is capable of occurring only in the paradoxical or negative form of relentless scourging of the weak and foolish. Once again, it may be asked, to what "other" sympathy does the poem offer recourse?

The Fox and the Ape begin by appealing to the sympathy of a shepherd, presumably a good one, since after the Ape's mournful recital ("that same he weeping sayes,"[44] the shepherd "was grieu'd, as he had felt part of his paine."[45] The good shepherd, we take it, feels an authentic compassion for the purported victim, and goes on to supply the relief that the situation calls for, albeit thus setting himself up for exploitation. Yet even if we took it that we are here called on to distinguish between authentic and spurious sympathy, a distinction reinforced by all the traditional and Biblically loaded distinctions between the shepherd and the predators that ravage his flock, we would still have to notice the *reflexiveness* of the act of sympathy: the "his" in line 260 implies not just compassion for the other, but a possible "discovery" by the shepherd of *his* own pain in a manner similar to that of the Ape earlier in the poem. The insidiousness of sympathy is thus implied in the very language that seemingly extols it, and the reader can appreciate the joke if s/he has even for a moment thought that a legitimation of sympathy was under way in the exchange between the fox and the good shepherd. What good meaning could it *ever* have for a shepherd to be drawn into sympathy with a fox? Is the shepherd culpably unsuspecting, or does he become a fox himself – employing the vagabonds as substitutes with no questions asked so that *he* may take a holiday from his ordained duties?

We expect that the shepherd will return after his unexplained (unjustified?) absence to find the flock massacred and the pseudo-shepherds gone. The expectation is almost fulfilled when the flock *is* massacred and the "shepherds" flee; all that remains is for the shepherd to return and be confronted by the results of his folly. To anticipate this moment, sympathizing with the shepherd in this predicament, would however be to sympathize with gross negligence if not with self-serving deviousness under the guise of compassion; the figure of the negligent steward is superimposed on that of the shepherd as if to make the point.

Throughout the poem, the successes and various outrages of the Ape and the Fox become not only functions of the incapacity or corruption of those they delude, but also question the forms (or is it formalisms?) inhabited by those they outwit, for example, those of legitimate pastoral or courtliness. Their own egregiousness and "formless" improvisation also come perilously close to representing the true if normally unacknowledged dynamic of the society through which they move. At no level of that society do they fail to find themselves at home. Nor does their "impersonation" ever fail until they turn against each other, or before the Ape in particular, having recklessly forfeited the services of his manipulator, stands "vncased ... like as a Puppit placed in a play,/ Whose part once past all men bid take away."[46] (Poor Raleigh?) If there is an emergent point to the "satire," it is that the successful careers of the Fox and the Ape are practically definitive of the successful career as such in the context of Elizabethan cultural politics; the question then, *pace* the *Variorum* editors, is not: "to whom in what circumstances might the poem refer?" but rather, "to whom in what circumstances does the poem positively *not* refer?" Ironically, indeed, if the poem as good satire declines to name names, confining itself to general abuses, the flip side of that decorum (or testimony to the power of censorship) is that the abuses *are* generalized as those of the system (or simply "encode" themselves in the poem), and practically anyone in appropriate circumstances becomes a candidate for identification. (Raleigh as upstart, monopolist, fortune-hunter, performer and notoriously overweening courtier? Burghley as upstart "mock-king,"[47] self-aggrandizing influence-peddler and alleged destroyer of the old nobility? Leicester as relative upstart, *miles gloriosus*, and would-be power behind the throne? Edmund Spenser as ever-plaintive victim successfully orchestrating his own rise to poetic pre-eminence?)

To read the poem in this way is implicitly to deny its own or the poet's ability to *differ* significantly from the cultural-political order in which they arise, or to gain access to anything but the real, political forms of power, privilege, and success constitutive of that order. "Representation" accordingly becomes a kind of tautology such that the power of representation is also the representation of power in a closed circuit from which the "other" is always excluded, or included only in a devitalized form. Any claim to poetic autonomy, particularly one resting on the notion of sympathetic representation, appears to be foreclosed in these circumstances. Yet for Spenser this foreclosure is precisely the point to be resisted.

The question which the history of the Fox and the Ape elicits in the poem is this: "what ultimate cause, or ultimate abdication, creates the vacuum in the 'animal kingdom' that allows crime to mount up to a reign of terror and permits moral agency only in a negative or inverted form?" With this question, a turning away from the poem's field of political *likeness* is effected, and "another" scheme of things, albeit incomplete or deficient in the present, is reintroduced for consideration. This scheme is at once allusively imported into the poem and allowed to remain unfulfilled in the story of the "good" shepherd. We do not come to the *end* of that story in the poem; the shepherd merely does not return, and a revisionary ending isn't excluded in principle. The figure of the in-adequate shepherd typologically prefigures that of Christ as the fully adequate one, not only moved by compassion but incapable of being deceived on that account. Any prediction or assumption that the Fox and the Ape are getting away with it is therefore premature; can never be anything but premature. No narrative, by the same token, can be taken as concluded even if the personalities around whom it seems to revolve come to the end of the line; the narratable is always of necessity the unconcluded or inconclusive.

The poem's completion is accordingly played out in an allusive context of incompletion, a fact that tells harshly against the protagonists who hubristically assume that they have come to the end when they have merely reached the top, completing a success story. While the poem's own dénouement might seem subject to the same limitation, as might Mother Hubberd's narrative insofar as *she* assumes that it is all over once she has shown the predictable downfall of the protagonists, that dénouement may nevertheless be said not to foreclose all further possibilities, nor does it necessarily oppose the law of temporal incompletion and/or typological fulfillment.

What appears to mark the limit to the operations of the two predators is a surprising return of sympathy in the poem, or return of the poem *to* the power of sympathy. A sheep, who has been promised favor by the Fox, comes to court to complain:

> How that the Wolfe her mortall enemie
> Had sithence slaine her Lambe most cruellie;
> And therefore crau'd to come vnto the King,
> To let him knowe the order of the thing.[48]

There is no question here of the sheep's innocence; as a humble client of the Fox in a manifestly "unnatural" relationship, she does not exist outside the network of patronage and corruption. But if there is a deepening of the appeal for sympathy and natural justice, hence for a restoration of proper order that the abdicated Lion-king seems to have forgotten, that may partly be because complaint is voiced by the female persona, and partly because the Wolf has appeared on the scene. Significantly a "cousin" to the Fox, the Wolf does not possess the mischievousness and charm that the Fox still inherits from the Reynard tradition to which the poem owes something, but is a figure of unmitigated rapaciousness and ungovernable savagery, the wholly "uncivil" creature. It is moreover the natural enemy and figurative Biblical assailant of the sheep. The Fox thus gets himself in deeper when, defending his cousin, he sends the sheep packing "with heauie hart."[49] The moment in which he does so to the sheep and "so manie more" is also the one in which Jove finally takes note of what is happening.

We cannot say that it is simply on account of the sheep's appeal that

Jove intervenes. In fact, if Jove finally takes cognizance of the situation it is because the strife in the animal kingdom threatens to cease being the division that enables him to rule passively and to become a form of misrule threatening to his own. Yet in acting for himself, Jove also acts for the reader – or on behalf of the reader's presumably continuing (or in-need-of-reawakening) sympathetic concern, however childish, about the fate of the poem's animal victims. In despatching Mercury to restore order, Jove sends one who does *hear* "complaints"[50] without obviously appropriating them as his own, and who does see into rather than through the complainants:

> And through the power of that, he putteth on
> What shape he list in apparition. . . .
> Thenceforth he past into each secrete part,
> Whereas he saw, that sorely grieu'd his hart,
> Each place abounding with fowle iniuries,
> And fild with treasure rackt with robberies.[51]

Such, finally, is the poem's "other" – other sympathy, other theatricality, other poetic, other form of power – and what secures the difference is a transcendental origin or determination either lacking or "forgotten" elsewhere in the poem.

If it may seem to us that this other is always the same as what it opposes – theft against theft, violence against violence, sympathy against sympathy, power against power – and if moreover that "same" seems now to be invested only with a facile Spenserian narcissism mercifully absent in the previous sections of the poem, it is also a repetition that may come to be taken as heuristic rather than affirmative. A saving difference, and by the same token a final and saving act of divine sympathy which is also, in the case of Mercury, sympathetic divination of the "secret part," is not foreclosed in principle, but rather typologically projected into a sphere beyond the poem, a possibility that arises in the Renaissance tradition of reading Virgil's fourth eclogue typologically as prefiguring the incarnation as well as in Boccaccio's allegorical rehabilitation of pagan fiction. Both completion and a saving difference await the finally imaginable if not representable "return" of the shepherd/pastor/poet, an exemplary figure now absent from the poem, but whose space remains and whose absence continues forever to be marked. Mercury, the embodiment of the poetic function, becomes not only an active figure but the single liminal one, passing between the world of the poem and that of the "other," but also, by virtue of sympathy alone, between self and other.

If it is possible to deal somewhat schematically as I have done with the poem's ending (one in which the transgressors are also unmasked) that is because the terms of its evidently allegorical or typological solution are of a kind familiar in Renaissance poetics. The solution isn't the particular point of interest, and in any case a "crisis" that may vitiate any such solution, either in the poem or as we articulate it critically, has been succinctly described by Robert Durling in an essay on Petrarch's "The Ascent of Mont Ventoux:"

> it is difficult to avoid projecting our own critical concerns into the texts of the past [but] I believe it is possible to demonstrate that Petrarch's letter...is based on a precise and clear problematic inherent in allegorical discourse [in which] one event "means" another event, either by anticipating it, foreshadowing it, or by recalling it, fulfilling it and thereby illuminating it. [But in Petrarch] the parallels are negative. In place of the integrative, resynthesizing process of Augustine's experience, we find disjunction, the dissolution of possible connections, negative parallels.[52]

If (or as) the cumulative, proleptic movement of "positive" allegory yields to the disjunctive, endlessly protracted movement of "negative" allegory, a certain loss of urgency, as Durling points out, comes to attend the arrival of what may be marked as crucial or terminal points (a fact of some significance in accounting for the prodigious ["endlesse"] nature of *The Faerie Queene*).

The significant point in my terms is, however, that a virtually magical, compelling and transforming power of sympathy is reclaimed towards the end of the poem, both as the represented irresistible plea of affliction and as forceful intervention of the "other" in response to that plea. The poetic capacity to differ endlessly – endlessly to represent both the other and itself *as* other – seemingly exists only on the ground of a "sympathy" which, if it must always be marked as insufficient, continues nevertheless to *be* so marked in Spenser – but also to be marked as an unforeclosed possibility on which poetic representation as such depends. And the technical device that enables the poet to effect this representation of what is absent, silenced or other is named in the title to "Mother Hubberd's Tale" itself; it is the "prosopopeia" that Puttenham defines [under Hypotoposis] as the power to "faine any person with such features, qualities and conditions, or...[to] attribute any humane quality as reason or speech to dombe creatures or other insensible things."[53]

There is a final point to be made. If it can be affirmed (as I believe it can) that commitment to an always deeply problematical sympathy, or to sympathetic representation, constitutes the poetic version of keeping the faith, that faith is one accompanied by its own heresy. Insofar as sympathy enters into Spenser's poetic at the foundational, practically molecular, level, this heresy continuously shadows it, yet its very shadowiness and scandalousness make it such that its existence can hardly be proved according to the rules of scholarly evidence (in this case equivalent to those of legal incrimination). It is thus close to being no subject at all for scholarly research, and can best be dealt with in a postscript to the more readily admissible good faith of sympathy. The heresy in question is one that I will refer to as that of *aggressive* sympathy.

The existence of this heresy becomes perspicuous in Spenser's work once "sympathy" is established as an important general factor; the heresy then emerges as a special or particular case, albeit as one that threatens to take precedence over the general case. For this heresy to be detected, however, certain quite well-established premises concerning Spenser's work have to be accepted. One of these is the premise that Spenser's poetic representations, and particularly his representations of Queen Elizabeth, are powerfully charged with animus, this being the case in the highly theatricalized world of Elizabethan court politics. Spenser as *courtly* poet contributes, it has been argued, to the production of a political power that at once sustains and threatens his existence, thus doubleness is always a feature of his courtly–political representations.[54] The image of the queen is, for example, endlessly magnified (she is empowered) but also endlessly doubled, fragmented and dispersed (she is disabled) in the poetic operation that constitutes *The Faerie Queene*. The specifically heretical element enters the situation insofar as the Elizabethan courtly world resembles a masquerade of power in which the poet must also participate.

The transactions within that real-life masque must be supposed to occur between aggressive–defensive personae, and the penetration of the mask (unmasking of the actor) can be conceived by the poet (or by the reader, on whom the interpretation must depend) as the supreme terror but also the supreme desire of those engaged in the performance. The mask as a self-objectification, as a projection of power, and as a defense against aggression is also that behind which the self is forever imprisoned. Or rather behind which, given the eternal publicity of Elizabethan courtly–political life and the vulnerability of those involved in it, the self is doomed to perpetual solitary confinement. Spenser can accordingly represent, or be taken to represent, the queen in a mode of aggressive sympathy that ostensibly responds to her own *desire* for the mask of the eternal virgin to be penetrated, enabling recognition of her hidden fears and wishes; recognition of her "self." The quite remarkably persistent iconoclasm of Spenser's representations of the queen can accordingly be seen as a paradoxical function of sympathy, whatever its other determinants may be.

But how is this to be seen, let alone proved? For Spenser simultaneously to reproduce the queen's image and shatter it in the always public discourse of poetry would obviously be a delicate operation, one capable of being performed only "gently" and under fairly deep cover. I would, however, suggest that the "November" eclogue in *The Shepheardes Calender* (1579), in which the Colin Clout persona mourns the reported death of "Dido" while promising her immortality (even granting her a power of self-regeneration) can be so read. The poem does violence, in other words, by anticipating the aging queen's death.[55] To do so in as many words was of course politically out of the question for Spenser or anyone else, and could theoretically have exposed the author to the charge of treasonably "imagining" the ruler's death.[56] Yet in the masquerade of *The Shepheardes Calender*, very little is out of the question, including this and other forms of treason.

The plausibility of this reading is conferred partly by the poem's condoling with the great shepherd "Lobbin" (Leicester/Robin?) on his (anticipated) bereavement, and indeed the identity of "Dido" as well as the poet's stake in the order she sustains is suggested by the lines, inapplicable to anyone but Elizabeth, that read:

> The beastes in forest wayle as they were woode,
> Except the Wolues, that chase the wandring sheepe:
> Now she is gon that safely did hem keepe . . .[57]

And the celestial fields in which the poet-speaker eventually "sees" Dido regenerated are called, not without archness, "Elisean." The poem thus "responds," at least at a certain level, to the fears and wishes capable of being sympathetically inferred as those of the queen.

I would suggest, too, that the extraordinarily tender if oblique consolations offered to the mourning "Venus" in the Gardens of Adonis episode of *The Faerie Queene*, Book III, can also be read in this way, possibly as Spenser's public/private condolence upon the death in 1588 of an actual Adonis, the Earl of Leicester, for whom the queen's own mourning was reportedly intense but utterly private:

The news was brought to Elizabeth, and she received it in the way that was characteristic of her. Though public even to indiscretion in her pleasure and enjoyments, all her life she made a private thing of her grief. Only when she was old and weak, and had lost Burleigh, did the tears run down her cheeks when others named him; but usually she

wept alone. Over this friend, hid in death's dateless night, her silence at
last alarmed those about her. She retired into a chamber by herself;
hours, a day, a night, another day passed, and she would let no one in.
At last Lord Burleigh acted. Taking some of the council with him, he
ordered the door to be broken open.[58]

Although the few facts as distinct from sentimental inferences in this
passage are cited from the Spanish diplomatic correspondence, I have
quoted the passage in full since the sentimental intonations aren't
necessarily false, any more than the author's "vulgar"/unpolitical
assumptions are necessarily false; perhaps only incomplete. (Indeed, any
propensity of our own to suppress or displace these forms of pathos,
assuming the mutual exclusiveness of the political and the sentimental,
could itself result in historical falsification.) It is precisely in that nexus
between the political and the personal, the private and the public, that
the possibility of the sympathetic heresy arises.

Unlike Burghley who, supported by earnest, well-meaning courtiers,
broke down the door, Spenser enjoyed the possibility of simultaneously
keeping his distance and very "delicately" penetrating the sanctuary of
the queen's grieving self. In the Gardens of Adonis, and in her own arbor,
one impervious to the ordinary male-poetic violence figured by "*Phoebus
beams*" or "*Aeolus* sharp blast," Spenser's Venus withdraws to reminisce,
fantasize and mourn, but not to do so unseen by a sympathetic witness:

> There wont faire *Venus* often to enioy
> Her deare *Adonis* ioyous company,
> And reape sweete pleasure of the wanton boy;
> There yet, some say, in secret he does ly,
> Lapped in flowres and pretious spycery,
> By her hid from the world, and from the skill
> Of Stygian Gods, which do her loue enuy.[59]

Some malicious or "disabling" mileage can undoubtedly be got out of this
passage; that of a Plutonian Burghley, enemy to love and would-be captor
of the "passionate" queen, but also of a queen, whose virginity is hardly a
condition of known fact let alone of mind, now embalming her beloved in
necrophiliac fantasy. Yet the passage's power to manifest the truth of the
"queen's" condition as well as its offered consolation are still sympathetic
in the heretical terms specified above.

So if sympathy in the guise of "gentle" violence – of an endlessly
intrusive, presumptuous and irresistible *lèse-majesté* – informs these
particular examples, it can no less be taken to inform such extended
sympathetic portrayals as that of Britomart-as-woman in Books III–V of

The Faerie Queene. (Despite many testimonials to the success of Spenser's sympathetic representation of Britomart, the enabling conditions of that claimed success have not, to my knowledge, seriously been considered.) As an always deniable activity pursued at a very respectful distance (and who would have dared to make the accusation?) this heretically sympathetic representation may be described as the one humanizing possibility evident in an otherwise frigid courtly masque, recalling the one repeated daily in Spenser's fictional House of Busirane. Yet it is in recalling that place rather than the Gardens of Adonis, and in recalling the Evil Enchanter who imprisons and terrorizes Amoret by exploiting her own bleeding heart, that the irredeemably heretical nature of aggressive sympathy becomes evident.

Any claim to act for the good on the basis of such sympathy would depend on an impossibly drastic separation of the supposedly constrained public persona, of which even gender would have to be regarded as a mere function, from the hermetic self. It would also depend on the assumption of an underlying, transgeneric identity of selves and conditions authorizing aggressively sympathetic action (Scheler's "savagery" under the guise of perfect manners). And it would depend lastly on the forever impermissible presumption of acting violently upon another person at his/her secret or politically censored wish. Not only are all these assumptions questionable to say the least, but Spenserian aggressive sympathy can hardly appear to be other than sublimated rape, accompanied by the masculinist justification, forestalling any possible voiced objection, that it is his/her unspeakable or politically censored desire. Spenser's prolonged and repeated violation of the defenseless subject (even if s/he is the royal one in most cases) constitutes to all appearances an insidious and sustained form of terrorism, the ultimate power-play of the "political" poet. And if aggressive sympathy cannot ever appear otherwise, it cannot be reclaimed or professed, remaining merely the heresy shadowing poetic good faith.[60]

3
Countercurrents

In the previous chapter what I have called the quest for a crime had come up with a result inasmuch as a heresy had been uncovered, yet that unforeseen result wasn't quite equivalent to the discovery of a crime, nor is the archaic tribunal of inquisition (even of secular inquisition) the one to which this detective enterprise refers itself. And although Spenser had come under suspicion – or remained under consideration in a "hermeneutic of suspicion" – the need to pursue other leads was dictated by the developing contingencies of the profession.

The next three chapters were written almost as one. Although the foregoing discussion of Spenserian sympathy made some claim to be historically informed, and was actually informed by some historicist work cited in the notes, these chapters constitute a virtually compelled response, not to the beginning, but to the real breakthrough of historicism in the sixteenth-century field. Not simply being informed by historicism but taking explicit account of it had become critically necessary. The chapters thus reveal one of the major contingencies to which the criticism of sixteenth-century literature has lately been subject, but no less are they a tribute to the sustained initiative of the individual critics who brought about this result.

Simply as a record of events, my own narrative has no difficulty in assimilating the phenomenon of historicism, yet logical assimilation of this historicism to the critical concerns of the foregoing essays was, and remains, another matter. Insofar as that assimilation was possible, these chapters show the attempt to effect it, but always subject to the difficulty, verging on impropriety, of trying to have it both ways: of accepting certain historicist data and premises while trying to rewrite the history and redraw the conclusions. No transitional formula is proposed, but the issue of Spenserian sympathy does re-emerge under this historicist aspect as well as that of "representation."

In the meantime, and in chronological sequence, the next essay deals with Sidney. Considering the case of Spenser was always implicitly to consider that of Sidney as a parallel and/or counterinstance. As things progressed within the field, moreover, the additional need to read Puttenham's glosses on sixteenth-century poetry became ever more compelling. The historicist approach increasingly revealed what could be done with *The Arte of English Poesie* as a manual of courtly maneuver and above all of courtly dissimulation – as a work disclosing the rich political "subtext" of sixteenth-century poems formerly capable of being seen as pure aesthetic phenomena or at most as broadly ideological utterances. Puttenham's work seemed also silently to be displacing Sidney's *Apology for Poetry* as the major interpretive document of English sixteenth-century poetics. Precisely to the degree that Puttenham's *Arte* demystified the poetry in question – or gave the game away, in the idiom of detection – Sidney's *Apology* appeared to do the opposite by idealizing and hence obfuscating ("covering up") the practice of sixteenth-century poets. Not only did the *Apology*, unlike Puttenham's *Arte*, offer no detailed account of the functioning of poetic language in courtly settings – or of any material language in any material setting at all – but its exaltation of the omnipotent poetic mind could be taken as underwriting a persistent (and false) "idealist" conception of sixteenth-century poetry.

The substitution of Puttenham for Sidney as the authoritative English commentator on the poetry of his contemporaries could be taken as one striking occurrence in the brief history of the new historicism, but for the dislodgment of Sidney to have been effected it was also necessary for a sustained, general critique of critical "idealism" and/or "essentialism" to have occurred, as it did on the widest possible scale before and during the surfacing of the new historicism in the 1980s. Without, I hope, exaggerating the individual importance of Puttenham (or Sidney, for that matter) I took it that the implications of this shift, and the styles of reading that might emerge in consequence of it, remained fundamental issues for any critic of sixteenth-century literature.

I should begin by acknowledging a certain initial suspicion of historicism on account of what seemed to be its allegorical character – a suspicion capable of being repaid at compound interest as a counter-suspicion of invidiousness. It appeared to me, nevertheless, that the purported historicization of sixteenth-century literature, in the course of which such topics as those of ambition, of career management, of patronage and clientage, of authority and power, of social mobility and of *ancien régime* political styles rapidly became dominant, was often little more than an allegory of current professional life, or perhaps more accurately of a desired mastery of it as it was coming to be understood. In fact, the disconcerting speed with which this historicism and its favored topics gained ground suggested that it had virtually been a suppressed discourse awaiting articulation during the preceding phase of "theoretical" hegemony and/or of critical radicalism. However well-founded this historicism might thus seem, and however its arguments might be framed, its interest could hardly be described, even in its own terms, as purely historical. Its acknowledged theoretical reticence suggested, moreover, a certain unwillingness to consider what it was actually about.

Especially given the forthrightness of Stanley Fish on the nature and motives of the professional life – and on the professional life as one capable of being conceived forthrightly – it was possible to react with a certain impatience to this masked discourse of professional careerism; to see it as veiling its own fundamental interest, sometimes even from itself. It was also possible to anticipate a progressive, banalizing assimilation of major sixteenth-century authors to limited patterns of competition, clientage and career advancement (indeed, to limited conceptions of the political as such) that could more compellingly be identified in our own professional setting than in that of the authors in question. Yet my own initial repudiation came to seem premature if not unjustified. For me to profess an interest in Spenser, the ultimate allegorist, and in his political representations would not only be to incur a debt to historicism, but might also be to recognize, from an implicated position, the impossibility of "forthrightness," the complicated necessity of allegorical masking, and the pressure of the contingencies determining current historicist practice.

Instead of trying to address these issues, however (even if one perceived them to exist, it didn't necessarily follow that there was anything of great interest to be said about them), I found myself overtaken by another and perhaps more exciting interest, namely in the stories that historicism was telling (or perhaps newly authorizing) about sixteenth-century writers. The highly narrativized character of historicist criticism – its frequent express or implied recourse to authorial biographies, including psychobiographies, its dependence on historical narratives of mobility or crisis, its concern with paradigmatic careers – prompted me to explore a little further the stories being told, or capable of being told, about these authors in their particular situations. Given, that is to say, the premises and resources of current historicism, what else might follow? To what extent might the limits imposed by a self-allegorizing professional careerism be surpassable in these historicist narratives, enabling the possible strangeness, otherness, or even "truth" of the authors in question to be recognized? Pursuing such concerns would carry with it the risk of producing work that could be recognized neither as legitimate criticism nor as legitimate fiction (let alone as history), yet the now-uncontentious view that any critical act whatever implies an unfounded quasi-fictional narrative (of origin, of fall, of rise, of crisis, of rupture, or whatever) allowed some hope of leeway in this matter. It seemed possible, moreover, instead of theorizing further, to attempt something like critical counter-narrative in these circumstances.

The dangerous turn that my discussion had taken was, however, quite soon brought home to me. One reader of the following essay for an exalted journal wrote in terms unusually threatening in an academic context that "[he] had better mend his ways." "It isn't my style," said a professional colleague dismissively about another of these essays. "You seem to be trying to do things differently," said yet another colleague, failing to add whether that was a good or a bad thing. If I had begun innocently enough, I could not long remain so. I understood express or implied charges to include those of un- or anti-professionalism (the sorest point?), regression to conspiracy theorizing and/or fanciful biography, and perhaps a certain failure of the required attitude. Since it wasn't, and still isn't, clear to me whether criticism or merely error attracted this disapproval, the book goes on.

Historicism[1] and the romance of Astrophil

In a general essay, which deals with Sidney's sonnets among other English ones, Arthur Marotti lays down the principle that what looks like amorous courtship and performance (i.e. pure romance) in Elizabethan sonnet sequences must in fact be read as competitive display within a male-narcissistic peer group, as political solicitation within a paternalistic order, and as manipulation for political ends of the privileged cultural signs that constitute poetry.[2] The argument Marotti presents has political, anthropological, psychoanalytic and semiotic components, but it is also nevertheless an historicist argument, meaning that it calls for detailed reconstruction of the historical contexts in which Elizabethan sonnets were produced and meant to work, not to entertain. The phase of Elizabethan sonneteering is, in Marotti's argument, a temporally circumscribed one, and its reconstruction can be effected through a documentary approach to the period.

Like many arguments now classified as historicist, Marotti's is not, nor does it claim to be, historical. It involves, that is to say, no theory of history or historiographic rules whatever, and is unembarrassed by the lack. Typically of such arguments, furthermore, its procedures are mixed and it incorporates without apparent strain the methods as well as the results of work done in such non- or anti-historical disciplines as those mentioned before: semiotics, psychoanalysis and anthropology. Although not antipathetic to notions of theoretical rigor, the essay in fact dispenses with the rigor of any single discipline or method, and its accommodating nature is not untypical of historicism, which, as Louis Montrose observes, tends to be theoretically reticent – a formulation we could translate to mean self-indulgent.

Marotti's argument works through a series of categorical displacements as now one discipline and now another comes uppermost. The result, generically speaking, is that this particular historicist argument takes on the mixed, shifting character of romance, and even of inclusive Arcadian romance, despite its own apparent aspiration towards truth, scholarly virtue, and a no-nonsense treatment of flighty Elizabethan sonneteers. If there is a master narrative that governs the argument, it is the one supplied by Lawrence Stone in *The Crisis of the Aristocracy*,[3] which is to say a narrative of seemingly if not actually limitless political advance and/or class-mobility. It is a narrative which, I would suggest, has proved irresistibly seductive to many recent historicist critics, and its reinscription in historicism has been almost obsessive. Implicitly, too, this narrative, which I will call anti-romance (i.e. inverted romance), is always an allegorization of contemporary professional life, reimagined following the countercultural upheavals of the sixties and early seventies, as the restored life of an *ancien régime*. The Romance of the Stone thus appears to embody the new/old dream of our own professionalism.

Yet who are we (am I) to mock? To be free of this dream, or seriously to oppose it, may simply not at present be within our power. All that can reasonably be called for is a certain critical consciousness of what historicism is, how it operates, and what is implied in its now being "our" genre. The most I can practically undertake in dealing with Marotti's argument and with Sidney's poems is an attempt to trouble the romance of historicism a bit more than is normally done; the effect of my doing so, however, will hardly be to undermine that romance but if anything to diversify and intensify it. I will also implicitly ask whether any romance, including that of Astrophil, can be quite as narrowly directed towards a nameable goal or object of desire as some historicist arguments, positing "ambition" or "success" as master-terms, suppose it to be.

Before proceeding to the discussion of Sidney, I want to specify more fully what I think Marotti is saying, what would be taken as uncontentious in historicist criticism generally. It is that all the important Elizabethan sonnet sequences, whether written by Shakespeare, Spenser, Greville, Daniel, Sidney or others, constitute masked acts of political courtship in a patronage system in (or of) which, to quote Montrose again, the royal court is the "cynosure."[4] The "courtier" or "courtly lover," while making claims or revealing aspirations to gentility, will in fact be a client, perhaps an upstart (but who isn't in that world?) and certainly a careerist. The message of these politically *coded* poem sequences always concerns the political life of the courtier (its competitive conditions, its frustrations and its goals) and this is no less true when the dispenser of political favor happens to be a woman – Queen Elizabeth, Mary Sidney or any other putative patroness. While Petrarch, for example, may pursue the political and other rewards of the literary life in a strictly male world under the diversionary guise of courting an imaginary *mistress,* English sonneteers of high ambition can address themselves, if they wish, to real patronesses under the guise of courting *imaginary* mistresses. So even when nominally addressed to the various Stellas, Caelicas, Delias and Myras of the Elizabethan romance world, these sonnets may almost transparently address themselves as letters of courtship to putative patronesses in the real-political world of courts and powerful families.[5]

In addition to soliciting political favor and recognition, or as part of the process of doing so, these sonnets inevitably become records of the courtier's anguish and frustration in the political world he inhabits. They therefore become covert political autobiographies while still looking from the outside (an outside capable of being seen only by a naive middle-class reading audience?)[6] like the romance narrative of a pining aristocratic lover; the Astrophil-type. To conclude: the inside story, which is also the real one, is political, while the outside story is the hollow one of erotic romance. In general, the political discourse of the sonnets is masked from the world and can be understood only in the settings in which the sonnets were produced; in detail, that complex political discourse is coded in an "empty" language supplied by inherited conventions of amorous romance. (Or in a seemingly empty language of which the former political content has merely been lost or forgotten.)[7] There is nothing in principle to prevent the full political story from being "read" by a modern reader once s/he knows where to look for it, both in the poems and in contemporary records, and in principle the poems are capable of being fully decoded. The content of the sonnet sequences is a determinate political one rather than an indeterminate "aesthetic" or imaginative one, and any apparently nonsignifying flourishes or effects can be ascribed to the general imperative of competitive self-display, perhaps in what Eve Sedgwick has called a male homosocial system.[8]

It might seem as if this redefinition of the content of sonnet sequences leaves at least one major assumption untouched, namely that the sonnets are a record of passion (compulsive pursuit/quixotic endurance). What seems to change is only an understanding of the nature of the passion, or rather of its real goal and setting. Whereas it might once have been supposed in a naive, blinded, bourgeois way that passion is erotic, it now appears that authentic passion is political. The courtier's compulsive pursuit of socio-political rewards (ones seemingly offered and yet never fully given) becomes the sign and consequence of a passion inaccessible to explanation but also really needing none; we all know it at first hand – do we not? – and that is the knowledge that also tells us who we really are. Yet if it might still seem unacceptable that historicism should beg the question of this political "passion," thus substituting its own story of political antiromance for that of vulgar erotic romance on the retained unassailable premise of passion, there has also been a significant historicist effort to unbeg the question. The dynamics as well as the material rewards and punishments of the literary-political career have been studied with reference to its sixteenth-century cultural and political setting, one in which promises of limitless mobility and power are at least partly falsified by the stringent reimposition of hierarchical and other boundaries. Lawrence Stone's work, particularly *The Crisis of the Aristocracy*, has supplied the large framework in which the question can be treated with a certain critical consciousness, though not perhaps with enough to penetrate the core of the passion's mystery and power. Something is undoubtedly being exposed in Stoneian historicism, but something equally is being defended, left untouched. All this said, however, it remains unclear just what the consequences of political "passion" are in Elizabethan writing or what the apparently totalizing as well as linear dynamic of Elizabethan romance writing implies. I shall restrict myself to reviewing some of the things they seem to imply in Sidney.

In Marotti's view, the political antiromance of *Astrophil and Stella* cannot be overt, but has to be coded in the sense of being actually encrypted for the eyes of a courtly/coterie audience alone. The assumed point of the exercise is not so much the ongoing transmission of information or the relaying of a complex set of cultural and political instructions to future generations (one important sense in which "coding" might be understood) but rather the maintenance of romantic secrecy – of *open* secrecy in the community of readers to whom the political message is really addressed, of opacity to anyone else. This secrecy is negatively dictated by the possibility of censorship, inter-ference, reprisal, etc., and it is positively dictated by the need at once to mark the boundaries of the political "family" and to *constitute* it as an exclusive group of those who not only know, but stand to profit from their knowledge. We might characterize this state of affairs as Phase One political antiromance, namely the fully hermetic one of secrecy and espionage. This notion of antiromance needs, however, to be extended or modified in the case of Sidney.

Sidney's sonnets can undoubtedly be read as encrypted poems – famously so now that everyone recognizes the insinuated presence of Lady Penelope Rich, née Devereux (sister of the powerful Earl of Essex), as the real object of Sidney/Astrophil's devotion, and given that no such courtship can ever be taken as unpolitical in an Elizabethan courtly context. That there was a real "inside" community in which this secret was shared is suggested by the omission of sonnet 37 from the early published editions of *Astrophil and Stella*. This is the sonnet identifying with what might seem like vulgar obviousness (of parodied Chaucerian *fabliau*) Sidney's putative mistress:

> My mouth doth water, and my breast doth swell,
> > My tongue doth itch, my thoughts in labour be:
> > Listen then Lordings with good eare to me,
> For of my life I must a riddle tell.
> Towardes *Aurora's* court a Nymph doth dwell,
> > Rich in all beauties which man's eye can see: . . .
> Rich in the treasure of deserv'd renowne,
> Rich in the riches of a royall hart,
> > Rich in those gifts which give th'eternall crowne;
> > Who though most rich in these and everie part,
> > Which make the patents of true worldly blisse,
> > Hath no misfortune, but that Rich she is.[9]

Publication could presumably have been harmful in the 1590s to the increasingly exalted memory of Sir Philip, to the still living Penelope Rich, and possibly to many others, since as well as alluding to Lady Rich, the sonnet may also refer to Sidney's courtship of the old Rich Lady living in Westminster – Queen Elizabeth herself, a former mortal enemy of Sir Philip but somewhat reconciled to him before his death.[10] One of Sidney's editors points out that:

> The seat of the Riches was in Eastern England – at Leighs in Essex – so that the fairy-tale phrase "towards Aurora's court" has a direct reference; there may also be a sense of "near Queen Elizabeth's court."[11]

Yet even if the non-publication of sonnet 37 or its "misplacement" (it was included in the 1598 folio *Arcadia*) imply the existence of real secrets, and of an extended but still exclusive family in which Sidney's poems circulated, it is hard to take seriously the notion of actual encryptment. Such encryptment requires that the secret(s) be unambiguously readable by insiders, while to outsiders they must remain wholly opaque – or the cryptogram itself must paradoxically not be made available for decipherment. Such is the strict logic of encryptment, and if it applies in the case of Sidney's poems, the only conceivable motive would be to reaffirm the hermetic solidarity of the stable family and further exclude the excluded, who would not necessarily realize that they were being excluded. While such a motive isn't unthinkable, it *is* unthinkable that in the semi-public realm in which Elizabethan sonnets were produced and read an author could hope to maintain strict secrecy within a small family, or that a reader (virtually any conceivable reader of Elizabethan sonnets) would have settled for the romantic outside story. The fate of "restricted" manuscripts in the sixteenth century, which seems generally to have been to appear in print sooner or later, implies neither a strong desire nor a capacity to limit their circulation. Indeed, conflicting wishes for privileged insidedness and for *extended* family influence attained through publicity would necessarily result in an attempt to have it both ways: to hide and reveal the secret at the same time; to let the right outsiders become insiders. (Even historicists have not proved immune to being worked on by these clever poems.) Instead of strict encryptment, real secrets, perhaps there is only a flattering and seductive show of secrecy and the maintenance of "deniability," a term that Stephen Greenblatt has used in connection with Wyatt's *Penitential Psalms* and their apparent allusions to the sexual-political misbehavior of Henry VIII.[12] And if so, we are dealing with Phase Two of political antiromance, one that has to be regarded as a politically manipulative modification and successor to the fully hermetic antiromance of Phase One.

I would suggest on both logical and practical grounds, and even in the absence of sonnet 37, that the published *Astrophil and Stella* neither did nor was meant to conceal from any reader but an imbecile (or a hopeless outsider) the possible inside story of Sidney/Astrophil's courtship of Lady Rich. Who, in the Elizabethan semi-public realm which is in one sense just that of high literacy, would not have been tempted by the sonnets to identify the "real" object of Astrophil's courtship, and who would not have been able to take "rich" in several of the poems as a clue? Even before the publication of *Astrophil and Stella*, how successfully could the circulation of the sonnets have been restricted within a "family" that included Greville, Fraunce, Dyer, Daniel, Spenser, possibly Shakespeare, and no doubt two-thirds of the literary youth of England – and their "families," and so on, and so on? How seriously could the Sidneys as literary performers and power-brokers on the national scene have desired tight control over the circulation of their manuscripts? Their various disavowals imply only that they did seriously, hence threateningly, pursue power through authorship and patronage, and it now becomes increasingly possible to envisage Wilton, the estate of Mary Sidney, Countess Pembroke, as a counter-court.

What we seem to be dealing with, then, is not the narrow romance of encryptment and espionage, implying a hermetic fantasy of power – a high romance of letters, for the bold invention of which credit is due to Petrarch. Instead, we are dealing with a qualified version of that romance, in which the appearance of secrecy is manipulated for quite large public and political ends. In keeping with this hypothesis, another question follows: how seriously could Sidney or his sister have wanted to prevent general suspicion of his relationship with a nameable woman married to an *ipso facto* obnoxious rich husband? Wouldn't such a scandal (non-existent without names and circumstances) be incumbent, not just on a fictionally romantic Astrophil but on dashing, chivalrous "Sir" Philip, necessarily disdaining the pitiable taboos through which the bourgeois presume to legislate the existence of their betters? (Actually legislating it, of course, insofar as defiance of those taboos becomes "incumbent.") The Rich name is written out in sonnets 24 and 35 as well as in the already-noted 37, in which, to borrow a phrase from "Lycidas," it is "somewhat loudly" shouted. (Perhaps too loudly for the later hagiographic enterprise mounted by the Sidney "family" in publishing his works and variously memorializing him, though still important enough as information for the poem to be slipped in somewhere else.) The Devereux arms are, moreover, "encoded" in sonnet 13, and there may be many other "signs" that we don't recognize. How much more (or more direct) information would any conceivable Elizabethan *sonnet* reader have needed – perhaps especially a middle-class one wanting above all to be in the know? If the secret really was closed, surely it can only have been so to the illiterate or to those to whom it could not have had the slightest interest or importance.

It might admittedly be argued that it is not the mere fact but the details that are "deeply" coded, so that the mere identification of Lady Rich or the Rich Lady gives the outsider nothing – just a breath of scandal, domestic or courtly, and a romantic image of Sir Philip. The real inside story, then, may be one of detailed machinations and dynastic maneuvers. This assumption, which might lead to a revealing historical reconstruction of the dense political network in which Sidney moved, could be that of a serious and productive historicism. (It could also still be an unchallenged antiromance assumption, perpetuated to this day in such works as Paul

Fussell's recent one on class in America,[13] that any real aristocracy is virtually defined by its superiority to vulgar romance.) But even a serious, constructive historicism that investigated the inside story of Sidney's (feigned?) courtship of Lady Rich might come to the wrong conclusions, such as that the stakes and contexts of that courtship are the real, determinate content of the *Astrophil and Stella* sequence. How could it be established that that is so – or that that is the real inside story – without reference to some calculus or probability – perhaps even to some calculus of inherent interest, seriousness, or "richness?" Even given such a calculus, the difficulty that would remain in the case of Sidney's apparent courtship of Lady Rich is that the sonnet tradition includes, from the time of Dante's *Vita Nuova*, the figure of the screen woman,[14] the presence of whom tends at once to incite and forestall "discovery" of any single inside story.

In Dante, the apparent courtship of another woman masks, as the speaker assures Beatrice, his *real* love of her. The screen woman (screen romance) is necessary to satisfy public curiosity about Dante's lover-like behavior without allowing it any polluting glimpse of his chaste true love. Dante then tells the secret in print, making it "open." So never again will that device be able to work unsuspected, meaning that there will never again be an effectively screened One True Love, of whom the name is forever Beatrice. In *Astrophil and Stella*, there is quite simply more than one screen. Typically of Sidney, on whom no item in the sonneteer's inventory is wasted, the possibilities are multiplied. This multiplicity is not incompatible with the manipulative Phase Two romance I have attributed to Sidney, yet it is difficult to imagine how the potentially endless multiplication of appearances that becomes possible can be linked to any simple, determinate goal or *univocal* conception either of power or achievement. Merely listing some of the possibilities (not all of which are mutually exclusive) that arise may suggest the problem:

1 That the courtship of fictional Stella by fictional Astrophil (empty romance) screens but also reveals the courtship of Lady Rich and/or the Rich Lady by Sir Philip Sidney (political antiromance).

2 That the fictional Stella doesn't even qualify as a screen but remains a transparency, while the chivalrous courtship of Penelope Devereux as a screen woman masks but also reveals a real courtship of Queen Elizabeth. In this case, the courtship of Lady Rich (empty romance) may mask/unmask Sidney's true courtship of the queen (political anti-romance), but also his presumption, especially after having notoriously been rebuffed by the queen, and perhaps even the painful indecorum of having to court, for obviously political reasons, an ugly old rich woman, becoming the Miss Havisham of the English world by the 1580s.

3 That behind all these screen women there is yet another woman of whom the courtship and inside story (can it still be political?) remains to be discovered. One possibility, strong since the time of Petrarch, is of course that the true love solicited is that of the Muse, from whom the courtly lover may acquire a timeless superiority to conditions and persons to whom he must degradingly submit in the political present.

4 Behind a series of screen *women* there is a deeply screened man, even if he is only the imaginary object of a homoerotic passion that is still political (cf. the unmasking conducted in Shakespeare's sonnets).

5 Again invoking Shakespeare, that the real object of courtship is the self in an endless autoerotic transaction that at once promotes a powerful form of self-enclosure and a rich fantasy-life capable of being poetically embodied.

6 That an endless process of screening and self-mystification is itself the point, perhaps as a means to self-magnification in a political order in which no more than feigned subservience to self-denying goals and objectives can be afforded.

After the first screen woman has been put in place and then exposed as such, whether this happens once and for all in Dante or else begins all over again in any particular sonnet sequence, screens behind screens become all too easily imaginable, leading one to recognize that the real inside story or object of courtship may never be capable of discovery or may not exist. And if there is a single story, it now threatens to become very big and complicated; a story moreover on the inside of which the reader may find him/herself, wondering whether there is after all any "outside." S/he may also worry that s/he is still outside, excluded from an unpenetrated inside. And the very fact of penetrating any particular screen, a task more difficult in prospect than in retrospect, may itself become the "proof" that it cannot have been the real screen or have concealed a real secret; there "has" to be something more. Anyone who did assume that s/he had finally got the picture would risk being caught forever on the outside (i.e. an illusory inside) though that might forestall a good deal of further anxiety.

These possibilities are not simply academic, nor do I introduce them without consequence. What if Stella, Penelope Devereux, and Queen Elizabeth are all faked-out objects of romantic courtship, screen women? What could then be the inside story, and what, if anything, could still be getting screened? Before these questions even become askable, and thus potentially answerable, certain other assumptions have to be questioned. Did Sidney really not foresee that he would both threaten the queen and make himself unacceptable to her when he openly opposed her projected marriage to the Duc d'Alençon in 1580? (Interfering with *her* courtship, feigned or otherwise.) Did he, by the same token, really want to make his way back from rustication, himself considering it supremely desirable to pursue a public career under the queen's patronage? Do the sonnets in *Astrophil and Stella* really constitute a political courtship of that kind, the aftermath of Sidney's failure in and exclusion from the political world of which the royal court was the cynosure – the real star in the east on which Astrophil gazed entranced? Even if the answers to all of these questions tended to confirm that Sidney was a loser in the political game that he had chosen (or in "the only game in town"); even if, on top of that, we were to forget that Sidney's literary career or "unelected vocation" as a poet – as the one and only Sir Philip Sidney – was facilitated by his expulsion from public life; would it even *then* be possible to say that the Rich story is the inside story, and that Sidney is to be understood in terms of a prima facie commitment to self-advancement, public life, etc?[15] And perhaps the power relays are themselves more complex than they seem, the forms of indirection more subtle, the circuit not quite so short. Getting to the east, as we may recall from Donne, can involve travelling west, the opposite direction only in the short run. Might getting back to the queen depend on having developed something with which to get back at her? Last of all, *did* Sidney want what he knew he should want? Did he know what he wanted?[16]

These questions having been asked, which is enough for my purposes, I can now come to the point. If so far there are at least three putative screen women in *Astrophil and Stella*, who and what could still thinkably be getting screened? One possibility is that the deeply screened (but also deliberately unmasked) object of Sidney/Astrophil's courtship is indeed a particularly special woman, married, possibly unwillingly, to a possibly obnoxious rich husband. The unprintable name of the woman is that of Sidney's sister Mary, Countess of Pembroke. If she is the one, however, we may seem to have found ourselves substituting family romance as a putative inside story for political antiromance. Taking this possibility seriously for a moment, how plausible is the substitution?

There is some circumstantial evidence to support the incestuous supposition in addition to John Aubrey's well-known gossip about the Sidneys, reported by him as having been current during their lifetime:

> Sir Philip Sydney was such here [at Wilton], and there was so great love between him and his faire sister that I have heard old Gentlemen say that they lay together, and it was thought the first Philip Earle of Pembroke was begot by him, but he inherited not the witt of either brother or sister.[17]

The accident of Sidney's rustication, far from the royal court and the oppressive queen, is a little too convenient to be taken at face value. A scholarly claim that Mary was incestuously fixated on her brother has already been made in print,[18] and on the other side Sidney's possible *flight* back into public life and to a suicidal end at an early age is as compatible with the doubtful notion of intolerable stress as it is with the equally doubtful one of ambitious "passion." The trials of Astrophil, thwarted not just by a "rich" husband but by a real taboo, make more sense – acquire a real cultural content – if they are conceived to exist in the situation I have indicated. To read the whole sequence under this assumption is at once to recharge and transform practically every poem in it (one has only to try this) and it is also to recognize how really "impossible" it is for Astrophil/Sidney to enjoy or seriously to represent the truth of this love. At least for one long moment, Sidney's *Astrophil and Stella* does seem quite movingly to be about "loving in truth" and being "faine in verse [his] love to show," not just to be the empty rhetorical performance it has so often been found.

And yet, the situation may not be quite so serious – or even this seriousness may play back again into the larger inside story that I imagined earlier on. For one thing, as Arthur Marotti has suggested in discussion, but as others have also suggested, radical endogamy (incest) is the real story of the aristocracy, whose loyalty to and affection for kin surpasses any national, centralizing, or counter-dynastic interest. There is a sense in which for Sidney to have succeeded at the Elizabethan court, getting buried, at however high a level, in the state apparatus, would have been to fail, whereas his "failure" in that context enabled his return (or at least ready and sustained access) to the family center of Wilton. From this base, another kind of power could be promoted and substantial, inalienable literary property could be accumulated. There is also a sense in which exogamous political courtship, entailing the pursuit of an alien career and service to the queen, might have required Sidney's departure from the *desired* sphere of the family as well as his submission to persons and values at odds with those of the family.

Belonging to a family of relatively low gentry status on the father's side, and of limited means besides, there could also be no guarantee for Sidney that his service, however distinguished, would promote family interests. His father's fate as Lord Lieutenant of Ireland, harassed and impoverished, as he claimed, in the queen's service, might have sufficed as an object lesson. So we must question the widespread assumption that, in "failing" at court or in "failing" to live up to certain high expectations cherished for him by admirers, Sidney actually failed, or did not get what he wanted. He may also have felt that the maternal/matrilineal side of the family, that of the Dudleys (kin to Leicester), offered greater security, higher status, and something generally more congenial than the paternal/patrilineal one,[19] which apart from anything else figured the quixotry of public service. We may even want to say that Sidney could have felt a passion, apparently reciprocated, for his sister.

Despite these large contexts into which the question of possible "incest" (here as always more than simple erotic transgression) can be assimilated, there may also have been tactical reasons for Sidney to flaunt the possibility of his incest. For if Aubrey is to be believed (as he cannot be), gossip about the Sidneys was circulating in the sixteenth century. A moment's reflection may suggest that it could hardly have been otherwise – semi-public families could hardly have escaped prurient speculation – and to assume otherwise may still, despite the anti-hagiographic character of historicist criticism, be to fall for the myth of aristocratic immunity to vulgar speculation. An open secret or rumor of Sidney's possible involvement with his sister might have forced a response, though exploitation of the rumor might also have produced an effect akin to that of his rumored amour with Penelope Devereux. It could have helped to confirm the aristocratic status of that marginal gentleman, Philip Sidney, a knight only by virtue of the emptiest diplomatic formality.

Far more compellingly than chivalrous courtship, incest can mark a boundary between the gentry and those who are not; between those who can get away with it and those who can't; between those who dare to do it and those who don't; between those who are, by virtue of their peculiar exclusiveness, "fated" to do it and those who are not; between those who are culturally overawed and those who are not. Even if gossips can intrude, they cannot now, finally, go where their desire or curiosity leads them, or where wealth alone can take them. This peculiar distinction becomes especially important, if only in fantasy, when other sources of distinction are threatened or appear groundless, and it is also especially important to a marginalized or self-imagined gentry;[20] we need think only of "Lord" Byron parading the love that cannot speak its name across Europe. Incest embodies the dream, furthermore, of a return to ever-abundant nature and natural love *through* the most extreme and tormenting exile of artifice, class distinction, and high sophistication; it is no accident that in the one song (sonnet 8) in which Astrophil and Stella meet and acknowledge their love even if they can't consummate it, they are in a romantic grove, not a social setting. That open/secret place is one in which the meaning of "rich" gets revised by being made a phenomenon of darkness rather than of "all beauties which man's eye can see"; also, perhaps a phenomenon of lyrical simplicity as distinct from that of textured, public "richness" and dissimulation figured in the normal sonnet form of this sequence:

> In a grove most rich of shade,
> Where birds wanton musike made,
> May then yong his pide weedes showing,
> New perfumed with flowers fresh growing,
>
> *Astrophil* with *Stella* sweete,
> Did for mutuall comfort meete,
> Both within themselves oppressed,
> But each in the other blessed.[21]

An attempt on Sidney's part to forestall and even tactically reappropriate vulgar gossip (which could never have been silenced) is more than conceivable in *Astrophil and Stella*; it becomes almost necessary to assume it. But if that is the case, the correlative possibility arises of his writing those poems both in and *as* another Arcadia. The Arcadian story is definitively that of Philip Sidney, and the putatively ideal space of those poems, both songs and sonnets, is one that Sidney might hope to appropriate from Petrarch and others in such a way as to make it his own. But if he can put his distinctive mark on that space, he evidently cannot make it, perhaps any more than a real-life Wilton could be made, into an Arcadia; indeed, there is a sense in which the speaker is never *in* Arcadia but inhabits the position of the privileged witness or prurient spectator *to* it. Damagingly penetrated, in spite of everything, by gossip and scrutiny, riven by cross-purposes, oppressed by forms and values other than its own, and ultimately all the more frustrating for seeming to offer an ideal space of fulfillment (the *limitless* possibility at once given and withheld), *Astrophil and Stella* cannot become for Sidney/Astrophil an ideal place of secure privilege and total gratification. Nor can it be or represent a space in which all his most profound desires, infantile, narcissistic, heteroerotic, homoerotic, dynastic and literary come together in a single all-encompassing relationship.[22] What is lacking in the feverish sequence of *Astrophil and Stella* is any single poem of magisterial and completed fantasy that might sound like the following one:

> Mon enfant, ma soeur,
> Songe à la douceur

> D'aller là-bas vivre ensemble!
>   Aimer à loisir,
>   Aimer et mourir
> Au pays qui te ressemble! . . .
>
>   Tout y parlerait
>   A l'âme en secret
> Sa douce langue natale.
>
> Là, tout n'est qu'ordre et beauté,
> Luxe, calme et volupté.[23]

Neither Sidney nor, perhaps, the Protestant English sixteenth century could attain the rich decadence that would finally enable this conclusive poem to be written. Even where the dream image seems to materialize for Sidney/Astrophil in such a way as to be capable of possession, as it does in the "dark," exquisite and powerful sonnet 38 (which intriguingly follows, either as complement or antithesis, the "Rich" sonnet 37) it dissolves as soon as the waking mind seeks to possess it:

> This night while sleepe begins with heavy wings
>   To hatch mine eyes, and that unbitted thought
>   Doth fall to stray, and my chiefe powres are brought
> To leave the scepter of all subject things,
> The first that straight my fancie's error brings
>   Unto my mind, is *Stella's* image, wrought
>   By *Love's* own selfe, but with so curious drought,
> That she, me thinks, not onely shines but sings . . .[24]

Moving to possess the figure that possesses him (which would also be to possess the Baudelarian female poetic voice that would transform the poem) Astrophil wakes, however, and is left, as is the poem itself, to "nought but wailing eloquence." And in place of the soul's "douce langue natale," Astrophil hears (and is threatened with mere endless repetition of) the neoclassical babble of publicized courtship, really neither his own nor his "soul's" mother tongue.[25]

There is one poem in *Astrophil and Stella* that suggests that the word is already out in the family and possibly in public by the time Sidney writes the sequence, and that he must accordingly deal with the gossip by at once denying and appropriating it. This sonnet also places the very deep and much-screened secret, like the purloined letter, where it is most/least likely to be seen – that is to say, in the clear and on the surface. This sonnet is 83, the only one in which the author rather than the persona is named, and which begins: "Good brother Philip, I have borne you long." The subtle, intense and even obscene eroticism of this poem has already been well demonstrated by Daniel Traister,[26] so there is nothing left to be proved on that score. The speaker in the poem, putatively Stella, anomalously addresses *Astrophil* first as "brother Philip" and finally by the childhood diminutive "Sir Phip." In one way the secret is thus exposed and defused, but then also reappropriated and re-romanticized by "Stella's" denial. I shall now quote the poem in full, asking only for it to be imagined that Mary Sidney is in the "jealous" position of Dante's chaste Beatrice when she complains of a rival, one whom Dante can then claim is only a screen woman. Consider, in other words, both the possible jealousy and the ongoing "chastity" of the Countess of Pembroke, at once desiring and permitting liberties, denying the final conquest but also angrily warding off rivals, sinning all the way and sinning not at all:

> Good brother *Philip*, I have borne you long;
> I was content you should in favour creepe,
> While craftily you seem'd your cut to keepe,
> As though that fair softe hand did you great wrong.
> I bare (with Envie) yet I bare your song,
> When in her necke you did *Loue*-ditties peepe;
> Nay, more foole I, oft suffered you to sleepe
> In Lillies' neast, where *Loue's* selfe lies along.
> What, doth high place ambitious thoughts augment?
> Is sawciness reward of curtesie?
> Cannot such grace your silly selfe content,
> But you must needs with those lips billing be,
> And through those lips drinke nectar from that tong;
> Leave that Sir *Phip*, least off your necke be wroong.[27]

The story of romantic incest, which I have no desire to push against resistance or disbelief, simply rests on the displayed evidence – as I believe it can and must, since if the evidence isn't on the surface, it is nowhere else.

The conclusions to be drawn from this discussion can be summarized fairly briefly. They are, first, that the model of strict encryptment and belief in the hermetic inside story do not represent the strongest historicism, or perhaps the most compelling version of Elizabethan romance as practiced by major authors, though both hermeticism and encryptment may have to be taken seriously as the primary terms of romance and as the governing ones in some special cases, a possible one, suggested by Marotti in discussion, being that of Donne. Second, that there is no single, determinate story in or of Astrophil's romance unless it is the endlessly contradictory "story," at once imperious and threatened, self-revealing and self-occluding, of totalizing desire – that unlimited form of desire of which the strongest possible embodiment and gratification may finally be the literary one. Third, that the story historicism now tells is one that contains the historicist, and it is accordingly not to be expected that a powerful theoretical articulation of the historicist position will be forthcoming while any interest remains in simply retelling historical romances or romanticized histories, with whatever fantasized or real-political gratifications that may afford the teller.

4

The politics of theater (II)

If the "crime" of incestuous desire had in the previous chapter been brought home to Sidney, and perhaps to Mary Sidney, it was one that could hardly, since Aubrey's *Lives* or even since the appearance of *Astrophil and Stella*, be thought to require *detection*. This particular crime as open secret is, moreover, one that must be regarded as coextensive with the culture itself; to be precise, it is the imagined "criminality" (or form of incrimination) through which nature is reconstituted as culture, so its incriminating perception in any particular case rebounds upon the culture at large, or rather upon the problematic nature–culture opposition. If it is true that a very particular sixteenth-century history is always at issue in the case of Philip Sidney, it is also true that that history remains overdetermined by, or even a special instance of, the general problematic of cultural difference (differentiation). Nothing further to be said from the *detective* point of view.

The return to Spenser here is a return under somewhat expanded terms of reference now including, in addition to "theater," "sympathy," and "representation," "the career" and "the author." A reassimilating and resynthesizing attempt is thus being made here, one facilitated by the peculiarities (prophetic, as I suggest, of the mature Spenser) of *A Theatre for Voluptuous Worldlings*, the first work in which Spenser is thought to have participated. Although it has sometimes been remarked (not to my knowledge in published criticism) that all of Spenser is "there" in this work, this essay marks an attempt to determine *what* is there.

One of the conclusions capable of being drawn with the benefit of hindsight is that, if Sidney and Spenser can both be described as "political," Spenser is the truly political animal among English sixteenth-century poets, while Sidney figures not so much a losing politics (though perhaps that too) as a problematic and recurrent quixotry which like so many other things ("folly," "pícaro," "utopia," "Machiavel") is invented, named and embodied in this fabulously energized, strongly "poetic" time.

In contrast, the Spenser whom I have described as a political animal is not so much a thing without a name as a still somewhat indeterminate figure. A premature fixing of the lineaments is, however, one of the tendencies in Spenser criticism and indeed in Renaissance criticism against which this essay is written (*against* which I would like to think that Spenser's own poetry is written); the essay accordingly remains somewhat open-ended, and it relies periodically on forms of divination and/or wild analysis to reopen the question of Spenser's poetic and political character. If I have presumed as a rank amateur on the territory of art historians and specialists in emblematics in writing about the emblems in the *Theatre*, I have done so partly to reclaim the moment of relatively unconstrained *seeing* that those pictures allow (to forgo that moment at the bidding of any preemptive authority is to forgo a possible hermeneutic opening). I have done so as well because a certain institutionalized false consciousness is logically to be assumed even in high-Renaissance manuals of emblematic and hieroglyphic exegesis, in which case both the persistence and ubiquitousness of the particular interpretive "tradition" may tell against rather than for its authority in the present. (Etymologically speaking, tradition not only carries on but lies!)

In addition to laying down certain lines of approach to Spenser, this essay continues testifying to the rapidly developing historicist concern with the shape of Spenser's career as well as with the complex interplay of Elizabethan courtly politics. The essay does, however, reveal some critical dissatisfaction (for reasons that will emerge) with prematurely integrating or reunifying accounts of Spenser, sometimes pursued under the historicist rubric of "the career" or "the laureate career." Given that Spenser does, in important and highly visible ways, virtually reinvent in England the grand laureate career (as opposed to that of the gentlemanly amateur or the ungenteel professional writer),[1] what does this laureate conception of Spenserian authorship leave unexplained? Is his hetero-geneous poetic production fully and coherently explicable under that conception? Is there only one Spenser, or only one major authorial function corresponding to that name? And which Spenser(s) derive from models, careerist or otherwise, supplied, for example, by Homer, Hesiod, the exiled Ovid, Catullus, Chaucer, Langland, Gascoigne and Skelton (the English *Ur*-laureate recalled in the E.K. gloss to the first eclogue in *The Shepheardes Calender*)? Could Spenser write as gentlemanly amateur, as laureate and as ungenteel professional on separate occasions or all at once, endlessly manipulating the multiplying possibilities of Elizabethan authorship and literary management? Perhaps all of these Spenserian incarnations can finally be assimilated to a single model, even to a laureate one, but the tendency to effect that assimilation prematurely has manifested itself in some historicist accounts.

The risk entailed in pursuing my own previously stated concerns remained apparently undiminished. I had to postulate, courting the accusation of paranoia or perhaps of Robert Gravesian historicist fantasizing, an invisible – I would want to say "unofficial" – Spenser. And my questioning of historicism threatened to issue, not in further historicist knowledge but in something more like a divinatory *gaya scienza* of sixteenth-century authorship – in a "science" of the author's exhilaratingly exceptional or exaggerated revelation of existing cultural possibilities, ones for the very existence of which the ultimate proof would be the poetic text itself, not the by-definition limited confirmation available from other sources. Instead of seeking logically to derive the poetic text from the culture, in other words, and instead of regarding the poetic text as culturally *constrained* or merely symptomatic, this incipient *gaya scienza* would be bound to treat the poetic text as primary and unassailable evidence, available only through an act of sensitized reading which can then be redirected, so to speak, upon the cultural "text" in general. To engage in this potentially tautologous mode of inquiry – which I take, however, to be a procedure not wholly alien to historicism – would also be to risk "rediscovering" sixteenth-century authorship and cultural politics in all their forms of excess, disorder, savage intensity and perhaps dangerous powers of sympathy.   `

Spenser's work gives remarkably ample scope for the pursuit of this kind of inquiry. Can the seemingly earth-born ("Dionysiac") Redcrosse Knight, for example, in Book I of *The Faerie Queene*, embody an *ideal* both of his author and of patriotic English Protestantism in the sixteenth century without by the same token embodying the overreaching "imaginative" madness of both? Can these two possibilities be separated in Redcrosse's hallucinatory vision on the Mountain of Contemplation, where he "sees," not just the Geneva Bible's holy city of Hierusalem (*sic*), but a bizarre druidical father-figure, looking a bit like a hoary, sacred oak tree, who reauthorizes his quest and renames him St George, investing him with an unearthly pedigree? Does this almost unbridled fantasy of the clownish, lowborn "knight," received into the court of Gloriana and ultimately reconstructed as the patron saint of the kingdom, constitute an authoritative ideal – a legitimate ambition – or a symptomatic delirium of the imperialistic English sixteenth century? And how would one ever distinguish between the two? Does this episode in the poem at once specify the game and give the game away?

Spenser defends no doubt against this dangerous fantasy even while reproducing it in Book I of *The Faerie Queene*, and perhaps even while living it during his reception at court in 1590. Yet the possible "madness" of Spenser doesn't begin and end in Book I of *The Faerie Queene*, nor is a simple defense against explosive fantasies of this order (the politically unthinkable) possible to any major sixteenth-century author. In what I take to be a fundamentally important essay,[2] Louis Montrose has discussed the role of some astonishing erotic fantasies (dreams of impregnating Queen Elizabeth or of becoming her clownish beloved) in sixteenth-century cultural production, in particular Shakespeare's *A Midsummer Night's Dream*. Such dreams, Montrose argues, don't necessarily remain the property of isolated, mad dreamers, or result in self-destructive forms of criminal expression, but can decorously be articulated (covertly "played") by Shakespeare and others in such a way as to transform the existing meanings of monarch and subject, and of the relationship between the two. Yet if it could be argued on the basis of Montrose's essay that the difference between madness and sanity lies not in the culturally generated content of particular fantasies but in the authorial ability at once to defend against and productively to embody them – thus in a sense *binding* the culture or making it a hostage to its own phantasms – it is nevertheless true that this cultural production, including literary production, remains bound to forms of potentially destructive irrationality ("madness"). Neither the attainment of acceptability through work nor the fact of production is justifying in itself, nor does that production continue unaccompanied by inordinate excesses of violence and cultural erasure. If the destruction of the Bower of Bliss in Book II of *The Faerie Queene* does not suffice as a reminder of this, then perhaps Spenser's own *View of the Present State of Ireland* may do so.[3]

With all due acknowledgment of Montrose's seminal essay, then, it appears to me that its conclusions are prematurely sanitizing. It relies on a reading of what can be taken as a rather optimistic Shakespearean comedy; it conceives of a benign dialectic of cultural production in which forms of irrational excess either disappear or get absorbed; and the order of Elizabethan cultural politics is treated as virtually self-enclosed, allowing the essay to be written from an implicit standpoint of historical detachment. But to recognize the ways in which inordinate fantasies play out in the world of Elizabethan literature and cultural politics, at the same time acknowledging our critical implication, can't be to settle for "work" or "production" alone, and it may be to recognize the further need for an unsentimental science of the productive–annihilative dynamism and masked intensity of sixteenth-century authorship – phenomena which, if not beyond good and evil, exceed the rationale(s) implied by such terms as that of the laureate career or cultural production.[4]

Spenser's theater

Spenser doesn't of course have a theater unless we can count the "paper stage" on which he performs as a poet, and represents his own version of the world, as a legitimate instance of "theater." Yet an attempt to make Spenser, the major English nondramatic poet of the sixteenth century, into a dramatic poet on the basis of this verbal quibble might seem perverse, even if that particular quibble originates in the sixteenth century, and in a context not remote from Spenser's: Nashe invents the term "paper stage" to describe the volume written by Sidney and published as *Astrophil and Stella*.[5] But Spenser isn't Sidney, and the impropriety of assimilating him to Sidney and to any "paper stage" might seem all the more blatant in that a powerful antitheatricality manifests itself at many points in Spenser's work. So regarding Spenser as a playwright *manqué* may still seem less appropriate, even if we do acknowledge certain commonly recognized elements of theatricality in his work, than continuing to regard him as a purposeful author of epic and lyric poems.

The sixteenth century is, however, commonly designated as the "age of theater,"[6] deeply committed epistemologically and in its courtly–political life to the trope that all the world's a stage.[7] Presumably there are good reasons why "theatricality" does such heavy duty as a term in our present critical discussion of sixteenth-century literature and its contexts, so perhaps we should not too quickly rule out "theater" as a major or encompassing context for Spenser's work. To the extent that Spenser is antitheatrical, there is something there for him to resist, and perhaps resistance isn't all that Spenser's relation to theater entails. An actor, for example, apparently unmasks in the pseudo-Virgilian proem to *The Faerie Queene*, Book I, in which Spenser writes "Lo, I the man, whose Muse whilome did maske,/ In lowly Shepheardes weedes...,"[8] but who is the actor and why the unmasking? The *Muse* rather than the author unmasks or gets unmasked, and who is she, this inspiring pseudo-shepherdess? Is the masque now over, or is it just entering a new phase, with the players changing costumes? What is the relation of Spenser ("I ... the man") to this theatricality?

Perhaps the place to begin answering these questions isn't *The Shepheardes Calender*. Although this work constitutes Spenser's formal debut, it was published a full decade after his possible beginning, as the anonymous translator of a Dutch work by Jan van der Noot, short-titled in the English version *A Theatre for Worldlings*.[9] To begin with that work is indeed to recognize a theatrical beginning, but it is correspondingly to recognize the enormous scale of the interpretive problem that accompanies that perception. In this essay I can only call for the appropriate recognitions, doing so in a brief general prolegomenon to Spenser's theatricality followed by an equally brief specimen commentary on the first seven epigrams in *A Theatre for Worldlings*.

A "paper stage," belonging to an author other than himself, may have been the only stage of any kind available to Spenser early in his career – the only *paper* stage available to a nameless youth whose inferior social status as the son of a London tailor meant a lack of immediate access to the gentlemanly audience to which Sidney, for example, could appeal, and perhaps also the one possible *stage*, since the first public theater in England opened only in 1576. It is likely that, even when the public theater had been established, a paper stage was still the only one open to Spenser, since there would almost certainly have remained prohibitive aesthetic, class, ideological and even practical barriers to Spenser's pursuit of a career as a "vulgar" or "upstart" dramatic poet. Although there is some intriguing evidence that Spenser could as a schoolboy at Merchant Taylors' have participated in court entertainments (and have been dazzled by the image and milieu of the ruler?), difficulties experienced by Spenser's headmaster for reasons possibly including his relationship to the court might have been inhibiting.[10] We may also have to give passing recognition to the dubious proposition that Spenser's "genius" was not adapted to the public stage, although in the case of such an author as Spenser "genius" is fashioned as much as it is innate, and its development may entail recognitions of opportunity rather than reliance on passively received "gifts."

If not public theater, then why not court theater? Even assuming that that road might have been open to Spenser, it was the road not taken – or not *directly* taken – and the career of Lyly as court playwright suggests that as an apparently direct road to favor and success it really led nowhere.[11] It isn't too much to suggest that the eminently strategic Spenser might have foreseen this, but we can't proceed on that speculative assumption. It is safer to assume, on the basis of van der Noot's *Theatre*, that for the early Spenser the theatrical way just did not necessarily lead to the court, to the staging of revels, or to any physical theater at all.

Van der Noot's *Theatre* belongs in the first instance to the sterner, more militant, and implicitly less courtly (if not anti-courtly) world of Protestant diatribe in an urban setting of trade guilds and religio-political exiles from the Low Countries. Van der Noot himself, apparently a convert *ca.* 1563 from Catholicism to Calvinism, had fled from Antwerp in 1567 after an abortive attempt by the Calvinistic consistory to seize political power in that city.[12] In 1568-9 the *Theatre*, a manifestly violent, propagandistic work addressed to European Calvinists in general, was published from London, and from within the Flemish exile community, in three European languages. (With what looks like a certain talent for having it both ways, however, or for having it several ways at once, van der Noot dedicated the Dutch version to "Rogier Martens," Lord Mayor of London, while he dedicated the English and French versions to Queen Elizabeth.)

If it seems paradoxical that any form of "theater" should be invoked in that militant, polemical setting, given the common assumption that a radical antitheatricalism goes together with militant, neo-Augustinian Calvinism (not yet firmly designated "Puritan" in England by 1569), two points can be made: first, that a progressive hardening both of "Puritan" and antitheatrical positions occurred throughout the late sixteenth century, so that what might have been possible in 1569 would not necessarily have been so twenty years later; and, second, that theatrical tropes, including the one about all the world's being a stage, were already large commonplaces by the time Spenser's career began, and as such they imposed their own epistemological and rhetorical claims even on militant Protestants.

Just how compellingly they did so is apparent in van der Noot's *Theatre for Worldlings* itself. The English version, comprising emblems, poems (mainly imitated directly or indirectly from Petrarch, Marot and du Bellay by Spenser), and a long prose diatribe against certain worldly vices which are also those of Rome, acknowledges at a minimum the rhetorical convenience of the theatrical trope. The substance of worldly power in various guises (suggested in the emblems, for example, by a Greek colonnade and a pyramidal Egyptian obelisk as well as by a Roman triumphal arch) is at once displayed and annihilated in the *Theatre*'s paired emblems and poems, after which the visionary New Jerusalem alone remains to be seen in the final emblem (see p.96) as the sole form of truth, the sole reality beyond illusion, and the teleological goal both of the human pilgrimage and of a systematic Protestant pedagogy. The *theatre* for worldlings is thus one of only illusory substance, and the represented destruction of its most powerful forms – albeit by earthquake, thunderbolt or cataclysm – occurs with the annihilating suddenness, but also with the arbitrary repetitiveness, of successive *coups de théâtre*. Theater is, in effect, made to work against itself, and ultimately for the celestial city that lies beyond it.

Van der Noot's text anticipates further Protestant diatribes such as Thomas Beard's *The Theatre of God's Judgements* (London 1597), and it

I Saw new Earth, new Heauen, sayde Saint Iohn.
And loe, the sea (quod he) is now no more.
The holy Citie of the Lorde, from hye
Descendeth garnisht as a loued spouse.
A voice then sayde, beholde the bright abode
Of God and men. For he shall be their God,
And all their teares he shall wipe cleane away.
Hir brightnesse greater was than can be founde,
Square was this Citie, and twelue gates it had.
Eche gate was of an orient perfect pearle,
The houses golde, the pauement precious stone.
A liuely streame, more cleere than Christall is,
Ranne through the mid, sprong from triumphant seat.
There growes lifes fruite vnto the Churches good.

situates itself in a context of Protestant polemic in which the trope of theater is often invoked for partisan and didactic ends. Protestant antitheatricality is thus complemented by an attempted recuperation of theater and even its "pleasantness" for political–providential discourse. Not so anomalously, the Puritan Martin Marprelate's brilliantly successful attack on the episcopal hierarchy in 1589–90 relied on the devices of popular comedy, but also very precisely on his ability to turn the religious pamphlet into a paper stage on which the gross bishops and their witty antagonists became low-comedy buffoons.[13]

Even if the public theater as an institution came to be regarded by Puritans as irredeemable (partly because of the alleged "idleness" and petty criminality of the theatrical milieu), theatrical tropes, a politics of theater, and an epistemological problematic of theatricality, were all at a minimum recognized as inescapable by many Puritans. Whether or not we regard Spenser as having been from the start a "Protestant poet,"[14] his participation in van der Noot's text as well as in the propagandist context of its production plunged Spenser into a theatricalized *mise-en-scène*, not necessarily compatible with that of the court.

Once we have recognized this, however, we may have to take a step back and recognize at the same time that the context(s) of van der Noot's *Theatre* as well as the circumstances of Spenser's participation are exceptionally complex and obscure. Little can be taken for granted, not even Spenser's authorship, and the exact circumstances under which the English version was produced remain murky (even its ascription to the printer Henry Bynneman has been challenged.)[15] This obscurity goes together with contextual indeterminacy and a multiplicity of possible meanings. The romance-language poems, translated into English with the Dutch text as a possible intermediate stage, are mainly ones by Petrarch and du Bellay, and they thus "import" into the *Theatre* a context of extremely high literacy, literary ambition, and cultural prestige. Perhaps van der Noot believed that Calvinist propaganda could use some of that, or perhaps this way of putting it already makes the wrong assumption that Calvinist "propaganda" is normally indifferent to such considerations. Whatever the case may be, the Petrarchan poems and their multilingual translations also imply the entire problematic, now well recognized, of the sixteenth-century cultural *translatio* as one of nationalistic and dynastic appropriation of high-cultural emblems and goods. They imply, given the histories of both Petrarch and du Bellay, the further possibility of making exile or alienation in a "foreign" setting into a workable literary stratagem of indirection, one in which the detached, potentially disaffected position rather than the affiliated, "central" or incorporated one becomes the position of strength.[16] So even if the poems serve van der Noot's possibly complex polemical and didactic purposes, they may also serve other or additional purposes of their anonymous English translator. More than one possible context, more than one possible goal, and more than one possible reading, are implied by the emblems and poems alike.

In fact, contextual proliferation to the point of apparent contradiction becomes characteristic of van der Noot's *Theatre* and hence, *mutatis mutandis*, of its English translation. The emblems to which the poetic translations refer are ones that have their place in a high Renaissance tradition of hieroglyphic exegesis and humanistic hermeticism, yet as emblems they also invoke a tradition of elementary popular instruction.[17] This "contradiction" is not the only major one we have to confront in the *Theatre*, and it already begins to force the question: where *are* we – or, more to the point, where is Spenser – when we read this text?

Part of my undertaking will be to suggest that Spenser stages the problem of his own location, which is also that of his literary identity, in the *Theatre*, but it must be admitted that even that limited undertaking will remain beset by many uncertainties. The Spenser *Variorum*, for example, characteristically indicates a range of possible political reference for these early poems when they are reprinted as "The Visions of Petrarch" and "The Visions of Bellay" in Spenser's 1591 *Complaints*, and if they have by then become politically coded in relation to the Elizabethan court and aristocracy, are we to assume that they are not already so coded in their original setting? The entire tradition of poems by Petrarch and du Bellay implies just that possibility; Petrarch's repeated pun on the name of the patron-family of Colonna, as well as his coded reinscription of Roman imperial history involving such figures as Caesar and Hannibal, constitute a blank check for his successors. Something like a blank check, or one on which tentative entries may already have been made, appears to be displayed in the epigram that concludes the opening sequence, all of which is ultimately derived from Petrarch's Canzone 24, "Standomi un giorno . . .", in Spenser's translation:

> My Song thus now in thy Conclusions,
> Say boldly that these same six visions
> Do yelde vnto thy lorde a sweete request,
> Ere it be long within the earth to rest.[18]

The "lorde" of the song may of course be the divine one, but the "dream" of the anonymous translator may already involve getting taken up by a noble lord-protector, the name of Leicester possibly being capable of filling in the blank. In fact, the dream may be even more specific than that if we recall that the previous epigram concerns a "fair lady" somewhat resembling Eurydice in need of an Orpheus. The face of this "lady" is mysteriously (or is it allegorically?) veiled by a "darke cloude" above her waist, but it may be fair to assume that the "hidden" identity of this lady is that of the still fairly youthful queen as pastoral masker. Is it already Elizabeth and Leicester, with the nameless young English poet of the *Theatre*, still barely more than a translator, signalling his willingness to participate in a ménage à trois with the queen and her (new) lord-protector? Is Spenser as a young poet, one whom we would have to consider amazingly precocious (if the facts are right, he would still have been sixteen or seventeen years old), already fixing a distant but rapt gaze on the "cynosure" of the English political world?[19]

The question of political solicitation if not yet of full-scale coding within a network of English patronage evidently comes up from the start. Other codings, "political" in a different sense, have also to be reckoned with. It is hardly possible in our present state of knowledge to say, for example, in what ways radical protestant discourse of the sixteenth century may be coded rather than overt. An incipient anti-courtliness and even widespread regicidal fantasy or "plot" may, however, be implicit in the Calvinistic appropriation of emblems portraying the "vgly beast come from the sea,/That seuen heads, ten crounes, ten hornes did beare,/Hauing thereon the vile, blaspheming name,"[20] or portraying, closer to Spenser's home, "a Woman sitting on a beast/Before mine eyes, of Orenge [!] colour hew:/Horrour and dreadfull name of blasphemie/Fild her with pride . . ./She seemde with glorie of the scarlet faire,/And with fine pearle and golde puft vp in heart."[21] Alternative representations of the queen, as well as alternative class, ideological and party affiliations, may already be getting rehearsed under cover by Spenser in the *Theatre* – or rehearsed under a cover that already blows itself, obliquely disclosing a power of flattery and intimidation (eulogy and satire) wielded by the anonymous translator of the "epigrams."

In ways we are just beginning to see, moreover, the poems of Petrarch and du Bellay come to Spenser pre-coded as those of a rich (if still somewhat alien) continental humanism with its own cultural games to play; as those of a French nationalism and imperialism purporting to take over by way of *translatio* the assets of a liquidated Roman empire; and as ones embodying various poetic designs upon ruling dynasties as well as the political nation. If all that were not enough, Julia Conaway Bondanella has recently indicated how necessary it is to conceive of the poems in the *Theatre* as part of a large Renaissance "family" of visionary poems originated by the paternal figure of Petrarch.[22] And what is the nature of that "family?" Not only are the interpretive ramifications endless, but the particular poems of this visionary family call for and also threaten to defeat understanding of an ultra-high Renaissance poetic of vision and hermetic signification.

As we compile the impossible list of items to be dealt with if van der Noot's *Theatre* is ever to be mastered, we may also begin to recognize, for what the reassurance is worth, that we are indeed in Spenser country. The sheer multiplicity of contexts, determinations and overdeterminations, any or all of which may have to be taken seriously, point in the direction of *The Shepheardes Calender*, as does the structure of van der Noot's text, both "learned" and "popular," with its emblems, poems and prose discourse. All of this points, in other words, towards Spenser's first *volume*, with its emblematic "scenes" and its still unnamed and elusive poet masquerading in a variety of guises and contexts: some high, some low; some learnedly humanistic, some blatantly political; some visionary and some topical; some amorous and some satirical, some courtly and some ecclesiastical. The *mixed* volume rather than the single poem as a controllable unit of literary production is also prefigured by *A Theatre for Worldlings*, although the name of the author and hence property in such a volume (no matter how many translations or imitations of other people's work it may contain) is claimed by Spenser only in his 1591 *Complaints*.

A preliminary consideration of all this data suggests (1) that the *volume* rather than the poem may have to be taken as the basic unit of poetic production for Spenser as his career unfolds; (2) that it is the volume that comes to constitute the paper stage on which Spenser sets his various personae in motion, and, while representing himself and perhaps others like E.K., also retains the power of the invisible director; and (3) that appropriation of a multitude of voices and roles, poetic, scholarly and otherwise, becomes possible on the scale achieved by Spenser only when the *volume* is conceived in this theatrical manner. This theatricalization also makes Spenser's "career" into a major literary operation not simply identical with that of writing major poems, engaging in political courtship, or pursuing the "laureate" ambition; it finally makes possible the endless contextual *manipulation* and pro-miscuous inclusiveness of Spenser's poetic. Antitheatricality in Spenser may thus have to be regarded, whatever its local justification, as a grand gesture of disavowal that permits the operation to continue without necessarily appearing to do so, while an unacknowledged *fundamental* theatricality may have to be seen as that which makes possible Spenser's fluid movement between genres and hence between positions of affection and disaffection, identification and disavowal, flattery and intimidation, in relation to his represented objects.

In the crudest political terms, Spenser evidently tries to avoid getting pinned down in any single position in his "theater of the world," and he also tries to exploit in timely ways the advantages of various positions. This is not to claim that Spenser desires or engages in any "absolute" or "free" play within his theater, but rather that the symbolic transactions conducted (or is it rehearsed?) in that theater are also from the start ones that occur in, or in relation to, the cultural–political world that Spenser progressively "invades," acquiring a name and perhaps even losing some mobility as he does so.

These are admittedly large pre-emptive claims, and their defensibility as claims about Spenser's career in general can't be established all at once. With van der Noot's *Theatre* we can only make a beginning, in doing so considering the beginnings of what becomes the very large Spenserian enterprise – larger, perhaps, than even the *visible* evidence normally suggests. Two limiting considerations may, however, facilitate our approach to the *Theatre*.

The first is that the career of van der Noot himself, or rather the interpretive problems to which it has given rise, are suggestive for our reading of Spenser. It is possible to distinguish two phases in the modern critical assimilation of van der Noot.[23] The first is the one in which his role as patriot and Protestant reformer, but also as a possible timeserver who seems to have recanted his Calvinism in his latter days, is taken seriously, and his literary career (or mission) is interpreted in the appropriate contexts of European anti-Catholicism and Dutch–German politics. The second phase is the one in which van der Noot's enterprise is reinterpreted as that of a self-interested and high-powered operator, never just humbly serving the causes with which he identified himself, but exploiting the conditions of exile, publication, differing religious affiliation, etc., to promote himself, thus making possible his eventual return from exile to a literary career evidently to be pursued in contexts of aristocratic patronage.

The paper stage of van der Noot can thus be seen as one capable of being periodically reset, and also of being "translated" into real-political terms even if something inevitably gets lost in the translation. Van der Noot's history, like Spenser's, is one of increasingly ambitious publication, and his late "Olympia Epics" ("Olympia" being his counterpart to Gloriana, even if she cannot be identified with a living ruler as Spenser's Gloriana can) have been seen in certain ways to resemble Spenser's *Faerie Queene*.[24] (The ambitious *feint* of devotion to a supreme female figure, already recognizable for what it is since Petrarch if not Dante, apparently continues in the work of van der Noot and Spenser alike.)

The second consideration I want to stipulate before proceeding to Spenser's *Theatre* is that the *beholder* of all the emblematic spectacles in that text establishes his presence right from the first line: "Being one day at my window all alone . . . ."[25] The theater of the world (no less!) is thus occupied from the start by an audience of at least one, and our witnessing of the pictures is always mediated by the witnessing of the spectator, hardly visible and yet clearly visible. Hardly visible and yet also clearly visible is that spectator's appropriation of the passing images as *his* images, or as hieroglyphic pictures that do not speak until he speaks for them. The very form of the framed emblem is taken over by the speaker, who translates the frame of the picture into the frame of a private "window" through which he, and he alone in the first instance, sees the world as a particular succession of images. Finally, this "mediating" figure becomes potentially the all-powerful one, imagining and abolishing the spectacle of worldly power virtually at his own will. A kind of passive omnipotence or aggression is figured by the nameless spectator in the *Theatre*.

This paradoxical role of the spectator, at once impotent in a world overwhelmingly given under many aspects including political ones, but also omnipotent in reconstituting that world as illusion capable of being mastered – of being made subject to the individual mind – is the one into which Spenser could enter from the start, no matter how humble or excluded his position in the real world might have been. This ultimate spectatorial power, inseparable no doubt from ultimate delusion and/or ontological determination by the Divine Mind, is also the one form of absolute power conferred by the neoplatonism to which Spenser has traditionally been claimed to subscribe.[26]

Even in the terms in which van der Noot's *Theatre* presents itself, a purely contemplative or imaginary mastery of the world is not all that is at stake – or not what is at stake at all – since a mastery of visual and poetic representation is also involved. And since that mastery implies ongoing transactions in or with the world, and in relation to one or more audiences, a representational politics of the poet becomes inescapable for Spenser – a politics constituted by the power, not to originate any privileged representation in or of the world, but to transform any such representation and in doing so to transform its audience. So in reading Spenser, beginning with the English version of the *Theatre*, we can watch an imaginary kingdom or paper stage being transformed (usurped?) from within and then progressively "translated" into the worldly terms that we can loosely call those of Spenser's career. It is no doubt for us to judge how successfully or otherwise the translation was effected, since Spenser's own complaints of failure or obstruction in the world are also per-formances to be interpreted, not objective data.

These stipulations having been made, we can begin at the beginning.

To begin now is, however, to recognize the impossible omnicompetence called for if even this early Spenserian work is to be mastered, and it is simultaneously to recognize how successfully Spenser (or simply the Spenser-situation) dictates commentary in the "limited" style of E.K. The patchy, half-informed academic subtext, non-threatening to the author, may be the soundest possible commentary on Spenser; more so than any madly attempted total commentary or any prematurely reductive one – and what reduction will not seem premature? (To say this is not to mystify Spenser as the supreme genius of all time or of the culture itself, but rather to acknowledge his quite extraordinary passive–aggressive "weakness" for everything culturally and politically given to him.) Yet while succumbing to what the situation apparently dictates, and hence proceeding in E.K. style, I shall focus even more limitedly than E.K. on what I take to be moments of distinctively Spenserian recognition or self-definition in the first or "Petrarchan" sequence of the *Theatre*, namely epigrams 1-6. The second or "du Bellay" sequence needs to be considered extensively in connection with "The Ruines of Time" and the "Visions of Bellay" in the *Complaints* volume, and so does Spenser's destruction of the *sequence* in the *Complaints* volume by splitting the "visions" of Petrarch from those of du Bellay and dropping the last four apocalyptic emblems, no doubt untimely in 1591.[27]

The first emblem (p.104) shows two deer being hunted, the top one seemingly having been caught. The narrative that links the two instances as episodes in a single chase is, however, supplied only by the poem, which thus temporalizes two spatially discrete, synchronic events in the pictured hunt. (A not uncommon pictorial technique often used when the narrative is an established one, e.g. the Life of Christ.) Already the spectator does more than watch, though whether he invents the narrative or merely articulates a legitimate inference drawn from the picture isn't clear. (Whether this difference, which could be characterized as one between invention and interpretation, can ever be established in the context of the *Theatre*, and whether it would make any difference if it could, remains in question.) The narrative also reverses the right-to-left trajectory of the chase, making the picture "read" from left to right, but also from the bottom upwards. We see the deer's haunches being "pinchte" in the emblem, but only the poem can give the information that the deer "vntimely dide."

The locale may have to be regarded as one of pastoral or of the noble deer-park rather than of nature, since a city (church? despoiled abbey?) appears in the background, and the spectator watches through his window. Yet if it is a city it may already be celestial, situated as it is

Being one day at my window all alone,
So many strange things hapned me to see,
As much it grieueth me to thinke thereon.
At my right hande, a Hinde appearde to me,
So faire as mought the greatest God delite:
Two egre Dogs dyd hir pursue in chace,
Of whiche the one was black, the other white.
With deadly force, so in their cruell race
They pinchte the haunches of this gentle beast,
That at the last, and in shorte time, I spied,   10
Vnder a rocke, where she (alas) opprest,
Fell to the grounde, and there vntimely dide.
Cruell death vanquishing so noble beautie,
Oft makes me waile so harde a destinie.

"above" the field of action, and the entire sequence may occur, perhaps only as a Petrarchan visionary-heuristic one, on the other side of a stream that the observer cannot cross, or fears to cross. (cf. Petrarch 323 and 190, with Durling's annotation of the hind as traditionally sacred to Diana, beloved by Caesar, etc. See also Wyatt's imitation of 190, "Whoso list to hunt . . . ," that transforms the visionary poem in a Henrician courtly-political setting into one of male sexual rivalry, erotic pursuit, terrorized and terrorizing "possession.")

line 1 The anonymous spectator is simply there on the scene before anything (else) appears. This *passive* self-constituting *fiat* of the solitary spectator, observing but also observed, and thus situated in a liminal space between the image and the reader, ("strange things hapned me to see," line 2), is also an implicit denial of any *limiting* identity, relationship or social determination. The condition of spectatorship is thus paradoxically unconditioned, hence capable of being acted upon almost without limit and also capable of being transformed almost without limit.

lines 4–6 A highly charged opposition between the beautiful deer and the vicious dogs appears to be subtended by an "empty" diacritical opposition between the "black" and "white" dogs. What representational or other problematic inheres in this double opposition? Which is the privileged or "serious" opposition? Is it the beautiful object of the chase, or fraternal rivalry between the dogs, that excites violence and energizes the narrative? Who is this "hind," apparently not the same as the one who has an identifiable human face (Laura's) in Petrarch? Who, protected (or is it always really unprotected, as in Chaucer's *Knight's Tale*?) by Diana, takes the *place* of Laura in this particular scenario? If it is already a political scenario, does it imply something about the position of the unprotected young woman or even of a young queen in a world of male aggression and rivalry?

line 10 "In shorte time" meaning in a few minutes or in short Time itself, as in ". . . for short time, /An endlesse moniment."[28] Does the *poem* narrate a slice of the action, or does it as *epi*gram (superscript) at once rehearse, memorialize and rise superior to the completed action, concluded by the death of the deer? Is the status of poetic narrative and/or the position of the narrator always double?

line 11 The spectator's affective investment in the scene becomes manifest even if it is still parenthetically isolated from the action: "(alas)". The primary and indeed sole acknowledged response of this formerly unmoved spectator is sympathetic; this ostensibly labile spectator or unlocated sensibility feels, in other words, *for* the hind (female), into the suffering form of which he apparently projects himself in his first move towards self-disclosure. In doing so he identifies himself, sympathetically but also narcissistically, with the one creature in which, we have been told [line 5], God delights.

Apparently in the process of establishing himself as a sympathetic observer in a theater of violence, does the speaker not yet recognize, or does he fail to acknowledge, his possible investment, even if only as a narrator, in the other side as well – in the cruel but noble if not "gentle" chase; in the possibly empty competitive pursuit of the defenseless hind; in the violent torment and destruction of that in which God must be thought to delight? Is sympathetic identification with the wounded "other" to remain a mask behind which a ruthless self continues to tell its own story of violent pursuit? Or is a "gentle" self-fashioning and sympathetic representation of the other capable of being effected by the spectator?

line 14 The epigram concludes as a poem of static mourning for the hind and of proleptic mourning for whichever "Laura" the hind now represents. It is also by the same token a poem of self-mourning on the part of a spectator who explicitly identifies himself with the afflicted. Although the speaker's identification with the hind and with a beauty that passes seems complete at the end of the poem, the pathos is still incipiently that of one who is fated to destroy as well as be destroyed in a destiny that is not just doubly "hard," as the emblem may suggest, but perhaps inescapably *double*, and hence also duplicitous.

In the next poem-emblem pair (p.107) the entire narrative arises from within the poem, since all we see is a stationary ship on an apparently calm sea. Everything else may be implied in the pretty picture, an emblem, no doubt, of vanity, but these implications (the invisible rock beneath the surface) must be elicited by the narrator, who thus articulates what the picture can only incompletely and perhaps un-availingly suggest. In place of the empty scene, frozen in an instant of time, the poem offers a full temporal scenario concluding in the loss of the ship.

lines 1–3 The black and white of poem 1 are now perhaps "colored" with vanity, but to no apparent avail; the spectrum of colors still lies between the extremes, repeated in the poem as those of storm and calm.

line 4 "Seemed" emerging as a key Spenserian term of opposition between appearance and reality, and hence of a systematic antitheatri-calism? The ship seems also to be an image of singleness (a single image) as distinct from the image in the first emblem. Yet this singleness, which is also singularity, is false; the ship is almost literally spectral, it belongs to a *class* of vain objects, it comprises many separate parts (hull, ropes, sails, etc.) and it is only foregrounded as a single or singular form, since in

After at Sea a tall Ship dyd appere,
Made all of Heben and white Iuorie,
The sailes of Golde, of Silke the tackle were:
Milde was the winde, calme seemed the sea to be:
The Skie eche where did shew full bright and faire.
With riche treasures this gay ship fraighted was.
But sodaine storme did so turmoyle the aire,
And tombled vp the sea, that she, alas,
Strake on a rocke that vnder water lay.
O great misfortune, O great griefe, I say,   10
Thus in one moment to see lost and drownde
So great riches, as lyke can not be founde.

the background we can already see the double image of storm and calm. In order even to appear single, the ship must also exist in an ostensibly separate locale to which it alone is adapted. This locale is of course the sea, apparently separated from the land as well as from the setting in which the other emblems appear, but the separation is illusory. The whole scene is viewed by the observer from his "window," and the land-form of the fatal rock is merely hidden.

line 6 The "noble" mercantile ship of state, in the allegorical identification of which Puttenham's *The Arte of English Poesie*[29] may help us?

line 8 "Alas" no longer parenthetically isolated, but becoming integral to the narrative process. "She," alas once more, elicits the sympathy of the spectator, but in drawing attention to what he *says* or must say ["I say," line 10], the speaker also allows that there may be other things that he doesn't or can't say – or has already said without seeming to do so about a "female" vanity.

line 12 "Lyke" meaning not only "equal," but "likeness;" also "body" (corpse) and even "human subject." Anticipating "Lycidas," this poem envisages a situation of utter loss or absence – of the body, of the image, of any trace – in the absence of the elegiac poet. A poetic-political role as maker of memorial likeness for the vain is conceived in this poem, but remains unfulfilled. What we have is a pedagogic "epigram," the satirical aspect of which remains uppermost.

In the third pair (p.109), the narrative may follow on from that of the previous poem, as it implicitly would in Petrarch, there becoming a narrative that records both the death and visionary apotheosis of Laura. The context, at once poetic and mystical, is the large one of a "fortunate fall" from the Edenic condition that is capable of being redeemed beyond time, but also in poetic language. Again, the picture cannot speak of all this, whereas the poem can. (If the maxim *ut pictura poesis* still applies in this sequence, it seemingly designates a complex process in which pictures are simultaneously elucidated and displaced by poems, images by writing, spatiality by temporality. Yet perhaps only a *desire* to effect this displacement of pictures can be enacted by their "creative" interpreter, since a dialectical return to the picture and to "seeing" rather than interpreting appears to be inescapable. The pictures also show us some things that the narratives don't tell us, and the narrative, with its instant abolishings and/or discrete phases may seem bound to the same representational terms as the pictures.)

lines 3–4 In the act of seeing the "other" in the guise of the laurel tree, the passive spectator metamorphically becomes identical to what he

Then heauenly branches did I see arise,
Out of a fresh and lusty Laurell tree
Amidde the yong grene wood. Of Paradise
Some noble plant I thought my selfe to see,
Suche store of birdes therein yshrouded were,
Chaunting in shade their sundry melodie.
My sprites were rauisht with these pleasures there.
While on this Laurell fixed was mine eye,
The Skie gan euery where to ouercast,
And darkned was the welkin all aboute,
When sodaine flash of heauens fire outbrast,
And rent this royall tree quite by the roote.
Which makes me much and euer to complaine,
For no such shadow shal be had againe.

beholds: "Some noble plant I thought my selfe to see . . . ." This self-ennobling transformation into a sacred, supposedly eternal laurel, which also "plants" the speaker in a soil other than that of his birth, allows him to incorporate the song of many birds. The spectator has moved to the center of the action.

line 7 The "rauishment" of the spectator is at once a state of being passively mastered by the power of the vision and of being narcissistically fixated on an idealized self-image as that of the "other."

line 12 The "royall tree" or sacred laurel proves no more immune to a heavenly thunderbolt than it does in Marvell's "Horatian Ode." The shallow "planting," illusory aura, or perhaps even "upstart" presumption of the laurel make it possible for it easily to be uprooted, a point to be considered both in the politics of dynastic competition and of Protestant militancy. A point to be considered, too, insofar as the poet might wish to merge his own identity with that of the "royal tree," taken to mean either royal incumbent or her family tree.

line 14 "Shadow?" Is it to be understood that no such image, no such ravishingly complete and satisfying illusion, will ever again be entertained by a spectator who can *learn* from experience – and also teach? The shade/shelter of the laurel is also no longer available.

In the fourth pair (p. 111), a whole new scene, now getting elaborately fashioned as the definitive Spenserian one even while the picture is ostensibly just being glossed, is the subject of emblem and poem alike. If the three ladies pictured are not in the regular attitude of the three Graces, they anticipate the arrival of those three. The scene is now definitively pastoral, and at its center is the sacred spring rather than the sacred laurel, a *topos* culturally "older" in its evocation of Helicon than that of the laurel, but also newer in that it takes the place of the vulnerable laurel-*topos*.

line 2 "Mildness" as the aesthetic key to a situation otherwise fatally characterized by vain excess, "male" violence and recurrent loss?

lines 4–5 An absolutely exclusive version of pastoral (*sui generis*) as the new dream of the Spenserian "spectator"? A version of pastoral comprising *many* Muses, summoning up or fashioning a sympathetic chorus of female voices, and founding an exclusive, sympathizing community of noble women?

line 6 A "signature" line that will, as John Hollander has suggested in discussion,[30] recur in Spenser whenever this "primal scene" is rehearsed. The hypermetrical Alexandrine line enacts both a "sympathetic" tuning of the poetic voice to the natural, limpid, effortless, endless fall of water, but it also enacts a metrical mistuning (or mistake, as the *Variorum*

Within this wood, out of the rocke did rise
A Spring of water mildely romblyng downe,
Whereto approched not in any wise
The homely Shepherde, nor the ruder cloune,
But many Muses, and the Nymphes withall,
That sweetely in accorde did tune their voice
Vnto the gentle sounding of the waters fall.
The sight wherof dyd make my heart reioyce.
But while I toke herein my chiefe delight,
I sawe (alas) the gaping earth deuoure
The Spring, the place, and all cleane out of sight.
Whiche yet agreues my heart euen to this houre.

commentary supposes) that draws attention to its own artifice. This "gentle" sound is now the noble one, but it may also be a newly invented form of "feminine" nobility in a fallen world, in which other forms of nobility are ones of violent "masculine" excess. Again, poetic identification with feminine inspiration and *mise-en-scène* is revealed, yet the possible doubleness or duplicity of the speaker may only be intensified in this apparently complete abnegation of the male.

lines 10–11 "Alas," the gaping earth swallows up this consoling fantasy too. Yet if it disappears out of sight, it does not disappear out of mind, since it "yet agreues my heart euen to this houre" – an "hour" that presumably continues even after the entire sequence of emblems in the *Theatre* has passed in review: after the vision or "Sabaoths sight" of the New Jerusalem has been afforded to the spectator; and after the prophetic voice of St John has taken over as the authoritative one in the final poem: "I saw new Earth, new Heauen, sayde Saint Iohn..."[31] If the "gaping earth" devours everything of which the poem speaks, the spring itself merely goes back underground, and can re-emerge in due course.

In poem 5 (p. 113), as in poem 1, two discrete synchronic events in the emblem are linked in the poetic narrative, and the narrative itself is a "closed" one ending in the amazing suicide of the phoenix, apparently a case of *adynata* or impossibility that has nevertheless occurred. (The "single" phoenix is also doubled!) Although the self-regenerating but also self-regarding phoenix seems to take the place of the laurel and the spring as a figure of regenerative poetic power, its history and strange ending imply that it is less rather than more capable than its predecessors of withstanding destruction. Ironically, indeed, it alone destroys itself, in a fit of narcissistic pique.

line 2 This phoenix is also literally and metaphorically a bird of paradise: an emblem of the soul, of supreme holiness, and of powerful singleness, yet also of supreme vanity and narcissistic display. (It is the same mysterious bird that the speaker sees in Marvell's "The Garden.") The singleness of the phoenix-soul, although not necessarily false in principle, is fatally compromised by its appearance in a world of appearances and its participation in a temporal narrative in which we see it in two different phases. Perhaps the phoenix loses sight of its single/singular nature as it falls for its own image. Its suicidal act of self-wounding is virtually indistinguishable in the emblem from the act of preening, and suicide accordingly looks like preening gone wrong, or gone too far. The speaker who here thinks [line 4] that he is *seeing* some "heauenly wight" may be wrong, or may already be showing with sly irony that he knows better.

I saw a Phœnix in the wood alone,
With purple wings and crest of golden hew,
Straunge birde he was, whereby I thought anone,
That of some heauenly wight I had the vew:
Vntill he came vnto the broken tree
And to the spring that late deuoured was.
What say I more? Eche thing at length we see
Doth passe away: the Phœnix there, alas,
Spying the tree destroyde, the water dride,
Himselfe smote with his beake, as in disdaine,   10
And so forthwith in great despite he dide.
For pitie and loue my heart yet burnes in paine.

line 9 Apparently and perhaps wrongly anticipating its own destruction as it contemplates (also from the position of the spectator?) the
destruction of the tree and the well, which do after all remain *visible* in
the emblem, the phoenix pre-empts and thus seeks to control its own fate
through the absurd ruse of suicide. In doing so, perhaps it forgets itself –
forgets who it really is – or has succumbed to its own superficial
appearance as a highly colored bird of paradise. The narcissistic "despite"
in which the phoenix acts against his own nature and destiny gives only
an illusory nobility to his self-inflicted end.

line 12 Is it for the foolish phoenix, or for something else that he still
remembers, that the speaker's heart "yet burnes in paine?"

The sixth (p. 115) is another "double" emblem of which the narrative, this
time one concluding in apotheosis rather than death, is supplied by the
poem. Is *this* the double image that has possessed the spectator's mind
even as he recited the unhappy history of the phoenix? (The second line of
poem 6 virtually repeats the isolated concluding line of poem 5.)

A number of questions arise in connection with poem 6: why is the
lady (if it is only one lady) simultaneously shrouded and not shrouded?
Why is the shrouded face hardly less visible than the unshrouded one?
Does this pairing of emblem and poem finally teach us to read
allegorically, to understand the "dark conceit," rather than to see with
eyes that may have been dazzled by the superficial beauty of the bird of
paradise – or of the beautiful woman? Or does it function anti-
allegorically, teaching us to penetrate the mystification in which the
"lady" seeks to shroud *herself*? Does this emblem, finally, embody strong
version(s) of "doubleness" in contrast to previous weak ones, implying
narratives ending only in death?

line 3 Here and later in the Eurydice allusion, the lady seems to have
become a virgin "queen of the shepherds;" but also to have become one
capable of thinking her own thoughts ("pensiuely") and thus perhaps of
constructing her own fiction(s) and image(s). Does she need the Orpheus
who apparently offers himself in this poem as one who would be capable
simultaneously of immortalizing her and himself? Is there a place in the
system for an elegiac singer, memorialist, and even redeemer of the
"likeness" from oblivion? Is her Christian faith, or are her own pastoral
fictions, powerful enough to let her mount up "well assurde" even after
she is fatally snake-bitten while wandering unprotected through the
fields? Is the apotheosis capable of being effected *singly*, or only in a
double scheme incorporating both the singer and the female subject of
his song? And if there is no space for such an elegist, what space *is* there
for the speaker of the poem?

At last so faire a Ladie did I spie,
That in thinking on hir I burne and quake,
On herbes and floures she walked pensiuely.
Milde, but yet loue she proudely did forsake.
White seemed hir robes, yet wouen so they were,
As snowe and golde together had bene wrought.
Aboue the waste a darke cloude shrouded hir,
A stinging Serpent by the heele hir caught,
Wherewith she languisht as the gathered floure:
And well assurde she mounted vp to ioy.   10
Alas in earth so nothing doth endure
But bitter griefe that dothe our hearts anoy.

line 7 Rather oddly, the dark cloud shrouds her only above the waist – what may be incapable of concealment is her vulnerable gender. This vulnerability, incapable of being masked even if it is covered, also constitutes an opportunity for the ruthless spectator. If the cloud is *her* attempt at self-mystification, it succeeds only partially or not at all, and is portrayed as virtually transparent.

lines 11–12 Perhaps the only thing to which the epigram as a Spenserian form can finally *testify* is loss and grief, though it may also persist in an unacknowledged (or only generically hinted) aggression that perpetually unmasks or even threatens to annihilate its objects. As a form committed indistinguishably to grieving and grievance, it remains at once highly "sympathetic" and the reverse.

In a theatricalized world in which apparently nothing (no single *thing*) endures, "bitter griefe," a double condition, does endure and promises to generate its own successful forms even as it profoundly "anoys" all hearts. It thus becomes the sole possible basis for a developing if ambivalent and somewhat disturbing Spenserian poetic of sympathy that is also a masked politics. This development may be what we have to consider in and as the shape of Spenser's career; it is also the development we may have to trace as Spenser elaborates his own courtier-role in the theater of the world. The noble fiction of the courtier is also, as so many recent studies of sixteenth-century poetics have taught us, a form of dissimulation under which various political goals, including anti-courtly ones, may be pursued, perhaps simultaneously. Finally, Spenser's *Theatre* may teach us the meaning of the word "strategic" as applied to the literary career.

Afterword

After I had completed this essay, in which I had tried to work out a possible logic of Spenser's position as putative translator of the poems in van der Noot's *Theatre*, a helpful discussion of the Dutch author and his works by P.W.M. van der Sluijs appeared.

Conceding the still-preliminary nature of current research into emblem-and-poem relationships in sixteenth-century texts, as well as in the works of van der Noot, van der Sluijs makes this pertinent observation:

Another factor rendering investigation more difficult for the re-searcher of today is that people of the sixteenth century, particularly the learned, possessed a generally allegorical habit of mind that "translated" itself into literature and pictorial art [alike], and which is now as good as lost [unknown] to us.[32]

My own reading depends of course on the assumption that this lost habit of mind has to some extent been recovered in recent Renaissance literary criticism, especially where allegorizing is understood rhetorically as a process in which signification is at once veiled and "transported." Van der Sluijs's observation can, however, serve as an incitement to attempt "allegorical" reading (which can't in the nature of things be a safe enterprise at present) and as a caveat against any premature confidence in the results.

Van der Sluijs's mustering of precedents for van der Noot's *Theatre* as well as his interpretive application of Alciati and Sambucus should obviously be consulted on account of their intrinsic interest but also as a check on the kind of "wild" analysis I have undertaken. Van der Sluijs's discussion exemplarily refrains furthermore, unlike so many Alciatian applications, from canonizing itself as the authoritative "Renaissance" reading of the emblems and poems in question.

Exemplarily, too, van der Sluijs's discussion of the relationship, and above all of priority, between emblem and poem remains free of preconceptions that would arbitrarily privilege either image or text. Not only does he perceive the allegorizing habit to bear simultaneously on emblem and text, but he crucially observes that:

Similarities between emblematic and literary conception and execution do not necessarily imply that the author has borrowed from the emblematist; a communal [common] origin can account for resemblance.[33]

Van der Sluijs also reviews possible meanings of "epigram" in the context of the *Theatre*. It can be a virtual synonym for *subscriptio*, that is to say, "an explanatory [clarifying] text devoted to untying the riddle locked up in the *pictura*, or to facilitating its solution." It can mean, according to others cited by van der Sluijs, "tersely and pithily composed," but, as van der Sluijs points out, this definition doesn't strictly apply to the poems in the *Theatre* although it may to some in van der Noot's *Het Bosken*. An important additional consideration from my own point of view is contained in another essay, by K. Porteman,[34] in which it is argued that the characteristic turn given to emblematization in Dutch cultural history is that of satirical representation. Presumably "epigram" can (how, in general, could it *not*?) participate in this change.

I should like finally to emphasize the significance, to which van der

Sluijs's essay attests, of emblem-books as poetic source-books and indeed as poetic *programs*. Noting incidentally that Spenser's *Theatre* has been identified by a number of critics as the very first English emblem-book, van der Sluijs allows us to consider the extent to which Spenser's subsequent career can be said to have been programmed by his early engagement in the van der Noot translation, as well as the extent to which the same "program" unfolds in van der Noot's own subsequent career and works. One crucial item in the program to which I want to draw attention, both as it relates to the foregoing essay and to the next two chapters, is that in which an eternal relationship of symbiotic strife between poet and emperor is emblematized:

> In the lower part of the triumphal arch, the poet is glorified through the representation of a solitary man[ikin] with musical instruments in the company of two swans on the river. The meaning of this is that the poet must withdraw into solitude, far from the din of the world, if he wishes to accomplish his creative work. The symbol of the poet is a white swan, image of poetic [the poet's] purity, on a blue ground; this in contrast to [that of] the Roman emperors, conveyed by a black eagle on a golden ground (signifying victory). Both poets and emperors have the noblest birds in their coats of arms, yet they are sons of two great but different gods who are also brothers, Phoebus Apollo and Mars.[35]

5
Discovery

As a narrative and logical conclusion to the book, this essay adheres to the conventions of detective fiction. It names a "hidden" criminal and discovers a criminal scheme according to the convention that connects grand criminality with the figure of the evil genius. If this solution sounds frivolous, it is partly because in so much detective fiction the evil genius is conceived as a particular kind of person (abnormally brilliant, infinitely resourceful, always invisible, criminal by strange predilection, etc.) But in the next essay, although the cheap stereotype isn't beside the point, the notion of evil genius is taken seriously as one constitutively entailed in any conception we may be able to form of the "strong" poet.[1] To say this isn't primarily to attempt a negative (re)idealization of the poet as master criminal, though that also comes into it, nor is an attempt being made to restore the master poet as "onlie begetter" and sole possessor of the work. On the contrary, a state of being inhabited or acted upon is contained in the very notion of poetic "genius," a term that doesn't in any case always apply to a person ("*genius loci*") but does always imply "something there" (or something other there) which is incapable of being fully assimilated to any category but its own, problematically signified by the term in question. This stubborn or powerful resistance to categorization is no doubt what provokes the designation "evil," and makes it easier even in poetics to think genius evil than to think it otherwise. Yet still less, I would suggest, than such terms as "the author" or even "the poet," is the term "genius" (perhaps the archaic *daimon* is better) capable of being negotiated away in wished-for discourse of poetics, and the point isn't necessarily to go on evacuating the term as an offensively mystified one, but to introject a content, perhaps now that of a culture that can hardly be thought innocent. (I take it that this "genius" is no longer capable of being identified with the classical Freudian unconscious, a phenomenon no longer in the least "alien" or "other," but on the contrary incorporated into a rigorous poststructuralist logic of which it is also the foundation.)

Although all these considerations apply to the following essay, I wouldn't claim that they were all fully present to me at the time of writing. This essay, like the first, was dictated to a very significant extent by the state of play in the Renaissance field, in which a scenario had been emerging whereby the sadomasochistic fantasies of the exiled [male] poet or laureate *manqué* could, under the particular conditions of Renaissance life, be translated into a political master plan. But my inclination to *tell* the story that follows has been reinforced by considerations other than its apparent timeliness. I have already named Leonardo Sciascia (p.13) as an avowedly fictional exemplar, and the point of my citing his work is that it at once fulfills and critically challenges the logic of detective fiction. The moment of discovery in his work (if there is ever a single moment) isn't one that vindicates the detective and the order that has been transgressed while isolating the criminal and exposing him to retribution. On the contrary, the process or moment of discovery becomes peculiarly unsatisfying – or subtly satisfying.

It may involve a *sure* knowledge, which can never legally be established, of the criminal's identity and of the conditions under which the crime will predictably be repeated; it may involve identification of criminals and/or a criminal situation that the political Left and Right each have their own stake in concealing; it may involve recognition of a criminality so minutely dispersed along a criminal chain, or socially so constitutive, as to defeat the operation of justice. (For Sciascia, it is precisely in the field of Italian cultural politics that all these possibilities arise.) It may, finally, confer on the investigator a knowledge dangerous to him but incapable of leading to any desirable outcome. And, almost inevitably, it must entail at least a long moment of sympathetic identification with the criminal or pariah figure, who is in a sense an embodied critic/critique of the order that condemns him (the killer in Sciascia's *Equal Danger*).

Still considering this essay as an ending, I would claim only that it marked for me the arrival at a certain logical and emotional terminus. This did not mean that I took any method or program to have been established but rather that a process of avowal, with its accompanying process of disavowal, had sufficiently been enacted. The need to enact this process is one that I take to have been contingent on some of the premises and concerns stated early in the book: principally that of an apparent situation of containment in which, with nothing new entering the system and with nothing capable of being expelled from it, all that may be possible/impossible is an attempt to incorporate, "profess," redeploy or rename certain elements in the system while purging or exorcising others. If anything can save this from being an exercise in futility, it is only the degree of clarification that may ensue (well short of "coming clean"); the sense that some distance may have been travelled en route; the possibility of extending the perceived limits to the field of operation; an enabling renewal of the critical promise.

The most excellent poet of our time: a dark conceit

Everyone working in the Renaissance knows that there has recently been an astonishing boom in Puttenham studies. The quaintly archaic *Arte of English Poesie*,[2] once regarded as a mediocre, derivative and perhaps mildly eccentric schoolbook, one from which no major English poets of the Renaissance visibly learned anything,[3] has suddenly revealed itself as the skeleton key to sixteenth-century English poetry. Since the publication of Daniel Javitch's *Poetry and Courtliness in Renaissance England*,[4] the work has been read as a manual of political courtship, an art of government, and a treatise on the relationship between the poet and the sovereign, in particular Queen Elizabeth. Another way of putting it is that from the moment historicists broke a major taboo and began reading the poetry of the sixteenth century as politically encoded discourse, Puttenham's work began to look like the most powerful decoding machine available. Puttenham's accounts of the poetic genres and rhetorical figures, even if not to be taken at face value and blindly applied, were regularly found to constitute a strong basis for discussion and in many instances to unmask the courtly masquerade. Puttenham has perhaps most brilliantly been used by Montrose,[5] but has also repeatedly been cited by other historicist critics.

Although no upward revaluation of Puttenham has explicitly been proclaimed, the use that has been made of him has lifted him from virtually nowhere into a position of amazing prominence. One result of this must be to raise the question all over again: *Who* is Puttenham, the nominal author of the *Arte*? Who, or whose interests, does he represent? Where on earth is he coming from? In the standard edition of the *Arte*, Gladys Doidge Willcock and Alice Walker sift the meager evidence both about possible authorship of this work and about the (negligible) literary life of George Puttenham, but a new effort of scholarly retrieval seems emphatically to be called for. Whether there is anything more to be found remains to be seen; perhaps there is nothing. Yet as soon as we start to think about the matter in the absence of fresh evidence, Baconian fantasies begin to sprout. Here is one: "George Puttenham" is a front for Edmund Spenser, and he is also the hitherto missing E.K. of *The Faerie*

Queene. Perhaps E.K. even warns us in the *The Shepheardes Calender* that something is afoot: in the Argument accompanying the "October" eclogue, he writes that "the Author hereof els where at large discourseth, in his booke called the English Poete, which book being lately come to my hands, I mynde also by Gods grace vpon further aduisement to publish."[6] No such poetics ever appeared – under the name of Edmund Spenser. But did he write the *Arte,* singlehandedly or in collaboration? If not, did he effectively dictate it, perhaps only in its final form, in such a way as to serve his own interests?

Not a case to be proved in the absence of further or corroborative evidence, but perhaps a thought to be risked and an historicist story to be told since, if my supposition is correct, there may precisely be no more evidence forthcoming, at least not the all-important smoking gun. All I shall therefore do is point to some circumstantial evidence and indicate what I take to be occult (?) signs of Spenser's hand in the *Arte.* The nominal question and intriguing possibility will remain that of Spenser's putative authorship or dictation, but the question of anyone's individual authorship isn't the whole point; the nature of the literary system in a context of competitive authorship and patronage is more deeply the issue. Within the system, the *Arte* can be regarded as a work that prophesies *The Faerie Queene,* that pre-emptively unmasks it, and that finally remystifies both itself and the poem.

First, circumstantial evidence. Spenser's use of the E.K. front in *The Shepheardes Calender* is a major precedent for his critical "supplementation" of the poetic text. The E.K. subtext functions in many complex ways that have been discussed, but one of these is to exorcise or permit the simultaneous revelation and disavowal of possibilities that would otherwise radically threaten the pastoral *fiction.*[7] I would suggest that this particular use of the E.K. subtext is also an important precedent. And if we are entitled to *assume* that E.K. and later "Puttenham" are fronts, it is at least partly because in the *Arte,* Book I, under the heading of satire or "reprehension," we are allowed to see the poet-priests who rule an archaic commonwealth using masked "recitours" to deliver rebukes they cannot effectively or decorously deliver in their own sacred *propriae personae.* A mechanism is thus exposed; the poet-priest as an operator behind the scenes is also revealed. This could in principle be the mechanism of the *Arte* – but would that make the *Arte* into a *satire?*

Now for a strange coincidence. The *Arte* was published in 1589, just in time for the 1590 launching of *The Faerie Queene.* Critics have often been puzzled at the seemingly belated appearance of the *Arte,* since its citations refer mainly to poets of the mid-century and earlier. Both the belatedness and the citation of poets of *Spenser's* youth gain a certain intelligibility if we assume the guiding hand to be Spenser's. The citation of these earlier poets would also let Spenser out of making invidious references to his contemporaries – but it would more than invidiously diminish all of them, not least the Philip Sidney whose work is showcased in Abraham Fraunce's very "friendly" *Arcadian Rhetorike* [1588].[8] In that work, as is well known, the late Sir Philip is extensively anthologized and also made one member of a triumvirate of which the other two members are Homer and Virgil. Despite having written an Arcadian *Shepheardes Calender*, Spenser is treated as virtually non-existent. Sidney also "dares not allow" the legitimacy of *The Shepheardes Calender* in his own *Apology*. In the *Arte* the tables are turned.

Sidney, it is true, gets mentioned six times in the *Arte* – but could his name be omitted *entirely* from a survey of current English poets without violence to the facts and without "Puttenham's" tipping his hand a little too obviously? How fully, let us rather ask, would Sidney's sister and other hagiographers have been gratified by the following testimonial? What could they even have imagined it to mean? What, in fact, *would* it have meant in the wake of Sidney's elevation to the status of a major culture hero in Fraunce's book and elsewhere?

> And in her Maiesties time that now is are sprong vp an other crew of Courtly makers. Noble men and Gentlemen of her Maiesties owne seruantes, who haue written excellently well as it would appeare if their doings could be found out and made publicke with the rest, of which number is first that noble gentleman *Edward* Earle of Oxford. *Thomas* Lord of Bukhurst, when he was young, *Henry*, Lord Paget, Sir *Philip Sydney*, Sir *Walter Rawleigh*, Maister *Edward Dyar*, Maister *Fulke Greuell, Gascon, Britton, Turberuille* . . . .[9]

Here Sidney disappears into a gentlemanly ruck or band of women's men in which some seem to be actual noblemen and some not (courtly makers), some important poets and some not, but in which all seem abruptly to be leveled. If the stated objection seems only to be that their best work does not appear, meaning that it circulates in manuscript and not in the public domain of print, it also allows us to think that what they are really up to (their "doings") cannot be "found out." Clandestine activities may, in other words, be getting pursued by this set; activity threatening to the queen may even be getting pursued by her own fawning "servants." Either way, or in every possible way, Sidney loses, while the courtiers become either a band of emasculated servants (lovers) or else a group of palace conspirators.

All this may prompt us to reflect that, although we talk quite comfortably about the ambition and power-hunger of authors living in the highly imperialistic sixteenth century, we may not really permit ourselves to see what this might lead to, or to conceive the possible magnitude of the operations mounted by the Sidneys, Mary even more than Philip, and Spenser. And, fortuitously or not, the *Arte* at once clears and sets the stage for the final disclosure of the master, no longer the humble Sidney-patronized Immerito of *The Shepheardes Calender*, and one possibly capable of being seen, too late, by Mary Sidney as an appalling viper nursed in the extended bosom of the Sidney family. *Was* a large Sidney *corpus* memorially printed, or was it competitively rushed into print, starting with Fraunce's more than generous Arcadian preview in 1588 – the game having shockingly ceased to be one for gentlemen? Are there fronts everywhere, some the "beau semblant" type of Fraunce's innocent prattling, some the "false semblant" type of Puttenham's magisterial exposition? Maybe, or maybe not, but "Puttenham" warns us what to look for. *Qui nescit dissimulare nescit regnare* runs the virtual ruling maxim of the surely misnamed *Arte of English Poesie*: who knows not how to deceive, knows not how to rule. (One of the *Arte*'s own strange animated figures is that of the "Misnamer," formerly but now it seems incorrectly known as metonymy.)

In the much-noted Chapter XVIII, "Puttenham" embarks on his discussion of the figure of Allegory or "False semblant" (i.e. false face).[10] This, as is now well known, is the figure of extended metaphor, of "transport" and "alteration," of the upstart courtier himself. Allegory is of course master Spenser's figure, also the master figure of the *Faerie Queene*, wonderfully underexplained to 1590 rival Raleigh in the famous explanatory letter. It is in the context of "Puttenham's" discussion of allegory that we first hear the maxim about dissimulation being the basis of political rule: it is attributed simply to a "great Emperour," "who had it vsually in his mouth."[11] The suppressed but also well-known, disgraceful and threatening reference is of course to the Tacitean Tiberius. This capacity for dissimulation seems finally to be attributed (favorably) to the queen herself who, in Chapter XX, is seen to display a capacity for politic scrutiny behind a "gorgeous" exterior; also to be capable of addressing a word to the wise between the lines of her own poems. (Yet the advice in the quoted "ditty" (*sic*) attributed to her concerns the folly of siding with Mary Queen of Scots, not a burning topic by 1589.) Is Elizabeth then the successful Tiberian ruler?

She is the personification, it is true, of her own peculiar rhetorical figure of *Exargasia* or the Gorgious, but who ever heard of that one before, except perhaps in the name of the "feminist" Greek rhetorician Gorgias, and who knows what it means? Flatteringly, "Puttenham" explains or implies that it means everything; everything beautiful anyway, "beau semblant." The proud (gorge-ous) queen is the figure of figures, ornament of ornaments, poet of poets, subsuming everything that his text contains except perhaps the one who is speaking it, namely Allegory personified, false semblant. And if the "gorgeous" queen subsumes everything contained in that text of ornaments, she also subsumes everything in poetic art that "Puttenham" has exposed, shredded and reduced to an ostensibly teachable craft – a "mystery" only in that sense. And finally the queen is not a man and therefore not Tiberius even if she does mildly dissemble; she really deceives nobody, especially not after *The Arte of English Poesie.* Tiberius deceives, and he is the one who rules from exile in Capri (island/Ireland?), manipulating everything from afar, ruling above all through the letter. It is with a letter that he kills the seemingly powerful Sejanus (Raleigh?); and we hear about more letters at the end of the "Gorgeous" chapter. These letters are supposedly contained in a mysterious work "where we entreat of the loues betwene prince *Philo* and Lady *Calia*, in their mutual letters, messages, and speeches."[12] Mysterious indeed. Are these love-letters or threatening letters? Is there ever a difference? And is the *Arte* one of them? The *public* love-letter of which Tiberius to Sejanus is forever the model?

Not just some things but everything about the *Arte* indicates the presence of the master. For example: the complicated, virtually impossible or self-canceling instructions on how successfully to praise the queen, behave decorously in the presence of royalty, etc., as well as a perspicuous disabling of rivals, who are all, like the queen, figures *in* the book. Hyperbole, for example, renamed "the Overreacher," might as well be called "Raleigh," and "Puttenham" warns the queen in the course of discussing it against believing hyperbolic lies about herself. He thus kills two birds with one stone – three, in fact, since when he hyperbolically flatters the "gorgeous" one himself, she has been warned not to believe.

Next, the pseudo-learnedness of the *Arte*, its E.K. pedantry, contradictoriness, haggling over definitions, recital of the good old story of Orpheus, etc., are all vintage *Shepheardes Calender.* Yet something has changed. This is no longer subtext, no longer footnotes, but a putative master narrative and ideal anthropology of the culture in which poetic activity is constituted, and of which, to borrow or "transport" a term from Northrop Frye, poetry is "the great code." This, indeed, is Spenser's master narrative, that of *The Faerie Queene*, of the *View of the Present State of Ireland*, and also perhaps of the sixteenth century, obsessed with the cultural *translatio*. In "Puttenham," this master narrative is told with some visible Spenserian *entrelacement*, and despite its synthetic assimilation of a multitude of humanistic commonplaces, no "original" form or precedent for this totalizing cultural narrative has been found.

In this story, both counterpolitical and counterdynastic, the poets are the culture's originators, arcane founding priesthood, and first, best lawgivers, their pedigree stretching back to the time immediately after the Fall (or Babel) when Amphion and Orpheus rebuild "civility." Any poetic belatedness and outsidedness, as well as any subordination of the cultural to the political, is thus reconstituted as priority, insidedness and privilege – almost the first move in the game of Renaissance poetics and certainly the master move. While princes get hyperbolical – therefore exaggerated and obviously false? – praise throughout the *Arte*, the logic of the totalizing narrative is manifestly one under which the political order comes after the cultural one, and it is in the political order, which they inhabit as *aliens*, that the poets become degraded "Princepleasers."[13] Their legitimate power is also clearly usurped in and by the political realm of upstart dynasties, yet in the ongoing cultural order they remain the unacknowledged legislators of the world. Not only is poetic succession like an unbroken apostolic succession since Orpheus, but the ideal succession of poetic *forms* testifies to the unbroken "descent" of culture. The either usurped or perhaps only masked universal rulers may thus seek to reappropriate in the political world their expropriated power, and even seek the eventual restoration of a lost commonwealth from within the very heart of the political empire.

Not only is the *Arte* a manual of instruction about how to please rulers, but also about how to subvert and unmask them; how to restrain their tyrannical presumption. The genre of tragedy, for example, is explicitly anti-tyrannical, and the warning it gives to princes is that, although they may dictate their own representation during their lives, their image for posterity is in the hands of poets.

The *Arte* is also an exemplary negotiation of the extraordinarily difficult but historically indissoluble relationship between the cultural and the political orders: *translatio imperii translatio studii*. In each of these realms there is one master figure. The courtier (allegory personified) is visibly subordinated to the queen (gorgeous personified) in the political world, but the tables are repeatedly and visibly, hence threateningly, turned in the *Arte*. If the struggle goes on in the present, there can in the long run be only one master figure, and it is not that of "beau semblant" (the gorgeous) but of "false semblant" (the courtier). The cultural also prevails in the long run over the political; indeed, there is a sense in which only the culture is timeless, something the poets never tire of repeating, even if they are neither understood nor taken seriously.

The incapacitation of the queen as the rival poet (but also the inferior, pleasing poet) is ruthlessly pursued by "Puttenham," often or inevitably in the guise of flattery (false semblant). Consider the exemplary *blazon* quoted by "Puttenham" as *decorous* praise of Elizabeth, but which actually strips, sexually violates and even dismembers its object, also shattering the icon:

> Of siluer was her forehead hye,
> Her browes two bowes of hebenie,
> Her tresses trust were to behold
> Frizled and fine as fringe of gold.

And of her lips:

> Two lips wrought out of rubie rocke,
> Like leaues to shut and to vnlock.
> As portall dore in Princes chamber:
> A golden tongue in mouth of amber.

And of her eyes:

> Her eyes God wot what stuffe they are,
> I durst be sworne each is a starre:
> As cleere and bright as woont to guide
> The Pylot in his winter tide.

And of her breasts:

> Her bosome sleake as Paris plaster,
> Helde vp two balles of alabaster,
> Eche byas was a little cherrie:
> Or els I thinke a strawberie.[14]

If this freeze-frame approach hardly promotes the smooth flow of adulation, it also prompts us to ask why the momentum of the striptease is arrested at this point – or if it is so in the reader's mind once that particular momentum has been established. Is *that* what "decorum" means? And what is the result, for both observer and observed, of having the female breasts threateningly transformed into edibles? Whatever the answer to those questions might be, this "gentle" stripping might recall to the mind of the royal reader, to whom the *Arte* is after all addressed, the more drastic one in the first chapter of Book III ("Of Ornament"). There it is imagined that a court lady enters naked into a public assembly, thus being exposed to the most punishing imaginable humiliation. Exposure, as we see, is always possible, and "Puttenham" always sees through the "gorgious;" he also shows how easily gorgeousness can be reduced to nakedness.[15] (Compare Spenser's "Mutabilitie" Cantos in which the wood-god Faunus sees Diana/Cynthia naked and then carelessly, unforgivably, *laughs*.[16] Or consider even more tellingly the episode in *Faerie Queene*,

Book VI, in which Serena is stripped naked and prepared for ritual butchery by a sinister druidical priest after he has prevented the savage people from sexually molesting her.[17]) And the very art of the *Arte*, mystifying, demystifying, remystifying, is that of allegory, but also now of terror – of Tiberian rule, perhaps a necessary evil in the political world the poet is forced to inhabit. Even the decorum that the work has so studiously taught and in doing so quietly disabled (the name of another "Puttenham" figure or "prosopopeia," characteristically infused with poetic energy, is "the disabler") – this decorum is finally repossessed as that which can never be taught. Decency, "Puttenham" finally tells us, is that for which many names exist in English and other languages, but to which no single thing, or no *thing*, corresponds. Perhaps only "Puttenham" knows the secret.

In sum, then, the misnamed *Arte* may also have a misnamed author, of whom the real signature is everywhere visible. Indeed, the irony is that even without the smoking gun it is so perfectly obvious that "Puttenham" is a front for Spenser, the *Arte* either written by Spenser or "dictated" by him in his own interests rather than those of any poet-contemporaries. The evidence is where it is least/most likely to be seen, which is right at the beginning and on the surface. (Not the queen's picture printed as a frontispiece; we are not to be deceived by beautiful images, pretty fronts.) Chapter 1 of Book I has as its caption: "What a Poet and Poesie is, and who may worthily be sayd the most excellent Poet of our time." *Our* time? 1589–90? The "time" of culture rather than of political rule?

Anyway, the most excellent poet of *our* time turns out to be the most ancient, wise, and prestigious figure of all, traditionally misnamed Homer, and perhaps surprisingly absent as a recognized major influence on an Edmund Spenser who knew Greek as well as Latin. This is the true culture-hero, as distinct from princepleaser Virgil who, living under the empire, is no more than half the man he imitated. To *be* Homer would mean that one was the very first and greatest of the epic poets (a good position to be in for the launching of *The Faerie Queene*), and it would mean having moved from the characteristic Renaissance–Spenserian "starting" position of belatedness, exile and outsidedness to the very origin and center. Who, then, is "Homer," and in what time is he living? Who, more pertinently, does *this* Homer, a poor private man, most resemble of the English Renaissance poets we know – and whose poetic achievement in English would by 1591 look most like the one described below as Homer's? Who, playing the role of Tiberius in the political sphere, could also have played the role of Homer in the cultural sphere, thus doubling his own poetic identity? Finally, how *did* "Homer" know all the things about which he seemed capable of writing, and to which it seems hardly possible that he could have had any access? Secret letters? Divine inspiration? Inspired divination? Or just the magnified and darkening fancies of an incipiently blind and pitiable old man, certainly devoid of "Sabaoths sight?" Here at all events is "Puttenham's" "Homer," undeniably one with a more subtle claim to equivalence than Chapman's gorgeous one:

> And this science in his perfection, can not grow, but by some diuine instinct, the Platonicks call it *furor*: or by the excellencie of nature and complexion: or by great subtiltie of spirits and wit, or by some experience and obseruation of the world, and course of kind, or peraduenture by all or most part of them. Otherwise how was it possible that *Homer* being but a poore priuate man, and as some say in his later age blind, should so exactly set foorth and describe, as if he had bene a most excellent Captaine or Generall, the order and array of battels, the conduct of whole armies, the sieges and assaults of cities and townes? or as some great Princes maiordome, and perfect Surueyor in Court, the order, sumptuousnesse and magnificence of royal bankets, feasts, weddings, and enteruewes? or as a Polititian very prudent, and much inured with the priuat and publique affaires, so grauely examine the lawes and ordinances Ciuill, or so profoundly discourse in matters of estate, and formes of all politique regiment? Finally how could he so naturally paint out the speeches, countenance and maners of Princely persons and priuate, to wit, the wrath of *Achilles*, the magnanimitie of *Agamemnon*, the prudence of *Menelaus*, the prowesse of *Hector*, the maiestie of king *Priamus*, the grauetie of *Nestor*, the pollicies and eloquence of *Vlysses*, the calamities of the distressed *Queenes* [!], and the valiance of all the Captaines and aduenturous knights in those lamentable warres of Troy.[18]

Some of "Puttenham's" readers might have recalled the *Aeneid*'s warnings against Greeks who come bearing gifts, and also about the fatal impiety of all performances in the Greek manner. Some, too, might have recalled that there is a dark and not fully understood phenomenon known as homeric laughter. But if they did recall such disconcerting things, neither George Puttenham nor, for that matter, Edmund Spenser could have been accused of indulging in them.

Epilogue: the way forward

This essay, not written for inclusion in the book and in fact written several months after I had considered the book to be finished, now serves both as conclusion and as epilogue. It is included here partly to mark the continuing passage of time in what is, after all, a chronological narrative of the critical profession, and partly because I realized in writing the essay that its logic remained fundamentally that of the book.

What the essay marks, among other things, is an at least symptomatically momentous occurrence, namely the extraordinarily rapid and widespread return to Shakespeare as the prime subject of critical interest in the English Renaissance field and maybe in the profession at large. This occurrence, either foreshadowed or already manifesting itself at the conference referred to at the beginning of Chapter 2, reveals an overwhelming (possibly "historic") impulse on the part of many professional critics to recenter themselves on Shakespeare as the figure of supreme cultural authority, explicitly reclaimed as such. The return to Shakespeare can by the same token be seen as an almost ceremonious termination of so-called marginal or countercultural enterprises, with whatever they implied.

If, from this newly recentered perspective, it may seem as if counterculturalism "from within" now stands revealed as having always been a mode of psychological denial rather than of transforming political vision, it may also be said that this return to the center definitively sticks us with what we are and have – or, to adopt a more precisely applicable Shakespearean locution, with what we will. Complaining of being stuck with Shakespeare may of course sound perverse, not to speak of philistine, yet a return to Shakespeare in the present context may have to be construed, not just as a pleasurable homecoming, but as a fateful event in which we make destiny our choice. At times this return also takes on the look of a theurgical occurrence in the increasingly sanctified field of "our" culture; the moment of return is then also one in which Shakespeare is recognized all over again as the master-spirit, whose will it is left to us only to interpret. (An outcome not necessarily undesired or unforeseen in a series of notorious puns by Shakespeare himself.)[1] Yet if criticism is not simply to be abandoned in the wake of these events, some sense of responsibility to account for, or at least to grapple critically with, this willed recentering of Shakespeare must accompany the current reclamation of Shakespeare as a figure of cultural authority. The assumption of responsibility plays, at all events, some part in this essay on *A Midsummer Night's Dream*. Given the premises of this book, however, the proper critical relation to the author of "genius" as well as the nature of critical responsibility remain rather vexed.

Although a detective element is yet again involved here, some attempt is made in the essay either to reconceive literary detection as cultural work rather than a matter of impulse, or to reconceive the work of the critic in post-detective terms. The question of the *playwright's* finding work to do, or of his finding the *proper* work to do, is one that I take to be significantly explored in Shakespearean comedy up to and beyond *A Midsummer Night's Dream*; in considering that issue, I came to perceive it as a possible one for the critic as well. Yet the terms in which this "propriety" might be established were not immediately apparent.

As an emergent topic in the Renaissance field (and no doubt in others as well), "work" appears increasingly to be situated in the nexus at which culture, poetics and politics meet, and at which anthropological, poetic and political discourses thus also meet. One apparent consequence of situating work in this configuration is still to oppose it to play, and to all the forms of idleness, wishfulness and willfulness that seem properly to belong to the field of play. It might seem, moreover, that only in the sphere of play does the so-called magical thinking allied to idleness, wishfulness, and willfulness belong, and that this thinking remains impotently if seductively opposed to any kind of work capable of producing real if limited cultural and political gains. This magical thinking, which for our purposes may be taken to include conjuration, daydreaming, metamorphic fantasy and romance narrative, may even seem incipiently pernicious insofar as it can be regarded as another *way* of working, one capable of producing extraordinary results without labor. Yet if all these stark oppositions are expressed conditionally here it is because, partly thanks to Shakespeare, they remain incomplete or questionable oppositions, and their polarities are periodically reversible.

Not only has a need to rethink these categorical oppositions become intense as the professional commitment to Shakespeare has revived, but the possibility of rethinking them has significantly been established in neo-Freudian discussion of the paradoxical dreamwork as "another way of working," or of conceiving work. And once poetic "making" has been introduced into the cultural–political nexus, the work–play opposition gets triangulated, and more complex permutations obviously become possible. It then becomes possible to speak, as we familiarly do, of the poetics of culture, but as we now also might do of a magical politics not fully opposed either to practical politics or to the notion of work. For all these possibilities, *A Midsummer Night's Dream* offers itself as perfect test case, and its utility as such has richly been suggested in the essay by Louis Montrose on this play to which I have previously referred.

Yet if the work of the critic can partly be conceived in the antithetical–complementary terms suggested above, the profession of the critic calls for something else as well, namely the unending work of discovery and disenchantment that aligns it with the task of detection as a putatively responsible one. By no means a *simply* responsible one, since the breaking of the criminal bond and hence the definitive withdrawal of criticism from its criminal complicities remains virtually unthinkable, and a possibly unwanted form of responsibility thus constantly accrues to the critic.

What has to be attempted, it seems to me, is a critical discourse or form of work at once participating in and counter to that of poetry – one neither high-mindedly alienated from the poetic impulse as so much theory claims to be, nor dead to it as so much historical scholarship actually is, but also not identified with the poetic impulse or "will" to the exclusion of that critical *resistance* summoned up by the stoic maxim *nil admirare*. If regular scholarly research, necessarily un- or anti-imaginative in some degree, might be seen as the existing, proper, and successful form of critical work (the only problem then being that of the individual critic's attaining the required level of performance), it remains to be said that when Shakespeare and other major Renaissance authors are in question, the nature, limits and immunities even of that form of work (or propriety) come on trial all over again. Not only research, but a critical discourse "proper" to these authors and to the unreserved profession of the critic has still to be attempted.

No formula is proposed here for a stable critical discourse or specific project fulfilling all the conditions specified above, though perhaps the serendipitous discovery or adventitious phenomenon of counter-narrative can permanently be included in the province of criticism. I will, however, suggest that professing criticism in our situation requires criticism, or, as I would prefer to say, the language of Anglophone criticism, periodically to be reclaimed – not as a culturally exclusive idiom, but as a *critical* language rather than a fully incorporated (perhaps just "corporate") one.

Why, it may nevertheless be asked, should anyone want to bring such matters as these to a head in dealing with a comedy as delicate, pleasurable and seemingly remote from burdensome concerns as *A Midsummer Night's Dream*? Could a sense of heavy earnestness ever have been more misplaced? One answer is that criticism rather than appreciation or performance is at stake here, and that the price of criticism may include sacrilege. Another is that, by an apparent law of contraries, some of the strongest modern discussions of Shakespearean tragedy have been conducted as if those plays partake of black comedy or tragic farce. Conversely, many strong modern discussions of Shakespearean comedy have noted their disturbingly unfunny characteristics. This law, which is also one of critical perspective, may operate for as long as strictly critical interest is professed. And if notions of critical seriousness or responsibility are at issue, it is in Shakespeare above all that established or generically predicted correlations between essence and form, affect and implication, are forever fascinatingly unsettled. No single way of being serious or responsible, or even of knowing what the terms might mean, can thus readily be established in relation to Shakespeare's dramatic works, all of which are also called plays.

The name of the game in *A Midsummer Night's Dream*

> So those word-warriors, lazy star-gazers,
> Used to no labour but to lose themselves,
> Had their heads filled with cozening fantasies,
> They plotted how to make their poverty
> Better esteemed of than high Sovereignty.[2]

Do the above wild, anti-intellectual charges, embodied by Thomas Nashe in *Summer's Last Will and Testament*, actually mean anything? Are there any to whom, in the Elizabethan period, they can seriously be taken to apply? Or is it just academic satire, spleen, rant?

In trying to answer these questions, I will be making an argument that depends on a set of premises that must be stated in advance, and then somewhat elaborated in the course of the essay. I don't hold these premises to be self-evidently true or binding, merely defensible, and if I give them a quasi-axiomatic status here, I do it for the sake of argument. In another argument, any or all of them might become the bone of contention. The tactical point of beginning in this way – axiomatically, as opposed, for example, to engaging immediately with the published criticism – will appear in the specific nature of the conclusions that are facilitated, but also in the conferred possibility, to be invoked later in the essay, of suspending *interpretation* momentarily even while engaged in it and acknowledging its inescapability.

First, then, I stipulate it as an accepted fact that *A Midsummer Night's Dream* comes after *The Comedy of Errors* and *The Taming of the Shrew* in the chronological sequence of Shakespeare's comedies.[3] Second, that arguments can successfully be made, if not for an evolutionary development in the chronological succession of Shakespeare's plays, then at least for intelligible processes of revision and transformation in that succession, however varied the circumstances (contexts, events) may have been under which individual plays were produced. A certain canonical logic, in other words, rather than a series of false starts or accidents is discernible throughout Shakespeare's production. Third, that Shakespeare's very early comedies, meaning *The Comedy of Errors* and *The Taming of the Shrew*, are to be regarded less as 'prentice works than as works of almost alarmingly ostentatious early mastery – and masterfulness.[4] It is accordingly not as works of deficiency but of excess, in which the hand is overplayed, that *The Comedy of Errors* and *The Taming of the Shrew* become subject to Shakespeare's revision. Fourth, and virtually as a corollary, that both these plays are marked by what might be called an excessive (despotic) will to resolve. In both plays the eventual outcome remains a matter of suspense to the end,[5] and in each play the resolution is coextensive with the annihilating prevalence of a single will, that of the invisible playwright in *The Comedy of Errors*, or of Petruchio acting "for" the playwright in *The Taming of the Shrew*. Fifth, and last, that both these plays begin to do their work only after staging preliminary, virtually extra-dramatic situations (prologue; induction) of aimlessness, helplessness or inertia[6] – of virtually empty pastime, or of time fruitlessly passing. The dramatic *work* the plays then find to do is reciprocally dependent on their progressive discovery (finding; revelation) of ends toward which they can direct themselves: final clarification (elucidation, theophany) as release from the bondage of error in *The Comedy of Errors*; the subordination of women and restoration of all contingently threatened "proper" roles and hierarchies in *The Taming of the Shrew*. Moreover, the definite article in the title of each play makes the play in question instantiate, in addition to "itself," a comic category (*the* comedy of errors) or a comic principle (*the* taming of the shrew); one may accordingly argue that the simple type or principle is in each case worked out to its logical conclusion – and to the point of exhaustion.

Given these premises, certain claims about *A Midsummer Night's Dream* follow almost of their own accord. It can be claimed, for example, that without ceasing to do the work or relinquishing the specific goals of either of these plays, *A Midsummer Night's Dream* embodies revised and above all qualified (mitigated) versions of the projects embodied in both, though the value and significance of that "mitigation" are far from clear at the outset.

The most striking instances of mitigation in *A Midsummer Night's Dream* are those in which the stark antitheses and ultimately anti-imaginative ("proper") resolutions of both the earlier plays are absorbed and attenuated. In *A Midsummer Night's Dream*, a relatively feminized or indeterminate "moonlight" realm, nominally that of Phoebe, is constituted both as a poetic space of fabulous brilliance and as a space "between" the hard, bright light and stupefying darkness of the earlier plays. It is within that "new" liminal space that the imaginative excesses of the poetic Nobleman in the *Taming of the Shrew* induction, excluded from the play "proper," can now be accommodated. No final closure of this indeterminate or, more accurately, contestable, imaginative space is effected at the end of *A Midsummer Night's Dream*. Puck, for example, although having served as Oberon's henchman, still identifies himself as one whose existence depends on the deferral of full daylight as well as on the perpetual motion and endlessly shifting identity of "Hecate triformis," the daemonic trinitarian female principle, who "[is] Proserpina in Hades; Diana (and occasionally Lucina) on earth; and Luna (or Phoebe or Cynthia) in the heavens":[7]

> And we fairies, that do run
> By the triple Hecate's team
> From the presence of the sun,
> Following darkness like a dream,
> Now are frolic . . . (V.i.369–73)

Mitigation is also evident in the discontinuous temporalities of *A Midsummer Night's Dream*. The distinction between the fictional time of the play and the real time spent by the spectator in the theater is marked in Puck's final, unmasked address to the audience:

> Think but this, and all is mended,
> That you have but slumbered here
> While these visions did appear. (V.i.410–12)

While advertising that the time of the play *is* fictional in relation to the real time lived or spent by the audience during the running of the play, Puck complicates or reverses the distinction as he makes it, since, if the play has been succeeding, the audience will have been unconscious of the passage of real time, and will have been living or spending the fictional time of the play: dream-time. References in the play to various *tempi* and/or temporal units further complicate its fictions of time and duration: "[the] everlasting" (I.i.85); "swifter than the moon's sphere" (II.i.7); "night's swift dragons" (III.ii.379); "lazy time" (V.i.41); "the heavy gait of night" (V.i.354). The "time" of the play eventually includes subjective time, full and empty time, timelessness, and subdivisions of time that, in the manner of Zeno's paradox, indefinitely postpone the end. In view of all that, one need hardly add that the play contains one glaring and well-known temporal discrepancy, namely the departure from an announced time-scheme in which the marriage of Theseus and Hippolyta will occur after four days and nights:

> Now, fair Hippolyta, our nuptial hour
> Draws on apace; four happy days bring in
> Another moon . . . (I.i.1–3)

In fact, it occurs after the single wild night that elapses in the play.

If these temporal contradictions and discontinuities can be called "mitigating," it is because they disrupt any purported single, normative, temporal axis on which all the events of the play can be plotted, and at the "end" of which a resolution might be claimed. These incommensurable *times* also can't be contained within a single, all-encompassing frame, on the existence of which the restoration of any single, unified order would depend.

Other "mitigations" in the play could be listed. Theseus and Hippolyta are represented, for example, as significantly more "gentle" (not to say genteel – *Duke* Theseus?) than their respective violent legends might suggest.[8] Theseus is also the one who buys Hermia some time and even gives her a soft option in the face of the unmitigated alternatives of the Athenian law that her father invokes:

> As she is mine, I may dispose of her;
> Which shall be either to this gentleman,
> Or to her death according to our law
> Immediately provided in that case. (I.i.42–5)

That Theseus, in finding a loophole ("abjure,/Forever the society of men" [I.i.65–6], still prejudicially comes close to *equating* female singleness with cloistral isolation, sterility and living death is culturally symptomatic in ways that now virtually go without saying.[9] A complacent and consistent masculinism of the genially overbearing kind (the very worst kind?) marks virtually all Theseus's acts, but his apparently well-intentioned patronage is exactly what would come under the heading of "mitigation."

If qualification and mitigation, with a contingent increase in complexity, distinguish *A Midsummer Night's Dream* from the two named preceding comedies, it may be assumed that nothing is going to be worked (or fought) out to the bitter end. What, then, is the game? What, perhaps more precisely, is the ongoing double game?

It must be admitted that, if one of the ends is still purported clarification and an end to error, that end *is* attained when Titania returns to her *a priori* proper fairy lover, as do the younger ones to theirs after a nightmare of sexual violence, crossing and doublecrossing. (Being "cross'd" (I.i.150) in love in ways more disconcerting than the "customary" (I.i.153) ones Hermia foresees; "[coming] to confusion" (I.i.149) more disconcertingly than Lysander likewise foresees.) If, on the other hand, the end is a reimposition of threatened male ascendancy and its contingent order, that too is accomplished when Oberon outwits Titania. Yet this gives the play two "ends," not a single hard-fought one, and both those endings are significantly weakened *as* endings by the events that precede them; by the forms of interminability to which they seek to put an end. Bad dreams can be "endless," nightmares can recur, and "monstrous" sexual fantasies are not under full voluntary control; the battle of the sexes likewise remains interminable for as long as the erotic interchange of courtship prohibits it from becoming total war – or a zero-sum game. The end(ings) of the play are thus apparently vitiated by qualification, and the relentless violence that might be applied in an effort to "strengthen" them by rendering at least one of them absolute, as in *The Taming of the Shrew*, is apparently withheld.

Here the questions already begin to arise. In *A Midsummer Night's Dream*, magic, not force, does the trick – but is the magic strong enough? Does it, strictly, accomplish anything? Can magic plus "good will" be partially substituted for an arbitrary violence and manipulation which they also mitigate – or does this substitution, on the contrary, mask a redoubled violence and arbitrariness directed to the same old ends? What is the real meaning of mitigation? Does the possibility of its exercise depend on the foregone certainty of absolute conquest, such as the one Theseus claims to have achieved over Hippolyta? ("I woo'd thee with my sword,/And won thy love doing thee injuries" (I.i.16–17). Or does it function politically to attenuate the "residual" antagonism of a conquest that can literally never be final? Even if Hippolyta were silenced, which she is not, what would that silence contain – or be thought by Theseus to contain?[10] How can Hippolyta be "silenced" as long as she, while *agreeing* with Theseus, can mean something different, as when she says, reviving the threat of feminine-virginal aggression even in relation to his anticipated triumph:

And then the moon, like to a silver bow
New bent in heaven, shall behold the night
Of our solemnities. (I.i.9–11)

Questions of this order are also strongly raised by the "mitigated" plotting of *A Midsummer Night's Dream. The Comedy of Errors* begins by establishing a foregone conclusion that is in fact the self-fulfilling prophecy and perverse wish of its subject: Egeon will die at sunset. In dramatically reversing the prophecy, the play also reverses a whole series of false prophecies and premature assumptions. The evidently good work of the play is thus accomplished by means of a very powerful plot, and indeed the play is virtually all plot. In contrast, the foregone conclusion of *A Midsummer Night's Dream*, that Theseus will wed Hippolyta, is an *a priori* desirable one that remains unaltered so, at this macroscopic level, suspense, surprise, and the justification of the master plotter simply drain out of the play. There is in fact no apparent need for a powerful plotter, and even if one more powerful than Theseus seems necessary for the young lovers "crossed" by Egeus, Hermia's father, to be united, the adverted conventions of romance, which we and the juvenile characters know all too well, guarantee the happy ending almost without need for anyone's potent intervention. Again, a trick will do it.

The plot element isn't just mitigated in *A Midsummer Night's Dream*, but the plotting function of the playwright is conspicuously transferred to operators in the play, Puck and Oberon. This transfer marks a step in a systematic disavowal of comic plotting in Shakespearean comedy – a systematic critique of the plotter's powers and motivations as well as of the results capable of being achieved in this way. The *errors* of the *Midsummer Night's Dream* plot become those of Puck, and Oberon himself begins to suspect malice rather than error in the process by which characters, especially young female ones, are at once cruelly exposed and vexed to the point of madness before being released. (The good work and good plot of *The Comedy of Errors* thus retroactively come into question.) And whatever is now accomplished in the plot(s) is accomplished by a tricky magic[11] that doesn't necessarily or permanently settle anything, since what has been in question is not only the seemingly interminable male–female contest for ascendancy but nightmarish derangement taking place in a "time" that will predictably recur, or that has in fact never ended.

It will be evident that another set of questions could now be posed about the meaning of mitigation, while yet another phase of instantiation could begin after those questions had been posed. Clearly that repetition must be arrested however problematical the results so far obtained. The point however is not just that some evidence has been presented and the question of "mitigation" raised, but that the questions have so far been posed as ones concerning the logic of Shakespeare's revision and transformation of comedy.

To speak of this logic of canonical–generic revision and transformation is to speak of that which alone can constitute an authorial canon out of a mere succession of works; it is that which enables us to speak of the authorial canon as a work in itself. To invoke this logicality isn't to represent Shakespeare as the subject of a monological fixation or as one possessed by an "inner logic" blindly getting acted out irrespective of times and circumstances.[12] (That kind of fixation is precisely what becomes the tragic one, the mark of the protagonist as colossal idiot, in the Shakespearean plays that we would always have to characterize as qualified, questionable or strictly unnecessary tragedies.)

To speak of Shakespeare's canonical logic also isn't to speak of a particular logical form or method, but rather of a logicality continuously being applied in, and with reference to, particular times and circumstances. Hence it is a logic of accommodation, adjustment, and recuperation, although no doubt one always threatened with "relapse" into being a monological fixation blindly pursued. If this logic of adjustment can now be taken as demonstrated in the comic sequence I have proposed, we need to pivot the discussion, with unavoidable inelegance, so as to come at *A Midsummer Night's Dream* from the complementary circumstantial side; in terms neither of "logic" nor of "circumstance" alone are the questions initially asked in this paper to be answered, but in terms of a dialectical interplay between them.

It would now go without saying that a complicated, historically specific sexual politics manifests itself in all the relationships of *A Midsummer Night's Dream*,[13] and we may include in that statement the relationship between the play (players) and the audience. The historical *circumstance* of a courtly setting and audience for *A Midsummer Night's Dream* is manifestly reinscribed in the play when Theseus, Hippolyta and the other gentlefolks become spectators of the mechanicals' performance, and when that performance displaces the more normal academic "revels" proposed by Philostrate to celebrate the duke's nuptials. There is moreover a strong editorial tradition, based mainly on the allusions in II.i. of the play, suggesting that *A Midsummer Night's Dream* was conceived specifically for performance in front of the queen – she, rather than the Christopher Sly of the *Taming*, is now the "normative" spectator – and there can hardly be any question that the postulated courtly setting and the particular royal witness are enormously enabling for Shakespeare.[14]

In the play, it is Phoebe, precisely, who constitutes the moonlight realm, the fairyland, in which a "noble" imaginative excess can at once be accommodated and put to work, and in which poetic operators like Puck, Titania, Oberon and the fairies, personified figments of the high-cultural as well as the popular imagination, can act and interact. It is in this imaginative space, moreover, that a devaluation of the plot can occur, and in which the self-imposing limitations of the lowlife Sly as spectator, of the inn-yard-turned-theater as a venue, and even of the philistine male-academic audience (possibly the "ideal" audience of *The Comedy of Errors*),[15] can be circumvented.

The enablement conferred by "Phoebe" begins to be established in the play from the very beginning, and it is so in the process of transfiguration in which Theseus's waning "old moon" (I.i.4), a "withering" dowager, his "cold, fruitless moon" (I.i.73), are first canceled out by Hippolyta's Diana-moon "like to a silver bow/New bent in heaven," and then appropriated and refigured by the young lovers, Lysander in particular:

> Tomorrow night, when Phoebe doth behold
> Her silver visage in the wat'ry glass,
> Decking with liquid pearl the bladed grass
> (A time that lovers' flights doth still conceal),
> Through Athens gates have we devis'd to steal. (I.i.209–13)

Moonlight: enough light now for the loving elect, and enough darkness for the thwarting reprobate. Pheobe: naively appropriated and refigured, since what Lysander apparently doesn't see is that the friendly Phoebe he names (imagines *he* is personifying) in order to co-opt, is potentially an all-annihilating figure, one whose projected image, the object of her own narcissistic fixation, is imprinted on the world without the slightest reference to his interests, or, worse, in ultimate opposition to them. This enabling figure of "Phoebe," who constitutes the poetic realm of fairyland, is one who, as recent historicist criticism has established, can practically *never* be named in Elizabethan literature without allegorical (i.e. incomplete, unstable) reference to the queen, hence to the circumstance of her particular rule.

This *allegorical* reference differs from immobilizing identification of the kind which, when attempted critically, merely seems arbitrary, trite, or comically philistine (it has been claimed, for example, with no doubt unintentionally obscene humor, that Bottom "is" the putative James I in the political allegory of *A Midsummer Night's Dream*).[16] Allegory allows not just for the continuous possibility, but for the inescapability, pleasure and profit of unfixed reference; it allows, moreover, for referential schemas to be set up in which those glancingly identified change places or names as the game continues, or in which exchanges can occur between figures in the work and those outside it ("outside" and "inside" also change places). If *The Faerie Queene* is the supreme instance in Elizabethan poetry of this referential mode, the mode itself becomes virtually literalized in the complicated shifts and "crossings" of *A Midsummer Night's Dream*.

Thus the Phoebe who shines generously for young lovers in the play is, in imagination or brute political fact, the supremely threatening figure outside it, not just to more perspicacious male lovers than Lysander, but to male poets (fiction makers) of "noble" imaginative excess. Hers are the obliterating image and dazzling light that threaten to eclipse all others, and not just because the queen is a woman but a particular one in particular circumstances; the sad reign of Mary Tudor, for example, leaves no legend of a fairyland or of noble imaginative excess.

Phoebe is threatening, without doubt, to Spenser and Sidney, but also no doubt to Shakespeare, though with the apparent difference that Shakespeare has a relatively autonomous base in the public theater, and can proceed in relative independence of court patronage, exploiting the riches of "fairyland" without necessarily becoming its captive. (Neither Sidney nor Spenser has an independent base, however energetically the fiction of possessing one at an Arcadian Wilton or in pastoral Ireland may be elaborated in their works.) Insofar as "fairyland," however, is the imaginative construction and/or projection of Phoebe, the male dramatic *poet* may also find that he has no place in it, or no real work to do in it.

Under these circumstances, it is not surprising to find a contest going on in the moonlight realm of *A Midsummer Night's Dream* between the king and queen of the fairies, ideally lovers but at present radically at odds with one another. *This* conflict, into which a good deal that is at stake in the play gets displaced, turns out to be a peculiarly Elizabethan one and also a peculiarly timely one if we assume that the play was written (not published) *ca.* 1594. One consequence of this displacement is that the interactions between Theseus and Hippolyta in particular are governed by, or remain a function of, this fairy interaction. So if Oberon and Titania can't be reconciled in the night-world of the play, the contingent reconciliation and marriage between Theseus and Hippolyta in the daylight kingdom can presumably also not take place, and no heir can be produced. The simple foregone conclusion of the play is thus not quite so simple and foregone. (This situation of dependency is of course anticipated in *The Taming of the Shrew*, where all the other marriages become contingent on the marriage of Kate to Petruchio.) If this "blocked" situation is apparent on the inside of the play, what is the situation outside? What exactly is the general situation, under which those inside and outside may be subsumed?

The quarrel between Oberon and Titania is a lovers' quarrel, but one throughout which we are aware that the choice Bottom perceives between playing a lover *or* a tyrant is probably illusory; to play one is to play the other.[17] The quarrel is literally, of course, about the ownership of a "changeling boy" that each of the fairies wants for his/her own purposes, but why does the conflict take that form under those particular circumstances?

At the beginning of II.i., the changeling boy is defined literally by Puck as:

> A lovely boy, stol'n from an Indian king –
> She never had so sweet a changeling. (III.i.22–3)

That literal if already ambiguous (changeling) definition is, however, preceded by Puck's revelation of one already-experienced effect of the contest for the changeling boy: that of reciprocal encroachment upon, and disruption of, the theatrical spaces occupied by the king and queen.

Both rulers, inveterate revelers, as it seems, threaten to invade one another's territory and disrupt one another's pastimes:

> PUCK: The King doth keep his revels here tonight;
>   Take heed the Queen come not within his sight. (II.i.19–20)
> TITANIA: And never, since the middle summer's spring,
>   Met we on hill, in dale, forest, or mead,
>   By paved fountain, or by rushy brook,
>   Or in the beached margent of the sea,
>   To dance our ringlets to the whistling wind,
>   But with thy brawls thou hast disturb'd our sport. (II.i.82–7)

At one level, then, the quarrel is about the separation of theatrical spaces and reciprocal encroachment upon them. (It must be emphasized that it isn't a quarrel about any particular, literal, place, but about any space immediately constituted *as* theatrical by the dominating, shaping presence of either Oberon or Titania.) The quarrel is also implicitly about differences of style: dancing in a ring *vs* brawling. The in-between Puck's only purpose, misconceived according to the eventual logic of the play and incapable of being effected anyway, is to keep the lovers as well as their respective styles and spaces separate.

These disruptions do, of course, have a theater-wars context. Given that *A Midsummer Night's Dream* is perspicuously a critique, reworking and *displacement* of Lyly's court-drama,[18] as well as a revision of Shakespeare's own, it is not too difficult to infer that the Titania–Oberon quarrel is informed by the historical invasion of courtly–theatrical space by an alien, would-be masterful figure from the "other" space of public theater, namely William Shakespeare.

Although this invasion may be accompanied by a manifold increase in the flattering power and brilliance of what can get acted out in the courtly–theatrical space, it also brings a new and threatening figure onto the scene, one who, unlike John Lyly, is capable of empowering the changeling boy-actors and of functioning as something more than an extension of the queen's own dramatic will; one capable of functioning, in short, as something more than one of her fairies. The seemingly infantilized world of Lyleian drama becomes one of intensified agon (brawling) in *A Midsummer Night's Dream*, and one of the threatened consequences for Titania in the play – but also for the queen outside? – is ravishment and even silencing. The latter possibility is one that her fairy defenders unite to conjure away as "Titania" (in *Metamorphoses*, III, 173, an epithet for Diana) falls asleep:

> Philomel, with melody
> Sing in our sweet lullaby. (II.ii.13–14)

Speaking conservatively, one can say, and need only say, that our understanding of the "changeling boy," defined literally by Puck, is inescapably preconditioned by his introduction in the context of theater-wars. Yet if we can speculate that the figure is highly charged in the way I have suggested, its being so would be consistent with the rich historical allusiveness (indeed, the virtual naming of names) that many editors and critics of the play have discerned in II.i. And since the changeling boy happens also to be a young prince, the contention about his ownership can't be without consequence in the future as well as in the present, and can't be without implication in the world of "fairy" succession.[19] Possession of the changeling boy implies significant control over the future shape of things theatrical, and perhaps over political repre-sentation more generally in a situation in which, given an aged, barren and unmarriageable queen, ever more powerful (and, it may be said, palpable) politico-dynastic fictions had become indispensable.

As soon as Oberon and Titania meet – "Ill met by moonlight, proud Titania" (II.i.60) – the famous quarrel ensues. Drawing to some extent on editorial tradition, but not only on that, we can safely say that the general ambience of this quarrel is not just that of theater-wars but increasingly that of the royal court in the late 1580s and early 1590s. Of a courtly "theater" that, despite the death of Leicester in 1588, remained one of continuing juvenile-romantic courtship of the aged queen but also now of violent recrimination, suspicion, "betrayal" and enraged retribution, all of which Raleigh's fall from grace in 1592 and somewhat vainly attempted comeback can be taken to epitomize.[20] This scene's image of lunar rage is both formidable and suggestive (sufficiently so to account for a placatory "Book of the Ocean to Cynthia" by Sir "Water" Raleigh?):

> Therefore the moon, the governess of floods,
> Pale in her anger, washes all the air,
> That rheumatic diseases do abound. (II.i.103–5)

In the idiom of *A Midsummer Night's Dream*, the spectacular public event of Raleigh's downfall made a profound "impression [on the] fantasy" (I.i.32) of Elizabethan authors; a traumatic impression, one might almost say, on the Spenser who keeps reverting to it, but an impression also, it would seem, on the Nashe of *Summer's Last Will and Testament*, probably staged and/or circulated in some form during 1592. In it, the fall of Raleigh is evidently a subject of frequent allusion:

> Lascivious and intemperate he is.
> The wrong of Daphne is a well-known tale:
> Each evening he descends to Thetis' lap,
> The while men think he bathes him in the sea.[21]

Significantly, however, this and other apparent allusions to poet-Raleigh's "betrayal" of the queen occurs in the play's general context of "changing times" and seasonal disruption, one remarkably akin to that established in these lines from the Oberon–Titania scene:

> The seasons alter: hoary headed frosts
> Fall in the fresh lap of the crimson rose; . . .
> The childing autumn, angry winter, change
> Their wonted liveries; and the mazed world,
> By their increase, now knows not which is which. (II.i.107–14)

Anxiety about the future and nostalgia at the passing of the Elizabethan "summer" (prefigured by the eclipse of "Sol") are widely manifest in *Summer's Last Will*:

> Fair Summer droops, droop men and beasts therefore:
> So fair a summer look for never more. . . .
> Go not yet away, bright soul of the sad year;
> The earth is hell, when thou leav'st to appear.[22]

Learning how to spend a season in hell is, however, one of Nashe's enterprises in the play as well as in *Pierce Pennilesse*, and Nashe's highly agonistic representation of Will Summer in the play effects a disruptive shift towards so-called satirical contentiousness ("brawling") in the closed form of the seasonal pageant. Nashe's work, possibly a direct influence on *A Midsummer Night's Dream*,[23] and certainly a theatrical counter-possibility to the charmingly devitalized plays of Lyly, may alert us to the political context(s) of the represented quarrel between Oberon and Titania. It is also one work among others that establishes the language of seasonal change and natural disorder as a satirical code in which reference can be made to political disorder, belied by ongoing appearances of stability and ageless juvenile romance, in the Elizabethan courtly–political world.

Titania's first extended accusation in the quarrel concerns Oberon's apparent faithlessness:

> OBERON: Tarry, rash wanton; am not I thy lord?
> TITANIA: Then I must be thy lady; but I know
> When thou hast stol'n away from fairy land,
> And in the shape of Corin sat all day
> Playing on pipes of corn, and versing love
> To amorous Phillida. (II.i.63–8)

Whatever else these lines do, they come dangerously close to effecting a quasi-identification of Oberon, the fairy king, with none other than Edmund Spenser, a willing or enforced fugitive from the fairy kingdom after his own (and Raleigh's) reception at court in 1590, the big event with which the publication of *The Faerie Queene*, Books I–III, had coincided. Corin admittedly is not Colin (and who is Phillida, what is she?), but that Spenser would not have occurred to Elizabethans as a possible avatar or changeling-form of Oberon here is practically inconceivable. And if Spenser *is* being invoked, at least one thing can be concluded, namely, that his case now figures a somewhat unsatisfactory possibility for the (over) ambitious Elizabethan courtier-poet of the 1590s.

Corin's absence from the fairy kingdom is either an indication of his rejection – of that "hostility" of which Spenser complains more tirelessly than most – or, more probably given the terms employed in this scene, of his "faithless" withdrawal from the consuming and annihilating presence of the Faerie Queene herself. And of his desired pursuit, by the same token, of his own imaginative or erotic object(s), although that pursuit is still enabled and perhaps inescapably governed in the long run by the queen. Two moments in the *Amoretti* will suffice to recall Spenser's self-perceived troubles in the mid-1590s, and if those troubles are dramatically exploited with characteristic Spenserian ruthlessness and resource, they are not necessarily to be discounted as real problems for that reason:[24]

> Great wrong I doe, I can it not deny,
> to that most sacred Empresse my dear dred,
> not finishing her Queene of faery,
> that mote enlarge her liuing prayses dead. (XXXIII, 1–4)

> After so long a race as I haue run
> Through Faery land, which those six books compile,
> giue leaue to rest me being halfe fordonne,
> and gather to my selfe new breath awhile. (LXXX, 1–4)

Alluding to Spenser, identifying him with Oberon, king of the fairies: these are undeniable possibilities for Shakespeare in *A Midsummer Night's Dream* – who else could have counted as the Oberon/*obermensch* of the Elizabethan poetic world *ca.* 1594? But to what avail could Shakespeare have invoked these possibilities?

For Shakespeare to have revealed Oberon's passage through multiple or successive poetic incarnations might on one hand have been to "expose" Spenser's extraordinary, veiled theatricality as that of yet another changeling boy, but it might also, and almost by the same token, have been for him to hint at the possibility of Spenser's replacement by a more faithful stay-at-home lover of equally noble imagination. The player-king can change roles, but the role can also accommodate a new player-king according to the apparent logic of an Elizabethan politics of supplantation,[25] and hints of this kind are by no means rare in the competitive, ever-changing world of Elizabethan poets.

Another point can be made about the reference to Oberon's pastoral infidelity, and this one holds good whether it is Spenser who is being identified (and supplanted) or whether Oberon's "infidelity" merely represents the incipiently typical case of the period: the fugitive impulse of Oberon reveals a possible "crisis" in the sexual politics of the Elizabethan court, one not just difficult for poets, but one implying that the courtly romance of Elizabethan life had taken a dangerously counterproductive turn in the early 1590s.

If we can assume that that romance had worked rather well for those who stood to profit from it up to the time of Leicester's death and/or Raleigh's transgression and fall, it is arguable – and, I would suggest, often evident in both poetic and political writings – that the romance must increasingly have been seen as belated and grotesque once the spell had been broken and the aging queen's stagy irascibility had become undeniable. (The extraordinary repercussions of Raleigh's disgrace, the hysteria in his own poetry as well as in that of others, need to be taken seriously.) Then again, we read in Act II of *A Midsummer Night's Dream*, in a language akin to that of *Summer's Last Will and Testament*, of Winter personified grotesquely masquerading in springtime blossoms, on the face of it an exceedingly threatening picture with which to confront the queen under present circumstances:

> And on old Hiems' thin and icy crown,
> An odorous chaplet of sweet summer buds
> Is, as in mockery, set. (II.i.103–19)

Are the Faerie Queene and her masquerade now brutally being seen through, being re-presented to *her*, despite the maintenance of courtly decorum, in the harsh mirror of Nashean satire? If so, the threat to her, albeit still partially masked and "mitigated," is extreme. At this stage, however, "good will" and poetic magic can still prevail, but in order that they may prevail, it is also necessary for some unmistakable messages about belatedness, barrenness, and a now-counterproductive sexual politics to be conveyed. ("Brightness falls from the air,/Queens have died young and fair," writes Nashe – meaning, perhaps, that they have died old while still masquerading as young and fair?) If all the "lovers" in/of fairyland are to be reconciled, however, as they should probably be in their own best interests, the real context and terms of the reconciliation have apparently to be renegotiated.

Since these suppositions may seem far-fetched, let us revert for the last time to the actual terms of the quarrel in the play before proceeding to draw conclusions. Oberon and Titania rehearse the notorious violence and infidelity (well documented in "the literature") of their respective protégés, Hippolyta and Theseus.[26] Yet the accompanying revelation of the fairies' power to manipulate protégés marks another kind of crossing, one in which the male speaker manipulates a female puppet and vice-versa, each of the fairy speakers proving capable of operating through one of the opposite sex in their respective power-plays. (On the part of both, this activity sounds remarkably like pimping.)

Even more disconcertingly, Oberon and Titania also accuse one another of what sounds like infidelity *with* their mortal protégés, though it may be that only favoritism is involved. (Would that "mitigation" make it better?) Oberon has, it seems, "come from the farthest steep of India" to bless the wedding of the "bouncing Amazon," his "buskin'd mistress and . . . warrior love," while Titania in turn has evidently manipulated Theseus' treacherous relationships with "Perigouna . . . Aegles . . . Ariadne and Antiope" (II.i.69–80). The additional possibility of sexual infidelity with their unwitting protégés would, of course, make the fairy king an incubus and the fairy queen a succubus in crossings that are, in Elizabethan terms, literally demonic; it would also turn the fairy king and queen into sinister possessors and contentious manipulators in a world otherwise inhabited by puppets – a *stage* world. An inflamed erotic possessiveness (tyrannical love) enters into the fight for possession of the still-ungendered and unpossessed changeling boy.[27]

To cut a long story short, the literal changeling boy is first referred to in a cultural–political context in which his meaning is doubly, trebly or multiply preconditioned,[28] and that figure continues rapidly accruing meanings and/or shifting through various contexts as the scene progresses. He is potentially the love-object of each fairy, implicitly the single "master–mistress" of each one's passion. He is also implicitly, as Titania virtually acknowledges (116), the contested child of bad, disruptive parents, both singlemindedly pursuing their own objects at his expense (116). He is incipiently a "henchman" (121) in the implicitly masculinized, hierarchical world of Oberon; he is incipiently an image of his mother and memorial to her in Titania's feminized world ("his mother was a vot'ress of my order ... And for her sake do I rear up her boy" (123, 36). (For *her* sake is also, of course, for Titania's sake, since the boy figures her own power to immortalize the mother.)

Like the young man in the sonnets, the changeling boy is potentially a father and image of his own father, the Indian king, or else "he" is one of whom, like that same young sonnet-man, it might be said that "thou art thy mother's glass, and she in thee, / Calls back the lovely April of her prime."[29] In Titania's view, moreover, he is the relict of a mother who, in imitation of the great ships, would "sail upon the land / To fetch me trifles and return again / As from a voyage rich with merchandise" (132–4); he is thus assimilated not only to a mercantilist vision of fruitful exchange, but to a parthenogenetic fantasy in which the "sails conceive, / And grow big-bellied with the wanton wind" (127–8).[30] In Oberon's view he evidently remains a pathic.

As a figure of relative indeterminacy ("changeling" is also an Elizabethan term, evidently coined by Puttenham, for the figure of *Hipallage*, or verbal criss-crossing with semantic change in a sentence),[31] the boy becomes the passive cause of universal disruption; the subject of fierce, overcharged possessive–interpretive impositions; the object of a conflict in which, finally, everything in the play and the courtly–political world outside it seems to be involved; the nexus of a difference that seems to go all the way down. Possession of the boy would, so it might be hoped, allow the sole possessor (or is it the possessed?) at once to stamp "the impression of his/her fantasy" on him and reciprocally to inaugurate or reconfirm an overpoweringly desired, fixed, gender-specific representation of the world which, as Shakespeare reminds us periodically, is (like) a stage.

Perhaps the *critical* temptation to be resisted here is that of being sucked into the vortex; of becoming the possessed–possessor; of blindly repeating in contemporary terms the activity of the fairy-principals, namely that of contesting ownership of the changeling boy by seeking interpretively to appropriate "him" and rigorously determine "his" meaning. (As phallus, for example, or as the paradoxically determinate figure of absolute indeterminacy prior to representation.) But if this temptation is capable of being resisted – if we have not always and already succumbed to it – what remains to be said?

My own undertaking here is simply to draw conclusions on the basis of the initial premises and the evidence of the play. According to the apparent logic of the play and of the generic–canonical line in which I have situated it, but also according to one possible construction of the courtly–political scene outside the play, the counterproductive quarrel between Titania and Oberon simply can't go on, or not in this disruptive, indecorous form. Perhaps disfigurement – a highly charged, repeatedly used word in the play – is that with which each of the contestants threatens the changeling boy, and the quarrel is, after all, still a quarrel of acknowledged lovers with an *a priori* common stake in reconciliation and further trading. Yet the quarrel can't *be* terminated unless one of the two parties graciously prevails without "winning" and the other graciously surrenders without "losing." This is the result Oberon evidently accomplishes by shaming Titania for her discovered love of ass-headed Bottom, but the defeat and surrender are whimsically mitigated ones, accomplished without the rough, systematic humiliation and thwarting of the second half of *The Taming of the Shrew*.

The one possible alternative to this "mitigated" result, rendered visible in the play, is not just reversion to the zero-sum form of the game but to fully malign "repossession" by the fairy protagonists of their agents from the worlds of classical mythology and English folklore – to rebarbar-ization, in other words, of Theseus and Hippolyta, to reactivation of the malignant fairies of which both folklore and contemporary demonology speak,[32] to a withholding of the good magic that sorts out crossed-up lovers, and finally to the sabotaging of any orderly albeit manipulated process of succession. The play is thus modeling a solution and specifying the terms on which civility can be maintained and adjust-ments can be made, but it is also displaying the consequences of failure, or refusal to negotiate. A very small dose of Nashean terror may be enough to force the settlement.

To put the matter in this way, or to articulate *this* logic, is of course to take the part of the man. What could be said from the other side is that the politics in question are simply those of systematic masculinist terrorism and blackmail, aggravated by insolent bluff, in which the inoffensive (?) ruses and mitigations of the play merely draw attention to the unrelenting savagery and increasing sophistication of the threat held in reserve. That the covert messages sent by the play are at once threatening to their subject and capable of constituting a newly "informed," hence alienated, courtly audience-as-political-community. That these messages are accordingly instruments, not just of intimidation and expropriation, but, adding insult to injury, of reconciliation still being offered at a bargain price. That all disavowals of plotting and displays of good will merely belie the reinscription of the *master* plot at a deeper level. And that even if this plot must be considered, not as a conceivable, perhaps blackly comic, *Realpolitik* of the Elizabethan world, but as the painful fantasy of the marginalized, ambitious male author (operand rather than operator of his own fantastic plot) the name of the fantasy-game is still blackmail.

It is this account that the "wild" accusations by Nashe, cited at the beginning of this paper, endorse, while my own discussion implicitly confirms Nashe's claims. And, to the question "To whom could those accusations have applied?", the answer, although not necessarily restricted to literary authors, appears to be: "Shakespeare, for one, and probably every single Elizabethan poet we designate as 'major.' "

Accepting that these charges can never strictly be proved although their grounds can certainly be displayed, and also accepting that there is never going to be a comfortable way round the stark possibility of blackmail, I shall conclude from what must inescapably be a masculinist standpoint. My point will be that the rational work of the play is principally that of delivering messages and modeling goodwill political solutions; the optative, counterfactual, epithalamic mode of the play's ending, wishing away both violence and disfigurement, is not simply to be discounted. The accompanying double game of the play, however, is always undeniably that of masking and unmasking, of prettily veiling and hideously unveiling the terror[ism] with which the play is fraught.

To associate the good name of Shakespeare with any such proceeding, particularly in a comedy as deservedly admired as *A Midsummer Night's Dream*, is to invite disbelief if not angry denial while the appearance of sensationalism in the reading may also provoke demands for some independent "historical" confirmation of an Elizabethan politics of systematic and sophisticated terror. The logic of the situation suggests, however, that this confirmation can never be forthcoming, since it is the essence of this terror that it remain veiled, unnamed, and above all civil. One of its goals, furthermore, is to increase the number of those who, wittingly or not, become silent partners in it.

Any attempt to disclose this blackmail, assuming that it could have been perceived as such during the Elizabethan period, would have been to risk the mighty counterpunch so mysteriously and permanently threatened by the Garter-inscription: *"Honi soit qui mal y'pense."* It might also have been to fall foul of what is, in the context of Shakespeare's comedies, a suggestive Petrarchan moral maxim, namely that it is better to will the good than to know the truth.[33] Yet even if this maxim were to be accepted as permanently valid, willing the good might now include knowing the truth about the historical Shakespeare. I would suggest, therefore, that the question of authorial blackmail can't be begged, nor can the logic of this apparent civil terror(ism) be denied.

If Shakespeare is there merely to be sanctified or (re)possessed as desirable property – as the *ultimate* changeling boy – then there can be no interest in this subject. But if "civility" is in question, or indeed "civilization," once the name of Shakespeare has been dropped, then primitive terror, capable perhaps of being mastered and reconstructed as a rational terrorism, is there to be seen in it. An extended critique of this terror (in which who, in our culture, does not *have* an interest?) might accordingly become one undertaking of an "unpossessed" Shakespeare criticism.[34]

Notes

Prehistory (pp. 1–18)

1 Stanley Fish's devastating and salutary attacks on anti-professionalism have appeared in various places, but see "Profession despise thyself: fear and loathing in literary studies," in *Critical Inquiry*, 10, 2 (1983), 349–64.
2 Stanley Fish, "The consequences of theory," in *Critical Inquiry*, 11, 3 (1985), 433–58. Having once written against being *against* theory ["Towards uncritical practice: Michaels and Knapp against theory," in *Critical Inquiry*, 9, 4 (1983), 748–59], I would be wary of re-entering that controversy (or of claiming to engage with what has been called the "new pragmatism") but I don't want to retract or modify the position I took in the essay named above. See, also, W.J.T. Mitchell (ed.), *Against Theory: Literary Studies and the New Pragmatism* (Chicago, University of Chicago Press, 1985) for the complete record of the debate.
3 Paul de Man, "The return to philology," *TLS*, December 10, 1982, 1355.
4 For example, "Poet: patriot: interpreter," in *Critical Inquiry*, 9, 1 (1982), 27–43, in which Donald Davie tries in various ways to imagine a "maverick" or expatriated critical position. The result, it must be said with regret, is the production of a neocolonial idyll in which Indian rather than Anglo-American readers of Spenser finally escape the professional net.
5 Rosamund Tuve, *A Reading of George Herbert* (Chicago, University of Chicago Press, 1952).
6 R.G. Cox, "The New Scholarship?" in *A Selection from "Scrutiny"* (2 vols.) compiled by F.R. Leavis (Cambridge, Cambridge University Press, 1968), vol. 1, 304–5.
7 F.R. Leavis, "Under which king, Bezonian?" in *A Selection from "Scrutiny,"* vol. 1, 166–7.
8 Cited by William Empson in "*Ulysses*: Joyce's intentions," in *Using Biography* (Cambridge, Harvard University Press, 1984), 208.
9 In "Other people's views," in *Using Biography*, 34.
10 The narrative framing of critical essays is hardly unprecedented: Stanley Fish's *Is There a Text in This Class?* (Cambridge, Harvard University Press, 1982) was for me the most significant recent instance. But the form of this book also owes something to that of Gascoigne's *The Adventures of Master F.J.* (1573), and in general the "problematic" of the book owes a good deal to the sixteenth-century English authors with whom it deals. For all the claims that literary texts are constituted by readers and/or interpretive communities, the possibility of dictating the status of the text (or the book) as well as the terms of the reading is one that the sixteenth-century authors in question seem particularly interested in

developing. (Whether one regards them as "real" authors or as bearers of a cultural code hardly matters in this context.) Spenser's career becomes a major study in this phenomenon, not only because of his possible production or manipulation of the apparatus accompanying *The Shepheardes Calender*, but because of the revealingly perspicuous move of "Colin Clout" from the position of the poetic singer to that of the self-interpreter in Book VI of *The Faerie Queene*. There is a real sense in which to write "sympathetically" about these authors is to accept their dictation.

11 Leonardo Sciascia, *The Day of the Owl* and *Equal Danger* (Boston, David R. Godine, 1984).

12 Jonas Barish, *Ben Jonson and the Language of Prose Comedy* (New York, Norton, 1970); Joan Webber, *The Eloquent 'I'* (Madison, University of Wisconsin Press, 1968); Stanley E. Fish, *Surprised by Sin* (New York, Macmillan, 1967) and *Self-Consuming Artifacts* (Berkeley and Los Angeles, University of California Press, 1972); Bridget Lyons, *Voices of Melancholy* (New York, Norton, 1974); Stephen Orgel, *The Illusion of Power* (Berkeley and Los Angeles, University of California Press, 1978).

13 Fish, "Consequences," *passim*.

14 Stephen Greenblatt, *Sir Walter Raleigh: The Renaissance Man and his Roles* (New Haven, Yale University Press, 1973); Paul Alpers, *The Poetry of "The Faerie Queene"* (Princeton, Princeton University Press, 1967); David Kalstone, *Sidney's Poetry: Contexts and Interpretations* (Cambridge, Harvard University Press, 1965); G.K. Hunter, *John Lyly: the Humanist as Courtier* (Cambridge, Harvard University Press, 1965).

15 Jonathan Goldberg, *Endlesse Worke: Spenser and the Structures of Discourse* (Baltimore, The Johns Hopkins University Press, 1981).

16 Stephen Greenblatt, *Renaissance Self-Fashioning: From More to Shakespeare* (Chicago, University of Chicago Press, 1980).

17 In "The subject of Elizabeth," delivered at Johns Hopkins University in 1985.

Chapter 1: The politics of theater (I) (pp. 19–34)

1 Some of the works in which this discussion has precipitated out are, Stephen Orgel, *The Illusion of Power*; Jonas Barish, *The Antitheatrical Prejudice* (Berkeley and Los Angeles, University of California Press, 1981); Jonathan Dollimore, *Radical Tragedy: Religion, Ideology and Power in the Drama of Shakespeare and his Contemporaries* (Chicago, University of Chicago Press, 1984); Jonathan Goldberg, *James I and the Politics of Literature* (Baltimore, The Johns Hopkins University Press, 1983); Louis Adrian Montrose, "The purpose of playing: reflections on a Shakespearean anthropology," in *Helios*, NS 7, 2 (1980), 51–74; also " 'The place of a brother' in *As You Like It*: social process and comic form," in *Shakespeare Quarterly*, 32 (1981), 28–54; also " 'Shaping fantasies': figurations of gender and power in Elizabethan culture," *Representations*, 2 (1983), 61–94.

2 Stephen Greenblatt, *Sir Walter Raleigh: The Renaissance Man and his Roles*; "Invisible bullets: Renaissance authority and its subversion," *Glyph* 8 (1981), 40–61; "Marlowe, Marx and anti-Semitism," *Critical Inquiry*, 5 (1978), 291–307; "Murdering peasants: status, genre and the representation of rebellion," *Representations*, 1 (1983), 1–29. Should it be remarked that in the phrase "Renaissance authority and its subversion," the subversion is suddenly possessed by authority and subordinated to it?

3 For example, in Alan Sinfield, "Power and ideology: an outline theory and Sidney's *Arcadia*," forthcoming in *ELH*. See also Alan Sinfield and Jonathan Dollimore, eds,

Political Shakespeare: New Essays in Cultural Materialism (Ithaca, Cornell University Press, 1985), the very recent appearance of which made it impossible for me to take it into account in this book.

4 Michel Foucault, *Les Mots et les choses*, tr. *The Order of Things* by Alan Bass (New York, Vintage Books, 1973), 262.

5 Johan Huizinga, *Homo Ludens* (Boston, Beacon Press, 1955), 5.

6 See, in connection with Puttenham especially, Louis Adrian Montrose, "Of gentlemen and shepherds: the politics of Elizabethan pastoral form," *ELH*, 50, 3 (1983), 415-60, and Daniel Javitch's seminal *Poetry and Courtliness in Renaissance England* (Princeton, Princeton University Press, 1978).

7 Antonio Gramsci, *Prison Notebooks, Selections* ed. and tr. by Quintin Hoare and Geoffrey Nowell Smith (London, Lawrence & Wishart, 1973), especially "State and civil society," 210-75 and *passim*.

8 To the extent that a political theory informs the *Arte*, it tends to be loosely that of monarchical "good government" underpinned by the secular priesthood of the learned, in which no real distinction is made between political and moral "good order." However contentiously or otherwise, neither an aristocracy nor the clergy is given a significant role; presumably the political phenomenon if not a theory of Tudor political centralism is that to which the *Arte* testifies, though the prompting of Sir Thomas Elyot's *The Boke Named the Gouernour* (1531) and *The Mirrour of Magistrates* (1559) can hardly be overlooked. (Particularly significant for my argument is Elyot's dictum that the effect of reading tragedies is to make men "execrate and abhor the intollerable life of tyrants," *Gouernour*, ed. H.H.S. Croft, 2 vols [London, 1883; New York, 1967], 1: 71.) Like many of his English contemporaries, Puttenham appears not to have been directly acquainted with the works of Machiavelli, and no criterion of *ragioni di stati* is acknowledged in the *Arte*. Insofar as political expediency is formally acknowledged in the *Arte*, its scope remains limited to the exercise of *courtly* dissimulation, a practice Puttenham justifies by invoking (without specifying its source) Tiberius's maxim: *qui nescit dissimulare nescit regnare*. The queen's own "courtly" rule exemplifies for Puttenham this justified deception.

9 The similarities include a commonplace humanistic concern with poetic origins and forms, as well as with the capacities of poetic speech to move and persuade. The dissimilarities are, however, more striking, since Puttenham's work is indeed a rhetoric – a manual of instruction and a functional analysis of the figures of speech rather than a contribution to the philosophy of poetry. Puttenham's invention of English names for the classical figures of speech has attracted recent attention as a revelation of the way in which his "translation" of classical terms is colored by the political imperatives of the English sixteenth century. Strong political readings of Puttenham have appeared in the essay by Montrose cited above and in Javitch's *Poetry and Courtliness*.

10 George Puttenham, *The Arte of English Poesie*, A Facsimile Reproduction intr. Baxter Hathaway (Kent, Ohio, Kent State University Press, 1970), 19-20. Despite the notoriety of Arber reprints, I have used this facsimile in preference to the "standard" edition edited by Gladys Doidge Willcock and Alice Walker (Cambridge, Cambridge University Press, 1936). Not only is that edition no longer state of the art, but, as will become apparent in the course of this book, there is reason to be wary of any "edited" version of this text.

11 Hathaway (ed.), *English Poesie*, 22.

12 ibid., 23.

13 ibid., 24.

14 Pastoral, which is very much the wild card in Puttenham's pack, threatens to

disrupt the entire "ideal" narrative of forms that I am rehearsing. See especially in this connection, Montrose, "Of gentlemen and shepherds."

15 *English Poesie*, 45.

16 Thomas Wilson, *The Arte of Rhetorike*, ed. G.H. Mair (Oxford, Clarendon Press, 1909), A. 8.

17 *English Poesie*, 46.

18 ibid.

19 The conception fundamental to both Sidney and Spenser's justifications of the "heroical" and/or "historical" poem, by which of course is meant the privileged form of the epic. Since it establishes the rationale of the poetic and dramatic forms, Puttenham's "History" must be included among the period's defenses of poetry, a fact that may account for his consistently maximizing his claims. In contrast to Sidney's forensic oration in defense of poetry, Puttenham's "history" of the poetic forms seeks to place the justification of those forms beyond the realm of dispute by merely displaying the necessity under which they exist in the world.

20 The subtitle of William Rankins's antitheatrical pamphlet *A Mirrour of Monsters* (1587) refers to the "infectious" sight of plays.

21 *English Poesie*, 47.

22 ibid., 48.

23 ibid., 30. Since "sovereignty" emerges as the common property of lawful kings and illegitimate tyrants in Puttenham's account, the distinction may seem to be quite seriously threatened. The ideal or nominal character of the sovereign is upheld in the *Arte* by Queen Elizabeth, whose idealized portrait (image) takes the place of a conventional book dedication. At the same time, however, the history of dramatic form decisively subordinates the political sovereignty of the "tyrant" to the hegemonic rule of the "priesthood." The *Arte* thus becomes a delicate exercise in having it both ways, and a warning is implicit in Puttenham's making the career of the dead tyrant into the definitive subject of tragedy. A powerful gloss on the whole question of the "sovereign/tyrant" in Elizabethan political life and especially in Elizabethan tragedy, of which I became aware only after having written this essay, is supplied by Franco Moretti, "The Great Eclipse," in *Signs Taken for Wonders*, tr. Susan Fisher, David Forgacs and David Miller (London, Verso Editions, 1983), 42–82

24 *English Poesie*, 49.

25 Sir Philip Sidney, *An Apology for Poetry*, ed. Geoffrey Shepherd (London, Thomas Nelson and Sons, 1965), 117

26 *Apology*, 118.

27 *English Poesie*, 49.

28 An English genre of "commonweal tragedy" has been posited by Joyce E. Petersen in *Curs'd Example: "The Duchess of Malfi" and Commonweal Tragedy* (Columbia, University of Missouri Press, 1978), and the notion of tragedy as a "defense of the commonwealth" against tyrannical incursions is not altogether new in critical discussion of Elizabethan drama. The "commonwealth" will however on Puttenham's showing remain the name under which more limited interests are served. Anxiety about the popularity of "tyranny" – about a conjunction between individual self-aggrandizement and widespread public admiration – is strongly manifested in William Rankins's *Mirrour of Monsters*, where the issue concerns not only the response of audiences to players in the theater but eventually of the public to a highly theatricalized monarchy. Anxiousness about the *unpopularity* of a hegemonic enlightenment is betrayed here as elsewhere by Puttenham.

29 A point to the confirmation of which Stephen Orgel's *The Illusion of Power* may lend itself. The royal masque (masquerade) tends to become a form of self-enclosed

fantasy rather than an *instrument* of effective government.
30 See, for example, Jonathan Dollimore, *Radical Tragedy.*

Chapter 2: Sympathy (pp. 35–69)

1 The argument concerning tragedy that I reproduce here, as far as I know still unpublished, was presented by Andrew Ross, now of Princeton.

2 Thomas Greene, "The end of discourse in Machiavelli's *Prince*," in *Concepts of Closure*, vol. 67 of *Yale French Studies* (New Haven, Yale University Press, 1984), 57–71.

3 Stephen Greenblatt, "The improvisation of power," in *Renaissance Self-Fashioning: From More to Shakespeare* (Chicago, University of Chicago Press, 1980), 222–54. But see also Jonathan Goldberg, *Endlesse Worke* (Baltimore, The Johns Hopkins University Press, 1981) and Angus Fletcher, *The Prophetic Moment: An Essay on Spenser* (Chicago, University of Chicago Press, 1971).

4 The connection both of knighthood and chivalry with rape is necessarily a huge topic and problem for Spenser. In the realm of sexual politics, the true knight is definitively one whose gambit is that of "rape declined," and saving the heroine from being raped is his definitive task in this realm, which in one sense *is* the realm of *The Faerie Queene.* This sexual politics is what the dominant tradition in Spenser criticism, that of "Christian humanism," characteristically refuses to discuss. The ability of Christian humanism to avoid this engagement depends partly on its recurrent privileging of Book I ("Holinesse") of *The Faerie Queene* as the paradigm for the poem. Following C.S. Lewis, who referred to it as the "perfect" book, this tradition refuses in effect to engage with the increasingly "vnperfite" nature of the poem – which includes its radical questioning of the premises of Book I. And even Book I tends to be read largely without reference to *its* sexual politics as well as to the clear possibility that the "weak," flawed Redcrosse Knight/St George is not, and never can be, the type or pattern ("patron") of true holiness. This possibility arises not just in the climactic episode on the Mountain of Contemplation, where Redcrosse is told that he is going to have to do it all over again, differently, but in the implications of Spenser's deriving the "patron of true holiness" from a *Catholic* source, the thirteenth-century Golden Legend ("legend"?). If there is a Protestant and *heuristic* point to Book I, it may be that the "patron" of true holiness is either absent, unthinkable, or else to be identified with Christ alone, allusively present and perhaps "acting" but incapable of being represented or even strictly foreshadowed in the book. The point isn't necessarily that Redcrosse, who is flawed like us and whom we therefore like, resembles or foreshadows Christ, or gets reconstructed in the image of Christ during the narrative, but that the Christ to whom the book alludes remains unthinkably other than Redcrosse – especially in the realm of sexual and power politics.

Book II, then, becomes the one in which a certain false consciousness ceases to prevail. Guyon, the knight of worldly Temperance, enters the poem as a seemingly autarchic and/or asexual being encased in steel. Such is temperance, or the well-tempered man, embodied in or *as* a suit of armor so complete that "from his head no place appeared to his feete" (II.i.6). For him to be moved into action, it seems necessary for him to get beside himself. The first but not the last occasion on which he does so is that in which Archimago and Duessa, the leftover conspirators from Book I, apparently find a chink in the armor. They stage a rape-scene, or rather pretend that Duessa has just been raped in a scene that Archimago graphically recreates, in doing so momentarily superimposing the figure of the raped virgin on that of the earth-mother, who is continuously the object of male violence in Book II and elsewhere in the poem. Guyon is "moved" by being made imaginatively a spectator and perhaps imaginatively a participant in this scene, the immediate result of which is indeed to set him off on a blindly fugitive quest for the rapist. Rape imagined and then declined becomes the primal scene of chivalry, and of the *writing* of chivalry, at least in Book II. The excitement of that imagined scene is what spins temperate Guyon violently off at a tangent, but to what eventual purpose isn't clear since the psychotically violent act of vandalism with which Guyon ends his adventures in this book remains a subject of critical debate.

5 Michel Foucault, *The Order of Things*, trans. Alan Bass (New York, Vintage Books, 1973), 23 ff.

6 On the general question of Pythagoreanism and its assimilation into Renaissance neoplatonic and poetic thinking, see among others S.K. Heninger, *Touches of Sweet Harmony* (San Marino, Huntington Library, 1974) and John Hollander, *The Untuning of the Sky: Ideas of Music in English Poetry 1500–1700* (Princeton, Princeton University Press, 1961).

7 Max Scheler, *Zur Phänomenologie und Theorie der Sympathiegefühle und vom Liebe und Hass* (Halle, Niemeyer, 1913); rev. ed. *Wesen und Formen der Sympathie* (Bonn, Friedrich Cohen, 1922, '26); (Frankfurt-am-Main, G. Schulte-Bumke, 1948); tr. Stephen Heath with introduction by W. Stark, *The Nature of Sympathy* (New York, Archon Books, 1970). If Scheler's treatment is, however, the single, ambitious, general one, the topic itself has been dealt with either directly or indirectly in various contexts – most pertinently for my purposes by Derrida in *Of Grammatology*, tr. Gayatri Chauravorty Spivak (Baltimore, The Johns Hopkins University Press, 1980), 171–92. See also, Pietro Pucci, *The Violence of Pity in Euripides' "Medea"* (Ithaca, Cornell University Press, 1980).

8 David Marshall, "The figure of theater: Shaftesbury, Defoe, Adam Smith and George Eliot," Diss. The Johns Hopkins University, 1980.

9 See, for example, Reginald Scot, *The Discoverie of Witchcraft*, repr. ed. Montague Summers (New York, Dover Publications, 1972), 170. Animals' friendliness or unfriendliness to man is often mentioned along with their other traits in such works as Topsell's *Historie of the Foure-Footed Beastes* (1609), though the situation is significantly complicated by the continuing tendency of Renaissance natural historians to distinguish between natural and monstrous races of animals and humans alike. See for example Rudolf Schenda, *Die französische Prodigienliteratur in der zweiten Hälfte des 16. Jahrhunderts* (Munich, Max Huber Verlag, 1961).

10 One of the clear primary sources for Spenserian sympathy as "gentleness" is the poetry of Chaucer, in which, for his major Renaissance successors, the phenomenon and problematic of poetic "gentleness" seems to be invented. This "gentleness" goes together with "sympathetic" representation of female personae, and both are no doubt indebted to a large medieval–Ovidian literature of complaint. Chaucer's staging of issues of sympathy, and of the *female* figure as mourner–complainant, become particularly important as Spenserian precedents once sympathy and "gentilesse" are explicitly interconnected, as they are, for example, in "The Squire's Tale," "The Franklin's Tale," and "The Wife of Bath's Tale." In "The Squire's Tale," the overwhelming importance of which for Spenser has been shown by Jonathan Goldberg in *Endlesse Worke*, the voicing of female complaint (indeed, an incipient poetic of female complaint) as well as the emergence of a pitying, feminized gentleness (nobility), depends precisely on the abeyance of normal, male-dominated court life. It is not long, however, before the language of female grieving in "The Squire's Tale" turns into one of bitter

grievance, even if a millennial conversion of the male is also anticipated – ironically so in a poem that breaks off short without bringing this millennium to pass. Among the important if somewhat tormenting possibilities that arise when Chaucer makes "pitee" characterize the "gentle" heart, is that of making cruelty or oppressiveness into a form of *vulgarity* – a crucial consideration in Spenser's conceptions of chivalry, and one that introduces an element of "poetic" sensibility into the otherwise arid ideology of *noblesse oblige*.

11 *Order of Things*, xv.

12 In general, the absolutist dialectic of same and other has to be abandoned in the discourse of poetics, or of poetic representation, inasmuch as "some" and "other" must always be conceived as the *absolutely* unrepresentable, and perhaps merely designated as the divine or, in the language of Foucault, as power. Poetics can therefore be conceived "between" these absolutist extremes, or against them, while they in turn may be conceived, at least in the case of Spenser, as the unrepresentable origin(s) or ground(s) of poetic representation. I would further suggest that unless the difficulties (which may be impossibilities) are recognized, as they often are by Renaissance poets, there is nothing to be gained by trying to think the unrepresentable categories of some or other *in* and *through* the discourse of poetics, which is why a very great deal of theologizing in the guise of Spenser criticism seems fundamentally beside the point. It should also be mentioned that speaking not about the "other" but from within it is a well-recognized feature of Foucault's work, beginning with *Madness and Civilization*. Both the distinct interest of such an undertaking and its problems are well discussed by Derrida in "Cogito and the history of madness," in *Writing and Difference*, tr. Alan Bass (Chicago, University of Chicago Press, 1978), 31–63.

13 *Order of Things*, 23–4.

14 ibid., 24.

15 *The Complete Essays of Montaigne*, tr. Donald Frame (Stanford, Stanford University Press, 1965), 139; also *Essais de Montaigne*, ed. Maurice Rat (Paris, Garnier, 1962), 204.

16 See among others in this connection, Barry Weller, "The rhetoric of friendship in Montaigne's *Essais*," *New Literary History*, 9 (1978), 503–23.

17 *Essays of Montaigne*, 314.

18 ibid., 317.

19 Michel Foucault, *Surveillir et Punir*, tr. *Discipline and Punish* by Alan Sheridan (New York, Vintage Books, 1979); Thomas M. Greene, "Dangerous Parleys – *Essais* 1:5 and 6," in *Montaigne: Essays in Reading*, vol. 64 of *Yale French Studies* (New Haven, Yale University Press, 1983), 3–23.

20 Marshall shows that for Smith, and subsequently for his commentators, a crux has been the nature and identity of the "impartial spectator" in whose absence no ethical theater and indeed no ethical judgment, in Adam Smith's terms, is possible. Smith's conception requires an array of terms including "bystander," "third person," "every attentive spectator," "every impartial bystander," "another man," "other men," "society," "mankind," and Smith's readers have added to the list. The question of the spectator rather than the spectacle is also important in the work of Spenser; see "Spenser's theater" in my Chapter 4 (p. 93).

21 Widely recognized in recent work on the Renaissance, but see especially Joel Altman, *The Tudor Play of Mind* (Berkeley and Los Angeles, University of California Press, 1978).

22 In accepting the commonplace that Renaissance poetry in general is conceived epideictically, that is to say, in the oratorical mode of praise and/or blame, one necessarily accepts the impossibility of any neutral relation to the object of poetic

representation. A prior affective investment also implicitly precedes the desired or attempted act of moral determination.

23 Forms of complaint (plaining, com-plaining) are a highly significant element in Spenser's medieval and Renaissance heritage; among the relevant names, in addition to Chaucer's, are those of Petrarch, Ronsard, Marot, du Bellay, Lydgate, Dunbar(?), Skelton and Wyatt. Having said this, one would want to cite references, but to the best of my knowledge there is absolutely no adequate treatment of this topic, this continuing to be the case despite such helpful works as Georgia Ronan Crampton's *The Condition of Creatures: Suffering and Action in Chaucer and Spenser* (New Haven, Yale University Press, 1974) and John Peter's *Complaint and Satire in Early English Literature* (Oxford, Clarendon Press, 1956). Among the issues to be considered are the passive–aggressive psychology of complaint; the relationship between complaint and self-constitution or self-aestheticization; complaint as the definitive rhetoric of the victim, "naturally" coded as feminine because of its ostensible reference both to a lack and to prior unjust deprivation, but also dilating the space of the mourning, vengeful subject. Whether medieval–populist "pitee" is successfully reinscribed or really lost forever in the work of Renaissance poets is an issue interestingly noted by T.S. Eliot in "Seneca," *Selected Essays* (New York, Harcourt, Brace & Co., 1950), 87. Referring to an exquisite translation by Heywood of some lines from *Hercules*, Eliot writes: "Nothing can be said of such a translation except that it is perfect. It is the last echo of an earlier tongue, the language of Chaucer with an overtone of Christian piety and pity which disappears with Elizabethan verse."

24 *Nature of Sympathy*, 53.

25 Thomas Greene discusses the nature of the word in Elizabethan English as a semantic complex in "Anti-hermeneutics: the case of Shakespeare's sonnet 129," in Maynard Mack and George Forest Lord, eds, *Poetic Traditions of the English Renaissance* (New Haven, Yale University Press, 1982), 143–62.

26 The most interesting direction of which I am aware is the one contained in an uncompleted study by David Baker of Johns Hopkins, which regards the *View* as an unmitigated document of sixteenth-century English political ideology. Spenser cannot think (or feel) "otherwise" because he is constituted by the ideological language he speaks, and nothing in the *View* escapes or contradicts that language. See also, however, Kenneth Gross's general account of the *View*, forthcoming in *ELH*, in which the problem of Spenser's "sympathy" is referred to his dividedness between Irish and English affiliations, the "heimlich" and "unheimlich."

27 Edmund Spenser, *A View of the Present State of Ireland*, ed. W. L. Renwick (Oxford, Clarendon Press, 1926; repr. 1970).

28 ibid., 102.

29 See for example, T.W. Moody and F. X. Martin, eds, *The Course of Irish History* (Cork, The Mercier Press, 1967), 174–89; G.A. Hayes-McCoy, "Strategy and tactics in Irish warfare, 1593-1601," in *Irish Historical Studies*, 7 (1941); Cyril Falls, *Elizabeth's Irish Wars* (London, 1950). Considerable interpretive differences emerge in these and other discussions of Elizabethan policy in Ireland. While Gross represents the Tudor administration as inept and the Irish "question" as a chaotic vexation, others have noted the systematic pacification of Ireland, despite setbacks, throughout the sixteenth century and have claimed relative success for the English policy of planting colonists (the course recommended in Machiavelli's *The Prince*, Chapter 3).

30 *View*, 104.

31 I don't use this term altogether unadvisedly, since something like a reflex action – i.e. an action prior to choice or below its level – appears to have been imputed to

sympathy right up to the nineteenth century. The discovery of the reflex arc and hence of a mechanical paradigm contributed significantly to the defeat of "sympathy" as an explanation for phenomena of physiological feedback and psycho-physical interaction. See Ruth Leys, "Background to the reflex controversy: William Alison and the doctrine of sympathy before Hall," in *Studies in the History of Biology*, 4 (1980), 1–66.

32 An intense rebound from sympathy into apocalyptic violence is evident not just in the *View* and in Book II of *The Faerie Queene* (a violence that can go either way, seizing on the apparent victim or the supposed aggressor but needing above all to be *expressed*), but also in revenge tragedy. (The failure of this rebound mechanism, and thus in one sense of sympathy itself, seems to be part of the "problem" in *Hamlet*, where lack of "nature" and natural sympathy has on occasion troubled critics.) See in this connection, as well as in the general one of sympathy-as-mourning, Peter Sacks, "Where words prevail not: grief, revenge and language in Kyd and Shakespeare," in *The English Elegy: Studies in the Genre from Spenser to Yeats* (Baltimore, The Johns Hopkins University Press, 1985), 64–89. Though not necessarily discussed under the rubric of "sympathy," phenomena of literary change in the decade in which the *View* was written have widely been recognized at least since C.S. Lewis's *English Literature in the Sixteenth Century* (Oxford, Clarendon Press, 1954). Disaffection from the Elizabethan regime and its constitutive fictions of pastoral order and imperial power coincides with a paradoxically enabling shift in poetics towards the representation of the oppressed, the victimized and the outcast. This contingent poetics of "madness," despair, revolt and extremity in various guises may be more evident in the work of some of Spenser's contemporaries than in his own – for example, in the work of Marlowe, Nashe and the Shakespeare of the tragedies – yet Spenser does not escape these changes, which indeed *compel* his reinscription of his own "proper" fictions of civility in a context in which their groundlessness and vitiating aggressiveness must increasingly be displayed. Spenser's projective capacity as an Irish settler to "change places" with the Irish victims, but all the more so his desired return to the Elizabethan order of cultural privilege and overwhelming power, are strikingly suggested in his "A Briefe Note of Ireland," addressed to Elizabeth, in *The Works of Edmund Spenser*, Edwin Greenlaw *et al.* (eds), (Baltimore, The Johns Hopkins University Press, 1947), vol. 9, 236: "receive the voices of a fewe moste vnhappie Ghostes, of whome is nothinge but the ghost nowe left which lie buried in the bottom of oblivion farr from the light of your gracious sunshine" (cited by David Baker).

33 For various identifications, including ones linking personae in the tale to Robert Cecil and to James VI of Scotland as putative ruler of England, see especially Charles Grosvenor Osgood and Henry Gibbons Lotspeich, eds, *The Minor Poems*, vol. 2 in *The Works of Edmund Spenser*, 350 and *passim*.

34 See Walter Oakshott, "Carew Ralegh's copy of Spenser," *The Library*, 26 (1971), 6. See also Conyers Read, *Lord Burghley and Queen Elizabeth* (London, Jonathan Cape, 1960); for the marriage negotiations, see 203–35. On Spenser's possible role, see *The Poetical Works of Edmund Spenser*, ed. J.C. Smith and E. de Selincourt (London, Oxford University Press, 1912), xxii–xxiii. On the general question of Burghley's alleged hostility and Spenser's other troubles, it has far too easily been assumed, as Jonathan Goldberg has argued in *Endlesse Worke*, that objective failure or opposition motivated Spenser's complaints. Spenser *was* more liberally pensioned by the queen, as far as we know, than any of his poet contemporaries. The constantly hinted antagonism of Burghley may partly be explained as one of Spenser's self-magnifying fictions – his name scarcely appears in works dealing

impartially with Burghley and his patronage. It would hardly be suspected from Spenser's works and traditional commentary that Burghley was a significant patron of letters; see, however, J. Beckinsale, "Lover of learning and patron of the arts," in *Burghley: Tudor Statesman 1529–1598* (London, Macmillan, 1967), 270–92. It is true that Burghley's patronage extended mainly to works of history, moral instruction and useful knowledge, so it may have been possible to consider him a philistine in the "Stoicke censur" mode. See also Richard Helgerson, *The Elizabethan Prodigals* (Berkeley and Los Angeles, University of California Press, 1976).

35 Nothing has ever been proved about Spenser's possible manipulation of editorial and printerly material associated with his poems. If what follows is therefore doomed to be speculative, it is nevertheless necessary to think what it would mean for Spenser to have (or *not* to have) controlled the physical presentation and timing of his works. The "Mutabilitie" Cantos, published posthumously in 1609, are of course accompanied by the rubric "TWO CANTOS OF *MUTABILITIE*: Which, both for Forme and Matter, appeare to be parcell of some following Booke of the *FAERIE QVEENE*, VNDER THE LEGEND OF *Constancie*. Neuer before imprinted" [394]. To cite the Longman *Faerie Queene*, ed. A.C. Hamilton (London, Longman, 1977), 714, "it is not known whose authority there is for the title, the division and numbering of the cantos (vi, vii, ['vnperfite']) and the running title 'The Seuenth Booke.'" Maybe Spenser, maybe not. It is logical, however, that the "Legend of Constancie" should have emerged in the course of the poem as the very one incapable in principle of being written or narrated. The "virtue" of constancy (would its gender be feminine, as it apparently is in Chaucer?) is opposed in absolute principle to change, temporality, seriality, etc., all of which constitute the very medium of the poem. Constancy accordingly emerges as *The Faerie Queene*'s unrepresentable and (hence) ideal "other." It is also the one name that can't be incorporated and undone in the shifting medium of the poem, and it is not the name of Elizabeth. The world of the poem (of poetic narrative) becomes, by the same token, that of mutability. If we owe this aesthetic dénouement to Matthew Lownes, Spenser's printer, or to time and chance alone, we seem to have found ourselves in a world of Greek romance in which miracles are the thing to be expected. If, on the other hand, Spenser is responsible, a good deal of consideration needs to be given to the status of "Mutabilitie" as an endgame – perhaps intentionally posthumous.

What also needs to be considered is whether the fragment could have been published during the lifetime of Elizabeth rather than Spenser; whether the fragment already makes gestures of accommodation towards Elizabeth's anticipated successor while "demystifying" her. There is not just the Faunus-Diana episode, in which the wood-god laughs at the spectacle of the naked goddess, but there are such stanzas as the ones in which Mutabilitie almost dethrones Cynthia by force (395–6; sts 14–41) and the one in which Cynthia's own mutability is shockingly manifest: "Euen you faire *Cynthia* . . . / We changed see, and sundry forms partake, / Now hornd, now round, now bright, now brown and gray" (405; st. 50). Mutabilitie, finally identified as nature's daughter, is the fairest one of all.

36 "Prosopopeia or Mother Hubberd's Tale," in *Poetical Works*, 495, lines 45–50.

37 "Mother Hubberd," lines 53–101.

38 *Nature of Sympathy*, 46.

39 The nature and availability of this theodicy can hardly be determined without detailed reference to contemporary Protestant theology and practice. I would, however, suggest that insofar as the issue is a poetic one, it can also be pursued in *Paradise Lost*, in which the "complaints" of the fallen Adam and Eve are the sign

and consequence of their full culpability as well as of their new psychology of denial. See, for a view of hardline sixteenth-century Protestantism, Alan Sinfield, *Literature in Protestant England 1560-1660* (London, Croom Helm, 1984), and Empson's still-pertinent *Milton's God*, rev. ed. (London, Chatto & Windus, 1965). In *The Prophetic Milton* (Charlottesville, University of Virginia Press, 1974) and *The Sacred Complex* (Cambridge, Harvard University Press, 1983), William Kerrigan has explicitly and persuasively discussed (indeed, has made a powerfully informed case) for Miltonic theodicy, in doing so necessarily conceding little to Empson, Waldock, and other old-fashioned anti-Miltonists. What ensues, however, is something like a sophisticated Panglossian totalization, Christian and Freudian, to which "we" as readers are continuously if not explicitly invited to submit. The sacred name (or "complex") that justifies this attempt is culture, a phenomenon essentially removed from the defining opposition to nature and also purged of political content.

40 "Mother Hubberd," line 197.

41 ibid., lines 199–202.

42 Although these indispensable terms have now virtually entered common critical parlance, they must be credited, along with all that they imply, to Stephen Greenblatt, especially his *Renaissance Self-Fashioning*.

43 Variorum, *Minor Poems*, 1, 571–610 and *passim*, on Spenser's possible involvement in contexts of ecclesiastical patronage and strife. The absence of a good cleric (and the nature of this poem's particular bad one) looks coded, and may also reflect on the consequences of the Elizabethan policy of suppressing the most militant, Puritanical but also presumably conscientious and articulate members of the Anglican clergy. However, an aggressive secular–poetic displacement of the "real" clergy even as the idealized clerical role remains a model for the poetic vocation appears to be one inevitable consequence of Spenser's poetic enterprise. Perhaps the same consideration applies in relation to the "real" nobility, whose place the gentleman poets also attempt to take.

44 "Mother Hubberd," line 254.

45 ibid., line 260.

46 ibid., line 930–2.

47 ibid., line 1091.

48 ibid., lines 1209–12.

49 ibid., line 1522.

50 ibid., line 1275.

51 ibid., lines 1289–90; 1303–06.

52 Robert Durling, " 'The Ascent of Mont Ventoux' and the crisis of allegory," *Italian Quarterly*, 18, 9 (1974), 7–29. Negative or disjunctive allegory does not of course imply any loss of urgency in the process of *writing*, but if anything a relocation and intensification of that urgency in the literary career as such, to which a constant and even aggressive perpetuation of differences is essential.

53 George Puttenham, *The Arte of English Poesie*, A Facsimile Reproduction intr. Baxter Hathaway (Kent, Ohio, Kent State University Press, 1970), 246. Puttenham also refers to *prosopopeia* as "counterfait" representation, and his definition is cited under "counterfeit" in *OED*, 4, to support the obsolete meaning "represented by a picture or image." Yet this limited meaning is questioned as well as supported by Puttenham, who refers to "something kindly ... counterfait or represented in his absence." Here "kindly" may be taken to imply "in its own kind," "naturally" and "sympathetically," while "in his absence" invokes the specifically poetic capacity to represent the unrepresented or otherwise unrepresentable. "Counterfait" draws, moreover, on complex, earlier meanings also cited. In addition to signifying "made

in imitation of that which is genuine; imitated, forged" (*OED*, 1) the word, in the spelling retained by Puttenham, recalls its Latin and Old French root meaning(s) of "[made] in opposition or contrast, hence in opposing imitation" (*OED*). Poetic imitation as counterfactual or counterpolitical rather than merely imaginary or "feigning" representation is thus strongly implied in the definition of *prosopopeia*, and that definition constitutes a poetics in a nutshell. It is a definition that also allows for poetic "feigning" to become the very form of the literal, insofar as the literal remains censored and/or misrepresented.

54 See, for example, Louis Adrian Montrose, " 'Eliza, Queene of the shepherdes' and the pastoral of power," *ELR*, 10 (1980), 153-82, and " 'Shaping Fantasies': figurations of gender and power in Elizabethan culture", *Representations*, 2 (1983), 61-94. I should also add that, having come to this point in my argument, I had the not uncommon experience of finding Harry Berger already there, especially in his essays entitled "Busirane and the war between the sexes," *ELR*, 1 (1971), 99.111, and "Orpheus, Pan and the poetics of misogyny: Spenser's critique of pastoral art," *ELH* 50, 1 (1983), 27-60. Deferring as I do to Berger, I question on one hand whether the logic of misogynist poetics can stop short of becoming the logic of generally misanthropic poetics (i.e. the logic of any poetic representation whatever) and on the other hand whether the so often represented battle of the sexes entails a suppression or misrepresentation of the common (single) quest for power.

55 The identification of "Dido" and her lover is at once obstructed and invited by the coy E.K. gloss: "The great shepheard is some man of high degree, and not as some vainely suppose God Pan. The person both of the shepheard and of Dido is vnknowen and closely buried in the Authors conceipt" (*Poetical Works*, 463.)

56 The act of "compassing or imagining the king's death" had been made treasonable by the statute 25 Edward III, subsequently extended and revised by other statutes, notably in the Tudor period. Some of the ways in which the statute was liberally interpreted are mentioned in W.S. Holdsworth, *A History of English Law*, vol. 8 (London, Methuen & Co., 1922-38), 309-16.

57 "November," *The Shepheardes Calender*, in *Poetical Works*, 462.

58 Elizabeth Jenkins, *Elizabeth and Leicester* (London, Victor Gollancz, 1961), 362.

59 *The Faerie Queene*, Book III, Canto vi, in *Poetical Works*, 176.

60 I don't suggest that this heresy is historically unconditioned; on the contrary, many of the conditions, including those of Protestant "selfhood," under which it can manifest itself in Spenser's work are powerfully established in Greenblatt's *Renaissance Self-Fashioning*. It would of course be interesting to know how the queen read Spenser, if she read him at all, or with any attention. The only extant Elizabethan "reading" of *The Faerie Queene* (Books I–III in the 1590 edition) is the one printed as *The First Commentary on "The Faerie Queene": Being An Analysis of Lord Bessborough's First Edition of "The Faerie Queene,"* ed. Graham Hough (Folcroft, Pennsylvania, 1964). This reading tends to confirm the mainline Protestant-nationalist-apocalyptic view of the poem as the canonical Elizabethan one, and it is understood to do so by Florence Sandler, "The Faerie Queene: an Elizabethan apocalypse," in C.A. Patrides and Joseph Wittreich, eds, *The Apocalypse in English Renaissance Thought and Literature* (Manchester, Manchester University Press, 1984), 148-74. This has to be mentioned as a control on my own argument, yet it proves nothing about how the work was read in the intimate court circle, nor does it even begin to contend with the multiple poet–audience–reading configurations represented in Spenser's poems. Nor does it account for the defensiveness of Spenser's authorial positions, for example in the Proem to Book IV and in Book VI of *The Faerie Queene*. Of what these phenomena are real evidence – perhaps only of Spenserian paranoia – is not easy to determine,

yet they do constitute evidence that can't be suppressed.

Chapter 3: Countercurrents (pp. 70–88)

1 By "historicism," otherwise "new historicism," I mean only the critical practice that has arisen within the past decade in relation to English Renaissance literature. The achievements of the "school" are brilliantly reviewed, and a useful bibliography is supplied, in Jonathan Goldberg's "Recent studies in Renaissance literature," *Studies in English Literature 1500–1900*, 24, 1 (1984), 157–99, and in "The politics of Renaissance literature: a review essay," *ELH*, 49 (1982), 514–42.

2 Arthur F. Marotti, " 'Love is not Love': Elizabethan sonnet sequences and the social order," *ELH*, 49, 2 (1982), 396–428. See also Peter Stallybrass and Ann Rosalind Jones, "The politics of *Astrophil and Stella*," *Studies in English Literature, 1500–1900*, 24 (1984), 53–68.

3 Lawrence Stone, *The Crisis of the Aristocracy, 1558–1641* (Oxford, Clarendon Press, 1965); also "Social mobility in England, 1500–1700," *Past & Present*, 33 (1966), 16–55.

4 Louis Adrian Montrose, " 'Eliza, Queene of the shepherdes' and the pastoral of power," *ELR*, 10 (1980), 153–82.

5 On some of the general questions involved, see Montrose, "Of gentlemen and shepherds: the politics of Elizabethan pastoral form," *ELH*, 50, 3 (1983) and Javitch, *Poetry and Courtliness in Renaissance England* (Princeton, Princeton University Press, 1978). The special case of the powerful woman within a paternalistic patronage system gives rise, of course, to a great deal of male (and perhaps female) anxiety, some of it resulting in what appears to be prurient fantasy of the kind associated by John Aubrey with Mary Sidney: "She was very salacious, and she had a Contrivance that in the Spring of the yeare, when the Stallions were to leape the Mares, they were to be brought before such a part of the house, where she had a *vidette* (a hole to peepe out at) to looke on them and please herselfe with their Sport: and then she would act the like sport herself with *her* stallions." John Aubrey, *Brief Lives*, ed. Oliver Lawson Dick (Ann Arbor, University of Michigan Press, 1962), 138. Alexandra Halasz, of The Johns Hopkins University, has pointed out to me the resemblance between this rumor and ones circulated about Catherine the Great, all of them implying significant anxiety about the threat of the too-powerful woman. This anxiety is represented as being almost overwhelming in Spenser's work, yet it is also paradoxically enabling. The "December" eclogue might be taken as a *locus classicus* in which the unnatural or violently irregular appearance of a comet (not a star) in the poet's sky seems capable of scorching all natural growth and of disrupting every natural regularity and progession. The poem Spenser imitates is Marot's "Eclogue au roi soubz les noms de Pan et Robin," in which the king seems to be a real father in a properly functioning paternalistic system.

6 Even if read as romance by this postulated audience, the romance will hardly be "pure." Quite apart from voyeurism, there is a political question about what middle-class readers might get out of aristocratic romance. This genre might on one hand excite a desire for social mobility that could be translated into practice, and it might on the other result in a fake-out of the reader fixated on the image. Either way, this romance would be doing the right work – that of encouraging *limited* social mobility and/or functioning as an anodyne.

7 Dynastic appropriation of medieval romance appears *not* to have been forgotten by Spenser, who extensively reappropriates it for the Tudors in *The Faerie Queene*.

8 In a talk delivered at The Johns Hopkins University during 1983. In this model,

women serve as counters or currency in male transactions of homoerotic bonding and fraternal rivalry. While Sedgwick's model functions well in connection with Restoration comedy and its social context, it functions, but less well, in the context of Elizabethan authorship. Such strikingly "empowered" women as Queen Elizabeth and Mary Sidney become far more threatening, even if only in male fantasy, than do the eighteenth-century ladies over whom rakes fight their cuckold-wars. See also Eve Kosofsky Sedgwick, *Between Men: English Literature and Male Homosocial Desire* (New York, Columbia University Press, 1985).

9 *The Poems of Sir Philip Sidney*, ed. William Ringler (Oxford, Clarendon Press, 1962), 183. Ringler's notes deal with the inclusion/exclusion of sonnet 37, but also of 24 and 35, in various texts of *Astrophil and Stella*, and also with the capitalization of "Rich" in the poem's final line.

10 An account of Sidney's unwanted advice to the queen on the occasion of her (feigned?) courtship of the Duc d'Alençon, as well as of the "banishment" from court that it earned Sidney, can be found in Dorothy Connell, *Sir Philip Sidney: The Maker's Mind* (Oxford, Clarendon Press, 1977), but also in other works on Sidney.

11 Katherine Duncan-Jones, *Sir Philip Sidney: Selected Poems* (Oxford, Clarendon Press, 1973), 218.

12 Stephen Greenblatt, *Renaissance Self-Fashioning: From More to Shakespeare* (Chicago, University of Chicago Press, 1980), 121.

13 Paul Fussell, *Class* (New York, Ballantine Books, 1983).

14 Dante Alighieri, *La Vita Nuova*, tr. Mark Musa (New Brunswick, Rutgers University Press), 7–8. I am grateful to Elizabeth Watson of The Johns Hopkins University for the implicit suggestion that Penelope Devereux is a screen woman. A clear major gloss on the question of "richness" in *Astrophil and Stella* is supplied by Terence Cave, *The Cornucopian Text: Problems of Writing in the French Renaissance* (Oxford, Clarendon Press, 1979). Here I will suggest only that although the generative powers of "copia" (variation, amplification, copying) are as evident in *Astrophil and Stella* as they almost necessarily have to be in any Renaissance sonnet sequence, Sidney's characteristic turn, as opposed for example to Shakespeare's, is to recharacterize "richness" in negative terms of covertness, absence, privation and darkness. The "copious" discourse thus becomes radically paradoxical and radically hollowed out in a way that differentiates Sidney's sonnets at least to some degree from Shakespeare's.

15 The claim that Sidney was a failure (a loser, as he has sometimes recently been called) is strongly and legitimately established as an anti-hagiographic one in Richard McCoy's influential book, *Rebellion in Arcadia* (New Brunswick, Rutgers University Press, 1979). Much credit is due to McCoy for the force with which he shatters the Sidney icon, thus making the author discussable. Any discussion of the problematic of the Arcadian world in Sidney (i.e. virtually *any* discussion of Sidney as an author) must also acknowledge a substantial debt to McCoy. The question of "failure" is nevertheless tricky with such authors as Sidney and Spenser, since not only is there no objective standard by which to measure it, but it also cannot be measured in relation to the possibly naive aspirations cherished on behalf of these authors by their friends (especially in the case of Sidney). And both authors tend to *represent* their forms of failure only in relation to an unlimited scale of perfection, thus making even failure a form of distinction.

16 It depends, of course, on what one means by "know" and "want." But biographical accounts of Sidney are numerous. M.W. Wallace, *The Life of Sir Philip Sidney* (Cambridge, Cambridge University Press, 1915) is sometimes described as the standard account; see also James M. Osborn, *Young Philip Sidney, 1572–1577* (New Haven, Yale University Press, 1972).

17 *Brief Lives*, 139.

18 G.F. Waller, *Mary Sidney, Countess of Pembroke: A Critical Study of her Writings and Milieu*, Salzburg Studies in English Literature, 87 (Salzburg, 1979), 100–1. What is almost amusing in this discussion is the assumption that the countess could have had no inkling of the real nature of her feelings for her brother.

19 In the "Dudley necrology" section of "The Ruines of Time," Spenser revealingly memorializes Philip Sidney as if he were sprung entirely from the maternal line. A secret complicity between an entire generation of sons and their mothers against strenuous, authoritarian, public-spirited fathers might be inferred from Richard Helgerson's *The Elizabethan Prodigals* (Berkeley and Los Angeles, University of California Press, 1976).

20 Incest isn't of course the only "mark" of the gentleman – the range of possible marks is almost limitless, and they can quite easily be invented. Indeed, one feature of poetry written by putative gentry in the sixteenth century is an almost frenzied attempt to inscribe such marks – vainly inasmuch as one prime mark of "breeding" is illiteracy, and another is a relentless stupidity. The idea that no clever man can be a gentleman (or vice versa) resurfaces in Fussell's *Class*. The best mark Sidney managed to inscribe may have been the quixotic one that implied the highest cost, that of an early death from a battle-wound, far away from the ostentatiously gentrified tournaments in which he also performed. Whatever marks caste must be visible and hence imitable (subject to appropriation), and this is especially the case with linguistic caste-marks, hence also poetic caste. Once that is recognized, perhaps all that can be done is to raise the cost of living up to the mark to the highest imaginable level. I wish to acknowledge a suggestive unpublished essay by Mark Rasmussen of Johns Hopkins on the marking of differences in pastoral.

21 *Poems of Sir Philip Sidney*, 217–18.

22 Needless to say, we may again seem to have been faked-out if we think the Countess of Pembroke is the One True Love; that screen pulls aside to reveal the mother and *maternal* incest ("I have borne you long"?) as the most deeply veiled objects of desire. Can we think our way through yet another unmasking? Even if not, *this* object of desire will also be one of supreme terror, possibly resulting in only a feigned *courtship* of it. Spenser's *Amoretti* and "Epithalamion" represent an attempt comparable to Sidney's inasmuch as they seek to make the space of "bourgeois" marriage one of full autonomy, of perfectly aligned interests, and of visible exclusiveness. Less quixotic than Sidney, however, Spenser conceives politic solutions; the *Amoretti* look so unthreatening as to have been found utterly flat and uninteresting by generations of readers. The continuing difficulty, however, of unifying conflicting interests continues to be represented. Apart from "Epithalamion," sonnet 74 might be taken as a *locus classicus*: in it, Spenser tries to line up the multitude of conflicting interests represented by the three Elizabeths, named in the poem, who at once confer and threaten his existence: mother, wife, queen.

23 Charles Baudelaire, "L'Invitation au Voyage," in *Les Fleurs du Mal*, ed. Antoine Adam (Paris, Garnier, 1961), 58. I discovered Barbara Johnson's essay on this poem and its prose counterpart too late to benefit from it here. See, however, *The Critical Difference* (Baltimore, The Johns Hopkins University Press, 1980). My citing this poem involves no supposition that it is unproblematical. On the contrary, it seems as if it would be possible to write a rule under which any attempted Arcadian totalization must simultaneously reveal the profound disturbances and contradictions that will make it "fail." A counter-rule might be that these disturbances must be reintroduced in order that the totalization *will* fail – that it is the ultimate

instance of the desirable and the undesirable together.

24 *Poems of Sir Philip Sidney*, 183–4.

25 If this sounds like a tired old story of the poet as poet, this "alienation" is exacerbated in the sixteenth century in two ways; first, by the assumption that literal language is prior to figurative, which means that the latter must always be wrenched away from a common or home base; and, second, that a conquest of the mother tongue is necessary for the progress of culture, the assumption of the imperial mantle, etc. In English rhetorics and poetics of the period, the conquest by Latin and/or Italian and/or French rhetoric of the vernacular (mother tongue) is at once widely feared and applauded. Practically any rhetorical text will exemplify this. In this connection, see especially Margaret Ferguson, "The rhetoric of exile in du Bellay and his classical precursors," (Diss., Yale University, 1974).

26 Daniel Traister, "Sidney's purposeful humor: *Astrophil and Stella* 59 and 83," *ELH* 49, 4 (1982), 752 ff.

27 *Poems of Sir Philip Sidney*, 208.

Chapter 4: The politics of theater (II) (pp. 89–118)

1 Richard Helgerson, *Self-Crowned Laureates: Spenser, Jonson, Milton and the Literary System* (Berkeley and Los Angeles, University of California Press, 1983); David L. Miller, "Spenser's vocation, Spenser's career," *ELH*, 50, 2 (1983), 197–231.

2 Louis Adrian Montrose, " 'Shaping fantasies': figurations of gender and power in Elizabethan culture," *Representations*, 2 (1983), 61–94.

3 See in this connection Stephen Greenblatt's important chapter on Spenser, concentrating on the destruction of the Bower, in *Renaissance Self-Fashioning: From More to Shakespeare* (Chicago, University of Chicago Press, 1980), 157–92. For Greenblatt, this act of destruction or "regenerative violence" is absolutely fundamental to the constitution of the (implicitly male) Renaissance "self," which also becomes the form of selfhood defining the uncompleted epoch in *western* culture that we inhabit. Not only is no difference allowed at this level between a male and female selfhood, but the text of *The Faerie Queene*, Book II, is made, uniquely in *Renaissance Self-Fashioning*, the one in which the gruesome law of our being is legible. I have seen no review of this book that comments on the extraordinary intransigence and confessional approach to the reader in this chapter, in which the fashioning of the self requires the *destruction* of the other. What is regularly taken away from this book is only a model of theatrical self-fashioning, yet the special treatment given to Spenser is one of the book's most compelling features.

4 If there is a single model or dialectic of production capable of assimilating these contradictions, I take it to be the one classically enunciated by Marx (not, for example, by Frederic Jameson, whom Montrose also cites). What Marx can fearlessly assimilate to the notion of capitalist production (rather than cultural production) is its unremitting vandalism.

5 Thomas Nashe appears to coin the phrase in his preface to the unauthorized edition of *Astrophil and Stella* (also containing poems by Samuel Daniel) published in 1591 "for Thomas Newman." See Nashe, *Works*, 5 vols, ed. R.B. McKerrow with supplementary notes by F.P. Wilson (Oxford, Basil Blackwell, 1966), III, 329. The point isn't that Nashe "tropes" the book as theater as many earlier sixteenth-century authors had done, but that he *literalizes* the conception with characteristic energy. The important distinction between literal and figurative thus recurs within this trope, not between it and some notion of literal theater.

6 The potential for trivializing simplification in this commonplace can be arrested by subjecting it to the kind of rigorous amplification and critique embodied in Foucault's account of the Renaissance *episteme* in *The Order of Things*, trans. Alan Bass (New York, Vintage Books, 1973), 3–77.

7 In *Homo Ludens* (Boston, Beacon Press, 1955), 5, Johan Huizinga characterizes the Renaissance conception of the theater of the world merely as an effete topos of neoplatonism, thus subjecting it to dismissive critique, if not amplification. In both Foucault and Huizinga, therefore, a conception of the plenitude or fertility of the Renaissance theatrical "mind" is inseparable from a conception of its incoherence and impotence.

8 Edmund Spenser, Proem to Book I of *The Faerie Queene, Poetical Works*, 3.

9 "A Theatre for Worldlings" in Charles Grosvenor Osgood and Henry Gibbons Lotspeich, eds, *The Minor Poems*, vol. 2 in Edwin Greenlaw *et al.*, eds, *The Works of Edmund Spenser* (Baltimore, The Johns Hopkins University Press, 1947), 1–25; commentaries 273–80, 611–27.

10 For Richard Mulcaster's apparently troubled relationship with the strongly Protestant governing body of the Merchant Taylors' School, as well as his pupils' playing before the queen, see F.W.M. Draper, *Four Centuries of the Merchant Taylors' School, 1561–1961* (Oxford, Clarendon Press, 1962).

11 For a discussion of Lyly's apparent failure and virtual humiliation as a "humanist courtier" in the guise of court dramatist, see G.K. Hunter, *John Lyly: The Humanist as Courtier* (Cambridge, Harvard University Press, 1965).

12 Accounts in English, even if incomplete, of van der Noot's career are supplied in the *Variorum* commentary and in *The Olympia Epics of Jan van der Noot*, ed. C.A. Zaalberg (Assen, Van Gorcum & Comp. N. V., 1956), ix–xiv. More extended treatment, to which I am strongly indebted, is given in Dutch in *Het Bosken en Het Theatre*, ed. W.A.P. Smit, Onze Oude Letteren Series (Amsterdam and Antwerp, 1953), 7–50. The question of Spenser's relation to the van der Noot text is also discussed there, as are some of the bibliographical peculiarities of the English and continental editions.

13 See *inter alia* C.L. Barber, "The May game of Martin Marprelate" in *Shakespeare's Festive Comedy: A Study of Dramatic Form in its Relation to Social Custom* (Princeton, Princeton University Press, 1972), 51–7; Raymond Anselment, *'Twixt Jest and Earnest: Marprelate, Marvell, Swift and the Decorum of Religious Ridicule* (Toronto, University of Toronto Press, 1980).

14 This familiar claim gets repeated with equally familiar lack of attention to what it might entail by Anthea Hume in *Edmund Spenser: Protestant Poet* (Cambridge, Cambridge University Press, 1984). Passing attention is given to the *Theatre* and its contexts.

15 See Smit, 37.

16 On the general strategy involved, see Margaret Ferguson, "The poetics of exile in du Bellay and his classical precursors."

17 Both these possibilities have been widely recognized in discussions of the emblem, discussions in which, however, I claim neither participation nor expertise. For some recent development in this field, see Peter M. Daly, *Emblem Theory: Recent German Contributions to the Characterization of the Emblem Genre* (Lichtenstein, Neideln, KTO Press, 1979).

18 Robert M. Durling (ed.), *Petrarch's Lyric Poems* (Cambridge, Harvard University Press, 1976), 11, st. 7.

19 Before dismissing the hypothetical precocity of the late-adolescent Spenser (already a student at Cambridge) as monstrous or simply implausible, we may have to consider whether we have or should be in quest of normal terms in which to

conceive of anyone's writing a poem as long, complex and in a sense relentless as *The Faerie Queene*, the facility of which is only apparent. We may further note that anxiety about the "monstrous" nature of poetic undertakings, related to their "imaginative" nature, is commonplace in Elizabethan literature, not excluding Sidney's *Apology*, and that monstrous or "unnatural" poetic genesis and rule are figured in the "du Bellay" emblems that succeed the "Petrarch" ones in Spenser's *Theatre*. Poem 8 in particular contains the "vision" of a Rome which "So many Neroes and Caligulaes / Must still being forth to rule this croked shore." These prodigious *wunderkinder*, of whom a succession, displaced from the city of origin, is foreseen, are also great artists *manqués*. Rome's decadence and corruption, which is also the condition of its regeneration, may have to be "lived" as well as its imperial glamor in a succession that passes from Augustus through Tiberius to Caligula and eventually to Nero.

20 *Variorum*, vol. 2, 22.
21 ibid., 2, 23.
22 Julia Conaway Bondanella, *Petrarch's Visions and their Renaissance Analogues* (Madrid, J. Porrua Turanzas, 1978).
23 For this history I am almost entirely indebted to Smit.
24 The *Olympia Epics*, parallels between the careers of Spenser and van der Noot, and parallels between these "epics" and *The Faerie Queene*, all lie beyond my scope here. Some discussion is included in all the pertinent works cited above, and the lavish, illustrated book containing the Olympia Epics is reproduced in the Zaalberg facsimile also cited above.
25 *The Minor Poems*, 5.
26 Here we stumble upon the possibility of an *epochal* fake-out, one in which neo-platonism, often taken to be synonymous with everything dreamily displaced, other-worldly, frustrated and rarefied in Renaissance thought, turns out to be the ground of an absolutist *Realpolitik* at once more real and more visionary than Machiavelli's – a *Realpolitik* that never finally unmasks, never lets go, and never disables itself even when it makes the gesture of doing so. Discussion of "visionary politics" (meaning something by no means antithetical to real politics) in the English poetry of the sixteenth century may be hampered by our want of a word corres-ponding to du Bellay's *songe*, with which Spenser is obviously well acquainted.
27 A disruption of teleological narrative and a (feigned?) loss of "Sabaoths sight" comes to characterize *The Faerie Queene*, Books IV–VI, and the "Mutabilitie" cantos. (Indeed, the "perfect" Book I of *The Faerie Queene* becomes the anomalous one of the poem; the "vnperfite" book of "Mutabilitie" the emergent normal one.) We can observe, accompanying this suppression and disruption, a new defensiveness on Spenser's part about such "noble" secular fictions as those of friendship, courtesy, nature and pastoral grace. The relentless Protestant iconoclasm of the *Theatre* sequence, perhaps timely in the early part of Elizabeth's reign and of Leicester's militaristic ascendancy, had probably ceased to be so in the latter part of that reign. A reaction against Protestant militancy and "vision" became increasingly apparent as Elizabeth's reign progressed, and as radical Puritans rather than Catholics became the internal threat to Elizabethan rule. But does Spenser lose "Sabaoths sight" and gain natural vision, or merely advertise a political suppression of the visionary at the end of "Mutabilitie?" Or both, or all at once, in an unusual case of double or multiple vision?
28 "Epithalamion," in *Poetical Works*, 579–84.
29 George Puttenham, *The Arte of English Poesie*, A Facsimile Reproduction intr. Baxter Hathaway (Kent, Ohio. Kent State University Press, 1970), "Of Ornament," ch. XVIII.

30 In a lecture given at The Johns Hopkins University in 1984.
31 *The Minor Poems*, 25, st.1, line 1.
32 P.W.M. van der Sluijs, "Invloed van Emblematiek, Hieroglifiek en Deviezenkunst in het Werk van Jonker Jan van der Noot," in *Wort und Bild*, ed. Herman Vekeman and Justus Muller Hofstede (Erftstadt, Lukassen Verlag, 1984), 53–73.
33 ibid., 53; my translation.
34 K. Porteman, "Nederlandse Embleemtheorie: Van Marcus Gillis (1566) tot Jacob Cats (1618)," in *Wort und Bild*, 1–7.
35 Van der Sluijs, 62; my translation.

Chapter 5: Discovery (pp. 119–29)

1 The notion of a poet's being "strong" is one so definitively associated with Harold Bloom that it is necessary for me to distinguish my usage from his and even in a way oppose it to his. For Bloom, strength is constituted within an oedipal and hence still family schema, whereas I would suggest that by keeping it all in the family and making it part of a process of legitimate even if parricidal inheritance, the notion of the poet is actually domesticated and weakened, while the project of the inheritor is narrowed down and rationalized. With Spenser partly in mind, and even within the frame of the family, it is clear that male poetic separation from fantasized maternal origins is at least as important as the relation to fantasized paternal ones, and probably a great deal more so. Whatever strength accrues to the poet in his fantasized familial transactions – and sibling transactions are hardly to be ruled out either – has to be thought both as excess "beyond" strength and paradoxically as a continuing form or function of deficiency as well; it is never a force proportioned to orderly succession. The violence of the inheritor accordingly becomes more difficult to circumscribe, characterize neatly, or legitimize. The conception of poetic genius also diminishes the significance of the family as a field or psychosocial locus of poetic action.

2 George Puttenham, *The Arte of English Poesie*, A Facsimile Reproduction intr. Baxter Hathaway (Kent, Ohio, Kent State University Press, 1970). It is in this phase of the discussion that the undesirability of using an edited and hence rationalized version of the *Arte* will become apparent. Anticipating my own argument, I should mention that the "courtly" figure of allegory is named "false semblant" in Chapter XVIII (197) but then listed in the index as "faire semblant" (318). The possibility of the courtier's [false semblant's] changing places with the queen [faire semblant], but also of a radical, threatening indeterminacy about who is, or who controls, the master figure of allegory (about who *is* the master-courtier) remains apparent throughout the text. It should also be mentioned that the *Arte* has been ascribed to Lord Lumley as well as Puttenham.

3 Who, after all, needed to be given English names for rhetorical figures known under their classical names to every schoolboy? However, they might to their surprise have learned of a secret master plot, or a possible succession of plots and counter-plots, in which they were all involved, wittingly or not. They might also have learned of the existence of a great code that we now call "culture" and that encoded them, making them bearers of the genetic instructions through which the culture perpetuates itself. Jonathan Goldberg, to whom I am indebted both for the tip about the "English Poete" in the October Eclogue and for important insights in *James I and the Politics of Literature* (Baltimore, The Johns Hopkins University Press, 1983), enables us to suppose that Jonson may have read Puttenham exactly right; the question of "Tiberian rule," raised here, is on Jonson's agenda. The "eight cancelled pages" from Jonson's copy of Puttenham, reprinted in the Hathaway

facsimile, also imply the possibility of Jonson's having got it right; pp. 123–4 bear the closest consideration, since they have to do with the playful "undoing" of the queen's name. Admittedly, in my own argument the whole of Book 2 ["Of Proportion"] remains an unassimilated mass, yet the possibility suggests itself that it is precisely a huge deadweight that the author intentionally drops on the entire Sidney-dominated topic of prosody. Not only would this chapter do it once for all, but would emphasize *English* rather than Latin prosody; it would also crush the legislative pretensions of the Sidney family, Gabriel Harvey and whatever might have remained in 1589 of the mythical, Sidney-dominated "Areopagus" of Spenser's early days.

4 Daniel Javitch, *Poetry and Courtliness in Renaissance England* (Princeton, Princeton University Press, 1978).

5 Louis Adrian Montrose, "Of gentlemen and shepherds: the politics of Elizabethan pastoral form," *ELH*, 50, 3 (1983), 415–60.

6 Spenser, *Poetical Works*, 456.

7 There is, for example, the violent disavowal of "paederastice" in the gloss to the January eclogue, yet homoerotic bonding and rivalry are, as every reader now sees, a part of the world of Colin Clout.

8 Abraham Fraunce, *The Arcadian Rhetorike*, ed. Edith Seaton (Oxford, The Luttrell Society, 1950).

9 *Arte of English Poesie*, 75.

10 It becomes increasingly possible to suppose that the master to whom Spenser owes an art of specifically English poetry is Gascoigne, still a truly invisible man of the English sixteenth century. Gascoigne in turn credits Chaucer, who has his own form of invisibility. The master text would not just be Gascoigne's *Certain Notes of Instruction* (1575), repr. Gregory Smith ed., *Elizabethan Critical Essays*, vol. 1 (Oxford, Clarendon, 1904), 47–57, but *A Hundreth Sundrie Flowers* ed. C.T. Prouty (Columbia: University of Missouri Press, 1942) notably including *The Adventures of Master F.J.* This text is indeed an *art* of courtship and manual of subtle indirection, in which the compromising power of the letter is fully exhibited. See in this connection Jane Hedley, "Allegoria: Gascoigne's Master Trope," *ELR*, 11 (Spring, 1981), 148–64. Discussing one of the poems in *A Hundreth Sundrie Flowers*, Hedley discovers, too, the plot that will become that of the *Arte*. A group of adulterous courtly lovers listens to the recital of a riddle-poem. Each knows perfectly well what the "answer" is, but no one, either man or woman, dares to acknowledge an understanding. The group is therefore bound together in criminal complicity, while the teller of the riddle becomes the terroristic master of the situation.

11 *Arte of English Poesie*, 196–7.

12 ibid., 256.

13 ibid., 32.

14 ibid., 251.

15 Two moments of naked terrorism, but by the same token naked terror, enter into the constitution of the rhetorical *mise-en-scène* in Book III (Of Ornament!). First there is the terror of the naked lady, humiliated in, but also profoundly threatening to, the male-imposed world of "ornament" – the decorous order of concealment under which "nature" and "woman" alike are buried. Then there is the second moment in Chapter 2, in which an old and toothless (castrated?) country gentleman makes a fool of himself when he gets up to speak in public. Rhetoric thus unequivocally and terrifyingly becomes necessary, and the "good" example is that of Sir Nicholas Bacon, successful politico, shown behind the scenes in his closet reading, of all things, Quintilian. On forms of poetic terrorism (terror) I want

to acknowledge the insight of Sydney Shep and Elizabeth Hanson, both of The Johns Hopkins University. Perhaps I should say finally, and no doubt unavailingly, that I do not consider my "story" to constitute a conspiracy theory – rather, it is about feigned or putative conspiracy that need never be more than the fantasy of a single author or perhaps a set of authors. I would, however, suggest that feigned conspiracy, perhaps capable of being translated in some degree into real conspiracy, is implicit in the very terms of Renaissance poetics as rehearsed by Puttenham.

16 Canto vi, 42 in *Poetical Works*, 399.
17 Book VI, viii, 41–5 in *Poetical Works*, 374.
18 *Arte of English Poesie*, 20.

Chapter 6: Epilogue: the way forward (pp. 130–51)

1 Readers inclined to doubt the seriousness with which Shakespeare's witty will can now be taken are referred to Joel Fineman, *Shakespeare's Perjur'd Eye: The Invention of Poetic Subjectivity in the Sonnets* (Berkeley and Los Angeles, University of California Press, 1986). This magisterial treatment of the sonnets, long awaited and well-argued, confers the highest imaginable seriousness on the Shakespearean "will." Yet in doing so it succumbs entirely to that will (or to one interpretation of it) and hence proceeds uncritically from start to finish. Assuming that the sonnets essentially tell one story, their own, in the metanarrative of the Young Man and the Dark Lady, Fineman amplifies and reconstrues that story as the story of western representation and the western "subject" *per se*. And although proceeding in terms of an essentially Lacanian schema, Fineman also places himself, Lacan, and everything else in poststructuralism inside Shakespeare, the new Leviathan. What is *uncritical* about this is Fineman's placing himself in the position of an analyst who accepts the story the patient tells about himself, ignoring all its suggestive disavowals and denials, as gospel. Do the sonnets, however, tell only one story or (at least) 156 different ones, and is there something they can't say except between the lines as their own counternarrative?

2 From *Summer's Last Will and Testament*, in Thomas Nashe, *"The Unfortunate Traveller" and Other Works*, ed. J.B. Steane (Harmondsworth, Penguin Books, 1984), 187–8. My questions are unaffected by the well-established derivation of this material from the Pyrrhonism of Cornelius Agrippa of Nettesheim.

3 I simply take over the sequence as published in *The Riverside Shakespeare*, ed. G. Blakemore Evans (Boston, Houghton Mifflin, 1974), 48–56. The arbitrariness of my proposed sequence, *The Comedy of Errors*, *The Taming of the Shrew*, *A Midsummer Night's Dream*, from which *Love's Labour's Lost*, for example, is omitted, can be justified only by my repeating that I have constructed it for the sake of argument. With *some* elaboration of the argument, *Love's Labour's Lost* could be included; I don't exclude it as troublesome evidence.

4 A sufficiently contentious premise, but not too startling or novel given the virtuoso development of the Plautine plot in *The Comedy of Errors*; the weaving of texts and sources in both plays; the relative refinement and funniness even of the brawling shrew-comedy, etc.

5 It can of course be argued that there is no real surprise in either ending, and that the audience's question isn't "what will happen?" but "how will he bring it off?" It doesn't, however, affect my argument that the suspense is merely conventional, since the point is that both plays are overtly linear and goal-directed in contrast, for example, to the sprawling *Merchant of Venice*.

6 That of the Duke in *The Comedy of Errors*, almost paralyzed by the law he cannot

alter; of Egeon and the Duke conspicuously passing the time in telling and hearing their own sad stories, none of which seems to make any practical difference; of the stupefied Sly falling into oblivion almost as soon as *The Taming of the Shrew* begins; of the eternally hunting nobleman, devising a plot of fantastic elaborateness to the trivial end of passing the time by disconcerting Sly, etc.

7 Cited from the Arden *A Midsummer Night's Dream*, ed. Harold F. Brooks (London, Methuen, 1983), 125. (All refs.)

8 Some of this material is incorporated in the text and notes of Louis Adrian Montrose's "Shaping fantasies: figurations of gender and power in Elizabethan culture," *Representations*, 2 (1983), 61–94. Both the ready availability of this essay and the increasing familiarity of this material make citation redundant here. Shakespeare's *gentle* Theseus comes at least partly from the Chaucer of *The Knight's Tale*, and it now increasingly appears that Chaucer's "courtesy" constitutes both a model (one regarded not wholly without suspicion) and an inexhaustible problematic for Elizabethan authors, notably Spenser and Shakespeare.

9 See Montrose, "Shaping fantasies," but issues of this order are widely discussed in feminist criticism.

10 On the question of what Theseus in particular hears in silences, see David Marshall, "Exchanging visions: reading *A Midsummer Night's Dream*," *ELH*, 49, 3 (1982), 543–76. Although Theseus is good at hearing what he wants to hear, it is also evident that he "hears" something more than that, since he evidently picks up silent melancholy in Hippolyta's responses to his celebratory rhetoric – or projects his own melancholy into them. "The pale companion is not for our pomp" [I.i.15], says Theseus, where "pale companion" stands for melancholy – moonlight – "fair" Hippolyta herself.

11 Tricky, apart from anything else, in that its nature and motives are suspect. The juice that equitably *reconciles* lovers comes from a flower that is, in Ovid, stained with the blood of Pyramus; the use of the potion thus in effect revives Pyramus's potency and may even revenge him. In *A Midsummer Night's Dream*, the flower has been stricken by Cupid's arrow, fired with "certain" (II.i.157) aim at "a fair vestal" who is also an "imperial votress," but which somehow misses its mark while she, oblivious, goes her way "in maiden meditation, fancy free" (II.i.164). This magical potion thus also reverses Cupid's failure, and functions to bring *down* the seemingly invulnerable "imperial votress." An appreciable quantity of male revolt, usurpation and/or revenge seems thus to be blended into the magic juice, the benign action of which may accordingly be more apparent than real.

12 The issue of monological fixation vs. occasion, variety, "adjustment," etc. arises in connection with Shakespeare's sonnets, as it has done with Petrarch's. Fineman's reading in *Shakespeare's Perjur'd Eye* tends, while acknowledging a shift after sonnet 126, to emphasize the uniformity of the sonnets.

13 Montrose, "Shaping fantasies;" Marshall, "Exchanging visions."

14 The issue of the queen as literal spectator, as distinct from merely being the idealized spectator-monarch of much Renaissance drama, is reviewed in the Arden *A Midsummer Night's Dream*, Introduction, lii–lvii.

15 Its first recorded performance was for the Gray's Inn Christmas Revels of 1594. Paul A. Jorgensen (ed.), *The Comedy of Errors* (Harmondsworth, Penguin Books, 1972), 7.

16 Edith Rickert, "Propaganda and satire in 'A Midsummer Night's Dream,'" *Modern Philology*, 21, 1 (1923), 53–87. Various other identifications are tried out or cited: the changeling boy "is" the dispossessed Earl of Hertford; the "little western flower" of the play "is" Lettice Knollys, Countess of Essex, etc. That the process of referring

should make sense, or that it can be seen as part of a poetic design as well as of a trivial if opportune political one, is apparently not required.

17 Marshall makes the point: "Exchanging visions," 554.

18 To some degree the process can be traced in the Arden footnotes. On some of the Lyly-Shakespeare connections, as well as for Lyly's tribulations as in-house humanist, see G.K. Hunter's indispensable *John Lyly: The Humanist as Courtier* (Cambridge, Harvard University Press, 1965). My own privative characterizations of Lyly in this context are informed by this work, but are not to be attributed to Hunter. Their privativeness is, moreover, determined by the context; I don't intend to beg the question of Lyly's own conceivable politico-allegorical designs. See Peter Saccio, *The Court Comedies of John Lyly* (Princeton, Princeton University Press, 1969).

19 Fairy succession, meaning *fictional* succession, which can't be accomplished singlehandedly (i.e. without the goodwill and consent of those who witness or assist in the manipulation), is a subject of brilliantly mordant irony and also of conspicuously displayed prowess in Spenser's poetry. *The Faerie Queene*, Book II, is a case in point; in Canto X, a long historico-dynastic recital of the reigns of British kings and queens is followed, for no apparent reason, by a narrative of "Elfin" descent (including the wars of the Elfes and the Gobbelines!), in which the royal line of "Elfe" and "Faye" passes through "Oberon" (Henry VIII) to "Tanaquill" (Elizabeth). Since the historical succession is manifestly interrupted at various points, and the elfin succession is not, it is presumably the more "uncompromised" one – also, given the strife over Elizabeth's legitimacy, it is the one that counts, rendering the historical narrative subordinate if not irrelevant. The notes to *The Shepheardes Calender* also reveal how dynastic games can be played, especially in those to the "Aprill" eclogue, in which Elizabeth's legitimate descent from Henry VIII/Pan is at once implicitly questioned and then re-established as a necessary fiction of the political world – and as one to be openly challenged only at mortal risk. Since only fictional succession (the production of a changeling heir) is possible in the latter part of Elizabeth's reign, there is a certain fantastic sense in which the continuation of the line depends on the "marriage" of the poet to the queen in the absence of any real husband/father, a point not lost on Spenser, whose own marriage poems model this solution to the dynastic question. (That a possible specific heir, such as James I, may allusively be designated in any particular case does not change the argument.)

20 Many accounts exist of Raleigh's fall from grace, but the analytically indispensable one for my purposes is Stephen Greenblatt, *Sir Walter Raleigh: The Renaissance Man and his Roles* (New Haven, Yale University Press, 1973), which exemplarily discusses the ensuing performance and draws attention to the Sir "Water" pun.

21 Curiously enough, these allusions don't seem to be picked up at all in R.B. McKerrow (ed., with supplementary notes by F.P. Wilson), *The Works of Thomas Nashe*, 5 vols (Oxford, Basil Blackwell, 1966), while G.R. Hibbard, *Thomas Nashe: A Critical Biography* (Cambridge, Harvard University Press, 1962), ignores *Summer's Last Will* entirely.

22 *Works of Thomas Nashe*, 150.

23 See Hunter, *John Lyly* and also C.L. Barber, *Shakespeare's Festive Comedy: A Study of Dramatic Form in its Relation to Social Custom* (Princeton, Princeton University Press, 1972), 58–157. For discussions significantly informing or anticipating my own, see Barber, 124–62; James Calderwood, *Shakespearean Metadrama* (Minneapolis, University of Minnesota Press, 1971), 120–48; J. Dennis Huston, *Shakespeare's Comedies of Play* (New York, Columbia University Press,

1981), 94–121; Robert W. Dent, "Imagination in *A Midsummer Night's Dream*," *Shakespeare Quarterly*, 15 (1964), 115–29.

24 Edmund Spenser, *Amoretti*, in *Poetical Works*, ed. J.C. Smith and E. de Selincourt (New York, Oxford University Press, 1970).

25 A politics now widely perceived to be enacted in Elizabethan poetic texts, but presumably not so enacted without hope of their being re-enacted in the world. Taking possession of another's "place" or "part" becomes a rationalized demonism of the Elizabethan poets.

26 Montrose, "Shaping fantasies."

27 Hardly "ungendered," it might be said, since he is a boy, and since he *is* gendered, the feminizing Titania will eventually lose even if she wins. But the cultural construction of gender – as distinct from sex – is implied in *The Taming of the Shrew*, in which Petruchio can whimsically make Kate turn an old man into a young virgin and back again. Petruchio, with an exhausted Kate at his mercy, arbitrarily chooses that the old man shall be restored to his "proper" gender. This unrestricted convertibility of male and female figures suggests, incidentally, why male figures can have reference to the queen in works like *The Faerie Queene*.

28 In all the ways already suggested, but in others connected with Elizabethan patterns of child-exchange, now a subject of research; with anxieties about supplantation in the line of legitimate succession; with romance-fantasies of dramatic upward mobility and/or movement from marginal to central positions in the culture (exploited by Spenser in the history of Redcrosse Knight in *The Faerie Queene*, Book I, Canto X); possibly with parental anxieties about marital infidelity and/or unruly children; certainly with parental disavowal of undesirable children, since, as *OED* notes, the child deposited by the fairies is normally "stupid or ugly."

29 Sonnet 3 in *Riverside Shakespeare*: 1750.

30 On such parthenogenetic fantasies, see Montrose, "Shaping fantasies," but also J.A. Barnes, "Genitor: genetrix: nature: culture," in *The Character of Kinship*, ed. Jack Goody (Cambridge, Cambridge University Press, 1973), 61–73.

31 George Puttenham, *The Arte of English Poesie*, A Facsimile Reproduction intr. Baxter Hathaway (Kent, Ohio, Kent State University Press, 1970), 182.

32 One well-known demonological source being Reginald Scot's *The Discoverie of Witchcraft* (1584), repr. ed. Montague Summers (New York, Dover Publications, 1972), especially Bk I, ch. iv; Bk IV, ch. ii; and Bk VII, ch. xv. Nashe's *The Terrors of the Night* (*Works*, vol. 1, 337–86), produced contemporaneously with *A Midsummer Night's Dream*, may be regarded as a middle term between the "straight" demonology of Scot and the full poetic assimilation by Shakespeare in *A Midsummer Night's Dream*.

33 Cited in David Norbrook, *Poetry and Politics of the English Renaissance* (London, Routledge & Kegan Paul, 1984), 22.

34 If this critique is called for, it is at least partly because of the evident connection in *A Midsummer Night's Dream*, and elsewhere in the work of Shakespeare and his major contemporaries, between terror and aesthetic power. It is a connection regularly posited, of course, in discussions of "the sublime," but generally without acknowledgment that "terror" possesses historical and/or cultural specificity, not to mention a local habitation and a name. This abstraction and distancing of terror is suggestively counteracted in Elaine Scarry's recent work entitled *The Body in Pain* (New York, Oxford University Press, 1985).

Index